THE EVIDENCE OF THINGS NOT SAID

THE EVIDENCE OF THINGS NOT SAID

JAMES BALDWIN
AND THE PROMISE OF
AMERICAN DEMOCRACY

LAWRIE BALFOUR

CORNELL UNIVERSITY PRESS
ITHACA & LONDON

First published 2001 by Cornell University Press
First printing, Cornell Paperbacks, 2001

Printed in the United States of America

Library of Congress Cataloging-in-Publication Data

Balfour, Katharine Lawrence, 1964-
   The evidence of things not said : James Baldwin and the promise of American democracy / by Lawrie Balfour.
      p. cm.
Includes bibliographical references.
   ISBN 0-8014-3751-2 (alk. paper) — ISBN 0-8014-8698-X (pbk. : alk. paper)
   1. Baldwin, James, 1924- —Political and social views. 2. Politics and literature—United States—History and criticism. 3. Political fiction, American—History and criticism.
4. Afro-Americans—Politics and government. 5. Afro-Americans in literature. 6. Race relations in literature. 7. Democracy in literature. 8. Racism in literature. I. Title.
   PS3552.A45 Z58 2001
   818'.5409—dc21

                                                                              00-010128

Cloth printing   10 9 8 7 6 5 4 3 2 1
Paperback printing   10 9 8 7 6 5 4 3 2 1

For Chad

Though there are whites and blacks among us who hate each other, we will not; there are those who are betrayed by greed, by guilt, by blood-lust, but not we; we will set our faces against them and join hands and walk together into that dazzling future when there will be no white or black. This is the dream of all liberal men, a dream not at all dishonorable, but, nevertheless, a dream. For, let us join hands on this mountain as we may, the battle is elsewhere. It proceeds far from us in the heat and horror and pain of life itself where all men are betrayed by greed and guilt and blood lust and where no one's hands are clean. Our good will, from which we yet expect such power to transform us, is thin, passionless, strident: its roots, examined, lead us back to our forebears, whose assumption it was that the black man, to become truly human and acceptable, must first become like us.

James Baldwin, "Many Thousands Gone"

As is the inevitable result of things unsaid, we find ourselves until today oppressed with a dangerous and reverberating silence.

James Baldwin, "Many Thousands Gone"

CONTENTS

PREFACE   *xi*

CHAPTER ONE
Speaking of Race   *1*

CHAPTER TWO
"A Most Disagreeable Mirror"   *34*

CHAPTER THREE
Blessed Are the Victims?   *60*

CHAPTER FOUR
Presumptions of Innocence   *87*

CHAPTER FIVE
The Living Word   *113*

AFTERWORD
Baldwin and the Search for a Majority   *135*

Notes   *141*
Bibliography   *171*
Index   *187*

PREFACE

James Baldwin credited his friend and mentor, Beauford Delaney, with showing him how to see. A painter, Delaney introduced Baldwin to the play of light and color and taught him to recognize, in grimy puddles and broken sidewalks, the life that had previously been invisible to him. I mention Baldwin's tribute to Delaney because Baldwin has served a similar function for so many readers. He certainly serves that function for me.

My interest in Baldwin is both scholarly and political. When people ask why a white political theorist would choose Baldwin as the subject of her research, the glib response I generally offer is that Baldwin chose me. But the answer is not really glib at all. What I mean is simply that Baldwin's words captured me, immediately and insistently. *The Fire Next Time*, in particular, enabled me to think through the complicated interrelation between democratic ideals and American racial history in a way that the traditional resources of the political theory curriculum had not. But his words speak beyond the concerns of political theory. By providing a moral vocabulary supple enough to contend with such issues as inequality, citizenship, power, identity, and the uses of history, Baldwin speaks to a wide range of disciplines and to the wider circle of concerned citizens.

The political impulse behind the project is a worry that the prevailing public discourse about racial injustice in the United States is sorely inadequate to its task. That I did not come to think seriously about questions of race and racism until graduate school—after many years of studying moral issues in politics—suggests that these questions are not receiving the kind of probing attention they demand. Baldwin, I argue, provides critical guidance for resisting the retreat from a national commitment to opposing racial injustice in what has been called the "post–civil rights" era. He would, I believe, have railed against the reliance on weak values like "diversity" and inquired instead into the forces that perpetuate white campuses and board rooms and neighborhoods. He would have insisted, furthermore, that women and men interested in disparities of power not cede the language of moral passion to conservatism. In a sense, this book represents an attempt to answer Baldwin's demand that we see and hear the world differently. If it accomplishes anything, I hope it is this—that more people will come to say about Baldwin what he said of Beauford Delaney: "At this moment one begins to apprehend the nature of his triumph. And the beauty of his triumph, and the proof that it is a real one, is that he makes it ours."

Although the nature of Baldwin's triumph as a democratic thinker seems obvious to me now, it was not always so. I was inordinately fortunate to have advisers who understood that a passion for Baldwin's essays could be a political theory dissertation long before I did. I still wonder at my tremendous good luck to have found not one, but four teachers, who were united in their encouragement of me and disagreed enough about everything else to force me to figure a few things out for myself. George Kateb, Alan Ryan, Jeffrey Stout, and Cornel West were essential to the definition of this project and continue to inspire the larger intellectual project of which this book is a part.

I wonder further at the generosity of the individuals who have read and commented on all or part of the manuscript or who have spent hours sharing their own perspectives on Baldwin's life and work. At the risk of neglecting the many people to whom I am grateful whose names do not appear here, I want to extend particular thanks to Judith Barish, Leora Batnitzky, Lelia DeAndrade, Robert Gooding-Williams, Amy Gutmann, Manfred Halpern, Michael Hayes, Jennifer Hochschild, David Kim, Florence Ladd, Toni Lester, Richard Newman, Jason Scorza, George Shulman, Richard Taub, and Kim Townsend. Special thanks are owed to Roxanne Euben, who scrutinized every word and walked me around Jamaica Pond until I got a few things nearly right. And to Dana Ansel, who furnished the necessary measures of moral support and calories to keep me going.

Crucial, early support for this project came from the University Center for Human Values and the Society of Fellows of the Woodrow Wilson Foundation, both at Princeton University. The staff, faculty, and fellows of the W. E. B. Du Bois Institute for Afro-American Research at Harvard University and the Center for the Study of Values in Public Life at Harvard Divinity School provided a wonderful environment in which to figure out how to turn a dissertation into a book. I am also thankful for the warm collegiality of the faculty at Babson College and for the generous support that I received from the Babson College Board of Research in the final stages of this project. My editors, Alison Shonkwiler and Catherine Rice, not only made the idea of writing a first book seem possible but gave wise advice about how to do it, and the anonymous readers at Cornell University Press provided indispensible direction along the way. Even where I departed from their advice, my thinking was improved because of it.

I am indebted to the James Baldwin Estate, which generously granted me permission to publish excerpts from all of Baldwin's writings except those essays collected in *Notes of a Native Son*. For permission to use material from *Notes of a Native Son* (copyright © 1955, renewed 1983, and introduction copyright © 1984), I thank Beacon Press, Boston. Additionally, I want to acknowledge the following publications for allowing me to use material that had already appeared in print: *Political Theory* 26 (June 1998), in which portions of chapters 1 and 2 appeared as "'A Most Disagreeable Mirror': Race Consciousness as Double Consciousness"; *The Review of Politics* 61 (Summer 1999), which published an earlier version of chapter 4 as "The Appeal of Innocence: Baldwin, Walzer, and the Bounds of

Social Criticism"; and *James Baldwin Now*, edited by Dwight A. McBride (New York University Press, 1999), in which a version of chapter 5 appeared as "Finding the Words: Baldwin, Race Consciousness, and Democratic Theory."

Finally, I want to thank my family. I owe a special debt to my parents, Dale and Bill Balfour, both for their faith in my aspiration to pursue such an impractical career and for their example, which has always been my inspiration. To my extended family on both coasts I owe thanks for the encouragement that sustained me throughout the writing process. I have Chad Dodson to thank for the West Coast half of the family and for much more. Unable to articulate adequately the substance of his enthusiasm, his kindness, his importance in the making of the manuscript and of a life beyond it, I have dedicated this book to him.

THE EVIDENCE OF THINGS NOT SAID

Speaking of Race

The Silences of the Majority

What could be more democratic than conversation among citizens about issues of national importance? What matter is in greater need of honest, thoughtful attention than the ongoing significance of *race* in American public life?[1] Though convinced that the appropriate answer to the first question is "nothing" and the answer to the second is "none," I have misgivings about the rage for racial dialogue. But why? One answer might simply be fatigue. Late in 1997, the *New York Times* summed up President Bill Clinton's national conversation on race with the following headline: "The Honest Dialogue That Is Neither." The article reflects the weariness many Americans feel about "the country's never-ending discussion of race."[2]

Yet weariness is an inadequate response when matters of injustice are at issue. And neither the inconclusiveness of the president's initiative nor the disconnection of the dialogue from substantive policy measures alters the urgency of the need for race talk. Consideration of Lani Guinier's call for "a broad public conversation about issues of racial justice" provides a threefold explanation why such a conversation is so crucial to the health of American democracy.[3] First, there is Guinier's own experience as a nominee for the position of assistant attorney general for civil rights. Among the lessons of her abandonment by the president and widespread public misrepresentation, certainly, is how the denial of the importance of race can serve to distort the efforts of anyone who aspires to address and oppose racial injustice. In the context of such denial, Guinier's efforts to imagine policies to achieve the promises of the Voting Rights Act of 1965 were read as a sign of an unhealthy preoccupation with race. Her ideas about how to ensure that a broader range of voters would have influence in political outcomes were, without examination, reported to be undemocratic. Perhaps if the nomination had taken place in a climate in which more Americans were willing to engage in an open discussion about the exclusion of African Americans and other minority groups from adequate political representation, Guinier would have been recognized to be supremely fit for the job. Perhaps, under such circumstances, there would have been a greater acceptance of innovative alternatives.

My disquiet with the prospects for racial dialogue does not stem from a quarrel with any of this, however. Nor does it reflect a belief that the circumstances of Guinier's aborted nomination have no broader political significance. For her call to conversation resonates at a second level: it reminds Americans that the very possibility of achieving racial justice is threatened by the inability to talk constructively about race. The susceptibility of Guinier's proposals to mischaracterization suggests a general unwillingness to probe the relationship between a racist history (as distinguished from a racist *past*) and democracy in America.[4] The susceptibility of Guinier herself to the racially coded epithet of "quota queen" indicates the dishonesty of claims that race does not matter in the "post–civil rights" era. For behind the drama of the nomination, a much larger story about race and exclusion was played out—and is being played out still. Despite the expansion of formal equality and the rise of individual African Americans to positions of power, a line between "white" and "black" Americans persists.[5] It persists in income levels, residential patterns, incarceration rates, life expectancy, and a variety of other empirical measures.[6] Furthermore, the existence of a color line in public opinion about the scope of racial injustice and the justification of policies designed to overcome it indicates how much still needs to be said.[7]

Guinier's call for dialogue also makes sense at a third and even more general level, the level of democratic theory. Like many contemporary democratic theorists, she endorses the idea that political accountability is enhanced by the inclusion of the widest possible array of voices in reasoned public deliberation.[8] This deliberative ideal has been championed both as a means of legitimating political decisions—ensuring that they are indeed democratic—and as a means of enlarging citizens' sense of their own powers and responsibilities. Where issues of racial injustice are concerned, the idea of public deliberation is especially compelling. It provides a way of rooting out violations of the promise that ascriptive identity, racial or otherwise, is irrelevant to American citizenship. Furthermore, the process itself can be transformative. Participation in public deliberation can provide an enhanced sense of agency to citizens whose experience of exclusion has alienated them from political activity while simultaneously undermining other citizens' obliviousness to their own racial privilege. Properly regulated, deliberation enables the participants to become their better selves by endowing them with an understanding of a common, rather than only their particular, good.[9]

If the call for public dialogue is a reasonable response to Guinier's own experiences, if it responds to what is perhaps the most intransigent failure of American democracy, and if it corroborates a central insight of democratic theory, what could possibly be troubling about it? This question generates an outpouring of others: How, I wonder, would members of a society with a history of denial about the significance of racial injustice even begin to engage in frank conversation? Should reluctant individuals be forced into the conversation? Would all voices be weighed equally? Or ought some voices to be recognized as more authoritative than others? Ought anyone to be excluded? Related to concerns about who would do the talking lurk even more unsettling questions about the character of the talk itself. What discursive resources are available to make honest dialogue possible? What limits, if any, ought to be placed on what is said? Ought racist considerations to be allowed in the name of open exchange? By what criteria would racist considerations be distinguished from non-racist ones?

What this by no means exhaustive stream of questions suggests is how complicated and delicate an undertaking racial dialogue must be. The stakes are high. When what is at issue in the conversation is the humanity of some of its participants, every word may do new damage. And when the issue has been such a subject of evasion as the significance of the color line, what is not said may be as revealing as what is said. The impact of this predicament on Americans' ways of talking to one another about race is that too often there seem to be only two, unacceptable, alternatives. The first alternative, "race-blind" discourse, not only fails as a solution to racial inequalities but also condemns to silence those Americans whose race does get noticed. By moving too quickly into the future, race blindness reinforces American racial innocence; it signals a refusal to grapple with the past and with the dilemmas of the present. Indeed, the pretense of not noticing race threatens to make Americans not so much blind as deaf and dumb: deaf to the anguish engendered by the color line and dumb about how that anguish relates to the promises of American democracy. Even when the demand for race blindness issues from a commitment to racial justice, it impoverishes public discourse and allows discussion of issues as disparate as welfare reform, multicultural education, affirmative action, and anticrime measures to serve as codes for an ill-defined complex of assumptions associated with race. It allows race, in turn, to be associated with blackness.

If appeals to race blindness stymie honest struggle with issues of racial justice, however, the second alternative may be worse. High levels of racial segregation in American neighborhoods and discrimination in American workplaces provide just two indicators of the vigor of what Judge Leon Higginbotham calls "the precept of black inferiority."[10] Perhaps under such circumstances, the subtler, subterranean forms of racism that lurk beneath the surface of public discourse ought to be left undisturbed. For what surfaces as frankness may simply be expressions of racism, formerly discredited, reemerging in a new guise. "Re-racing," according to Kimberlé Crenshaw, "is the thrill of today's social discourse." She continues:

> The process of having e-raced blacks now provides the moral distance from the racings of the past so that one can rest comfortably

in the belief that, although talking "honestly" now sounds suspiciously similar to the pre-civil rights justification for everything from sterilization to lynching, this race postreform discourse is different. Un-eracing is not old-style racing; it is merely putting certain commonsense observations and facts back into social discourse in the spirit of candor rather than prejudice.[11]

Because she has written so persuasively about the ways that the presumption of race blindness serves to undergird racial hierarchy, Crenshaw's warning is especially troubling.[12] Her reservations emphasize the dangers of bringing race, uncritically, back into public conversation. She shows how, in spite of the abolition of racial slavery and legal segregation, powerful assumptions about race and humanity remain unchallenged.

That these assumptions are so much a part of the fabric of everyday living makes this predicament a peculiarly democratic one. While racial injustices violate the promise of freedom and equality that is the birthright of all American citizens, these wrongs may be resistant to democratic remedy. This is not a new worry. It was, for example, the apprehension of Alexis de Tocqueville. Prophesying the impossibility of multiracial democracy, Tocqueville remarks, "It can happen that a man will rise above prejudices of religion, country, and race, and if that man is a king, he can bring about astonishing transformations in society; but it is not possible for a whole people to rise, as it were, above itself."[13] The acuity of Tocqueville's warning is borne out by the predicament of the post–civil rights era: the inadequacy of formal equality as an antidote to racial injustice. If the civil rights activism of mid-century redefined the boundaries of the imaginable, the limitations of the laws and court decisions impelled by that activism indicate the need to stretch those boundaries still further. Widespread acceptance of the *principle* of racial equality represents genuine progress. Yet resistance, particularly by white Americans, to mechanisms designed to implement the principle points to the limits of that progress. Despite tremendous gains, recent appeals for a national dialogue about race and the difficulty of engaging in such a dialogue signal the failure of the American people "to rise above . . . itself" simply by declaring race to be irrelevant to citizenship.

It is in such a context, I argue, that democratic theorists, and indeed anyone interested in the possibility of multiracial democracy, have much to learn from the writings of James Baldwin. Able to convey his experiences as a black citizen in a white-dominated society to readers of all races, Baldwin plumbs his own history for clues to the possibility of democracy in an environment where race figures so powerfully and, often, so silently. Relentlessly, he probes the exclusion of African Americans and struggles to create a language that will make the meanings of such exclusion real to a resistant populace. Although much of Baldwin's best writing was published in the postwar period, before the passage of the historic civil rights legislation of this century, he anticipates the limitations of such legislation. Understanding that Americans are capable of living with far more racial injustice than they are comfortable admitting, Baldwin identifies the underlying forces that have continued to deny African Americans the enjoyment of equal citizenship even after his death.

At bottom, Baldwin believes that the inclusion of African Americans as full members of American society requires a frank examination of residual, often unadmitted, traces of the assumption that blacks are somehow less than fully human. "We have all had the experience of finding that our reactions and perhaps even our deeds have denied beliefs we thought were ours," Baldwin observes. "And this is the danger of arriving at arbitrary decisions in order to avoid the risks of thought." Among the most vulnerable of those beliefs is "the arbitrary decision that Negroes are just like everybody else."[14] Refusing to mistake the spread of arbitrary beliefs for progress, Baldwin suggests an alternative approach, one that neither accepts the pretense of race blindness nor condones the kind of "un-eracing" described by Crenshaw.

Although Baldwin is an enemy of racism, and he made a substantial contribution to the undoing of overtly racist policies and institutions during his life, his greater triumph resides in his ability to identify and articulate the meanings of what I call race consciousness. As a descriptive term, race consciousness conveys the ways in which "whiteness" and "blackness" are noticed (or not noticed) in daily life.[15] Race consciousness describes the underlying complex of associations that shape Americans' sense of identity, influence everyday encounters, and frame responses to questions about racial injustice. Baldwin's unflinching evocation of the psychological, cultural, and moral dimensions of the color line reveals how "seeing by skin color"[16] fundamentally shapes Americans' outlook on the world.[17] Baldwin's exploration of race consciousness provides a way of capturing the mind-set of the women and men who inhabit a society in which, "without a racial identity, one is in danger of having no identity."[18] And it indicates why old attitudes cannot be, painlessly, superseded.

Listening for the unsaid that contradicts what has been spoken, Baldwin relies on his readers' awareness of a subterranean reality that exists "deeper than conscious knowledge or speech can go" and that, in some way, directs the course of their existence.[19] By retelling his own experiences, Baldwin conveys the both/and of race consciousness. He reveals the personal resonance of democratic ideals in a society in which "racism is both irrational and normal."[20] Defying racial orthodoxies, Baldwin holds that race is both meaningless, that is, a fiction, and meaningful, or real in its effects. Baldwin's approach is phenomenological, for it explores the ways in which racial divisions in the United States are lived and how racial injustices are felt. And it is hermeneutical, insofar as it accentuates the impossibility of escaping the bounds of context. At the same time, Baldwin is circumspect about the authority of the traditions and of the language within which he operates; his inquiry into the power of social meanings is oriented toward a future in which those meanings are transformed.[21]

By going to the level of assumptions and unacknowledged beliefs, the notion of race consciousness provides a way of casting a broad net and pulling in a wide range of conscious and unconscious associations between race and blackness, Americanness and whiteness. It enables Baldwin not only to criticize overt expressions of racism but also to describe phenomena that are untouched by the concept of racism as a consciously held creed or the idea of racial discrimination as a category of discrete, intentional acts. To say that Americans are race conscious in this sense does not necessarily entail a deliberate devaluation of black lives. But race consciousness coexists comfortably with such devaluation.[22] For it enables many Americans to sustain the idea that democratic ideals have been largely realized even as they know that not all citizens enjoy genuine free-

dom and equality—even as they know that these citizens are disproportionately black. Despite the widespread rejection of the beliefs
that upheld Jim Crow segregation, the ease with which the blame
for racial inequality is shifted to the shoulders of the disadvantaged
suggests the continuing force of the idea that blackness indicates deficiency.[23] The concept of race consciousness thus helps to articulate how racial injustices get taken for granted. But it also does more
than that.

As elaborated by Baldwin, race consciousness has not only a descriptive meaning but a normative meaning as well. If the persistence of a racially unjust status quo can be explained, in part, by the
silent workings of racial assumptions or beliefs, then opposing such
a status quo involves becoming conscious of those assumptions and
beliefs. Baldwin conveys the substance of race consciousness in this
second sense in a letter he wrote to Angela Davis in 1971, as she
awaited trial on charges of kidnapping, conspiracy, and murder:
"Some of us, white and Black, know how great a price has already
been paid to bring into existence a new consciousness, a new
people, an unprecedented nation. If we know, and do nothing, we
are worse than the murderers hired in our name."[24] Or, similarly, in
the closing passage of *The Fire Next Time*:

> If we—and now I mean the relatively conscious whites and the rel-
> atively conscious blacks, who must, like lovers, insist on, or cre-
> ate, the consciousness of the others—do not falter in our duty now,
> we may be able, handful that we are, to end the racial nightmare,
> and achieve our country, and change the history of the world.[25]

Consciousness, for Baldwin, is the active awareness and acceptance
of the ways that circumstances shape an individual's life and the attempt to make those circumstances articulate in order to bring
about change. Race consciousness in the normative sense thus entails the acknowledgment of race consciousness in the descriptive
sense. In this regard, Baldwin's conception of consciousness echoes
Antonio Gramsci's claim that transformation is only possible
through "'knowing thyself' as a product of the historical process to
date which has deposited in you an infinity of traces, without leaving an inventory."[26] Such a reckoning with history is a crucial first

step toward political change. And Baldwin, in describing his role as "a sort of an emotional or spiritual historian,"[27] implies that his own writing aims to plumb those traces for clues to an improved future. The kind of consciousness Baldwin advocates is morally and politically imperative as long as Americans' inability to talk honestly about race perpetuates racial injustice.

Two significant worries attend my use of the term "race consciousness." Amy Gutmann makes a strong case for substituting the term "color consciousness" for race consciousness, reasoning that the latter term perpetuates mistaken assumptions about the scientific basis of racial categories. While I share Gutmann's concern that "race is a fiction that often functions *sotto voce* as a scientific fact in the identification of individuals," I maintain that "race" is a fiction with a history too embedded in American experiences to be replaced by "color."[28] Baldwin would agree, emphatically, that biological conceptions of race—and the cultural notions of black deficiency that have superseded them—need to be thoroughly discredited.[29] But he would also argue that the survival of racial categories after their exposure as a fiction demands attention.

Another danger of defining race consciousness as I have is that it obscures the multiplicity of experiences compressed into the categories "white" and "black" and excludes those which it cannot subsume. The black-white line is not, by any means, the only racial division in the United States, and racial divisions are not the only cleavages. But insisting that American preoccupation with this line merits specific consideration is not to deny the power of gender, class, ethnicity, sexual orientation, and religion, or the ways that the multiple dimensions of identity intersect. Nor does it entail a hierarchy of suffering, obliterating or devaluing the experiences of other groups of Americans who have also been denied full enjoyment of the promise of equality and freedom. I argue instead that the ease with which Americans conflate race with blackness and Americanness with whiteness requires further investigation. Moreover, because the fates of African Americans have been so intimately linked to the definition of American citizenship from the time of racial slavery to the present, their experiences provide a crucial measure of the degree to which American democratic promises have been realized.[30]

In examining Baldwin's work, therefore, I neither offer an account of his historical significance as a public figure nor provide a new assessment of his literary achievements. Instead, I put to Baldwin the questions of a political theorist and read his answers as those of a moralist and social critic, a troublemaker with incredible rhetorical gifts and deep democratic commitments, recognizing all the while the pitfalls of confining Baldwin to a single label. My aim is to mine Baldwin's writings for an account of race consciousness in order to understand how degrading assumptions continue to prevent recognition and redress of black citizens' claims of injustice and to apprehend the political significance of those claims. To that end, I trace the development in Baldwin's writing of such issues as the kinship of racial hierarchy and American democracy, the importance of history to an understanding of present injustices, and the meaning of freedom and equality. And I argue that Baldwin's social criticism deserves careful attention for its insights into the dilemmas of the post–civil rights era. For Baldwin reminded his contemporaries and reminds his readers today that thinking about democratic politics involves investigating the silences and listening for the echoes that reveal the ongoing power of race in a society where white supremacy is supposed to have been permanently discredited and blackness is no longer an acceptable justification for dehumanizing treatment.

"I'm a witness . . . I write it all down."

James Arthur Baldwin was born in Harlem in 1924. The oldest of nine children living at home, Baldwin grew up in claustrophobic and desperately poor conditions. At war with his father, a laborer embittered by the struggle to keep his family alive and a minister who took "his conversion too literally" and viewed his son's intellectual ambitions as damned, Baldwin rebelled.[31] As a teenager, he rebelled by becoming a holy-roller preacher and outshining his father in the pulpit. Later he rebelled again by leaving the church altogether and moving to Greenwich Village with the determination to become a writer. Doubly alienated from the world of his growing up as an artist and a homosexual[32] and vulnerable to the deep injuries of race and class that followed him to the Village, Baldwin believed that he could neither work nor live in the United States. Hence, he followed the trail of Richard Wright and other black artists and fled to Paris in 1948. He spent the rest of his life, until his death in France in 1987, as a "commuter" to the United States.[33] Despite the flight, however, Baldwin never fully removed himself from American public life. Whether writing from Paris or Istanbul or Hollywood, he established himself as one of the most important intellectual forces of the civil rights era. And his insight extends beyond the specific struggles of the 1950s and 1960s. Anticipating the work that would remain undone after the achievement of access to the ballot and the end of legal segregation, Baldwin's writing endures as an acute inquiry into the character of American democracy.

Before turning to a more detailed examination of Baldwin's political thought, it is worth pausing briefly to say something about his career as a public figure and as a writer. Baldwin is rightly remembered as an energetic participant in the fight for black freedom. He took part in voter registration drives, went on speaking tours for the Congress of Racial Equality (CORE), the Student Nonviolent Coordinating Committee (SNCC), and other organizations, and made appearances with a wide range of black leaders that included Martin Luther King, Jr., Malcolm X, Angela Davis, and Huey Newton. Baldwin's political influence climaxed in 1963, when *The Fire Next Time* made best-seller lists, *Time* magazine featured him on its cover, and Attorney General Robert Kennedy sought his advice about black Americans' perspectives on American politics. But Baldwin's status suffered as the 1960s wore on. By the end of the decade, he was confronted by public assaults on his masculinity—and his blackness—by younger black nationalists and began to wonder if he that he had, in fact, been used as "the Great Black Hope of the Great White Father."[34]

To a significant extent, the decline of Baldwin's political fortunes simply reflected larger changes. It bears remembering that in this same period Martin Luther King, Jr., recognized the limitations of the Civil Rights Act of 1964 and the Voting Rights Act of 1965. Seeing that neither legislative triumph would mitigate entrenched poverty in the United States or address American militarism abroad, King was less sanguine about the possibility of realizing his dream.[35] Also at this time Malcolm X opened the door to collaboration with whites and SNCC split apart over a decision to exclude them. Moreover, the years after 1963 witnessed the killing of Malcolm and King and many others. Baldwin felt those deaths acutely, and he suffered, as did many partisans of racial justice, in the desultory decades that followed.

More fundamentally, Baldwin fell out of fashion politically because of his appreciation for the complexity of American racial dilemmas—an appreciation that had always made him an unlikely political figure. As Henry Louis Gates, Jr., recalls, "by the early '60s his authority seemed nearly unchallengeable. What did the Negro want? Ask James Baldwin." Yet, Gates adds, "the puzzle was that his arguments, richly nuanced and self-consciously ambivalent, were far too complex to serve straightforwardly political ends."[36] With equal vehemence, Baldwin rejected liberal calls for incremental change and militant demands for total opposition. And he found himself, as a result, alternately embraced and reviled by both whites and blacks, mistaken for an assimilationist and a racist. Refusing the choice between integration and separation as a false one, he showed that integration would amount to annihilation for black Americans until white Americans admitted the degree to which they too would have to change (hence the famous line attributed to Baldwin, "Do I really *want* to be integrated into a burning house?");[37] and, at the same time, he understood that separation required denial of the fact that the fates and futures of white and black Americans were already too intertwined to be uncoupled.

Not conforming easily to the role of a political leader, Baldwin made his signal contribution as an artist. "I want to be an honest man and a good writer," he announced at the outset of his career.[38] And, to that end, Baldwin wrote for almost his entire life. He published six novels, two plays, short stories, poetry, a children's book, a screenplay, and dozens of essays.[39] As the volume of critical literature devoted to his writing and the profusion of epigraphs bearing his name attests, Baldwin was extraordinarily successful. Although he saw himself as a novelist and hoped to become a great playwright, critics have generally held Baldwin to be a master of the essay and a good novelist of uneven achievement. While my focus is on the essays, I draw on Baldwin's fictional works for amplification of his ideas.

Much has been made of the impact of Baldwin's political activities on the quality of his writing. As Darryl Pinckney notes, "The darkening of the civil rights struggle coincided with a fall in Baldwin's overall critical fortunes."[40] But it would be a mistake to view Baldwin's career as an object lesson about the incompatibility of politics and art. That Baldwin wrote less prolifically in the years after 1963 is true. That the essays produced in those years lacked the acuity, the ambivalence, and the distance of Baldwin's earlier work is a more problematic claim. Indeed, what I find remarkable about the trajectory of Baldwin's essays across nearly forty years is their continuity. Without suggesting that Baldwin's life and writing are static or denying alterations in tone that diminish the rhetorical force of the later work, I emphasize elements of Baldwin's social critique that a reader can find in all phases of his career. I draw most extensively from Baldwin's earlier essays—for they are more completely realized than the pieces that follow *The Fire Next Time*—but I recognize moments of extraordinary power in the later essays as well. By focusing on continuity, I aim to discourage the impulse to read Baldwin's work as a before-and-after story that ignores, for example, Baldwin's stunning indictment of white Americans in one of his celebrated early essays: "The white man's world, intellectually, morally, and spiritually, has the meaningless ring of a hollow drum and the odor of slow death."[41] Likewise, I hope to challenge dismissive comparisons of an essay like *No Name in the Street* with Baldwin's more ambivalent, younger work by warning against readings that neglect the ambivalence in his concluding paragraph:

> To be an Afro-American, or an American black, is to be in the situation, intolerably exaggerated, of all those who have ever found themselves part of a civilization which they could in no wise honorably defend—which they were compelled, indeed, endlessly to attack and condemn—and who yet spoke out of the most passionate love, hoping to make the kingdom new, to make it honorable and worthy of life.[42]

My point is that Baldwin's essays are neither dated, stuck in a time that has passed, nor timeless. Rather, they perceive with enormous clarity the obstacles to multiracial democracy that bedeviled both his time and our own.

When asked to define his vocation, Baldwin calls himself a witness to the truth. He relates witnessing to artistic practice, explaining that the artist's job is to pierce the skin of society and uncover the turbulence disguised by the appearance of order on the surface. Taking explicit issue with Plato's strictures about the danger poets pose to the republic, Baldwin contends that the artist is an indispensable "disturber of the peace."[43] The artist bears witness to the precariousness of human lives and endeavors and the consequent necessity of embracing responsibility in the face of uncertainty and change. Baldwin's witnessing thus involves the investigation of the underlying forces that have sustained the color line. He uncovers the fears and the interests that promote the idea that racial identity provides a clue to a person's character. Such reliance on racial markers, he warns, assures Americans of the health of the polity by making racial injustice appear inevitable or natural. Consequently, Baldwin uses his rhetorical gifts to give public voice to stories—especially stories about the lives of black Americans—that belie the myths of American democracy.

To identify Baldwin as a witness to the suffering of black Americans is not to conclude that there is a single black experience or that Baldwin speaks for all African Americans. Indeed, Baldwin disavows the impulse to make him a spokesman. Accounting for what he sees as the limitations of Richard Wright's *Native Son*, Baldwin contends that Wright was handicapped by "the necessity thrust on him of being the representative of some thirteen million people." He reasons that "it is a false responsibility (since writers are not congressmen) and impossible, by its nature, of fulfillment. The unlucky shepherd soon finds that, so far from being able to feed the hungry sheep, he has lost the wherewithal for his own nourishment: having not been allowed . . . to recreate his own experience."[44] Baldwin's witnessing thus asserts no authority beyond that of his own life. "A spokesman assumes that he is speaking for others. I never assumed that I could," Baldwin explains. "What I tried to do, or to interpret and make clear was that what the republic was doing to black people it was doing to itself."[45] And the only materials Baldwin has to prove his case, he avers, are the details of his own experience. Witnessing entails "go[ing] through extraordinary excavations with your own shovel and your own guts."[46] Autobiography, by this account, becomes a critical, political act.

It is Baldwin's appreciation of his own singularity, no more singular than any other individual's but irreducible still, that enables Baldwin to call himself a witness. His background (urban, northern, and poor), his social position (male, gay, unmarried, black), and his language (moralizing and poetic) bespeak *a* black American experience. Baldwin at his most eloquent fights white Americans' embrace of him as *the* eloquent black man. This is not an appeal to idiosyncracy and it generally does not result in an indulgent form of self-exposure. Rather, Baldwin's perception of the singularity of all human experiences, in concert with an extraordinary capacity for description, enables him to link the unnoticed dimensions of the ordinary to the ambitious reach of the ideal and to demonstrate how, on the American terrain, race permeates both.

Allusive, vivid, complex, and, most crucially, aware of their own incompleteness, Baldwin's essays sustain the tension between general claims about the meanings of African American experiences and the singularity of individual experience. Baldwin thereby uses his life to convey what Theodor Adorno identifies as the fragmentary or the contingent character of all human lives:

> The relationship to experience—and the essay invests experience with as much substance as traditional theory does mere categories—is the relationship to all of history. Merely individual experience, which consciousness takes as its point of departure, since it is what is closest to it, is itself mediated by the overarching experience of historical humankind. . . . The essay . . . does not try to seek the eternal in the transient and distill it out; it tries to render the transient eternal. Its weakness bears witness to the very nonidentity it had to express.[47]

This appreciation of contingency and sensitivity to the particular is connected to profound moral commitments. Baldwin's power as a social critic resides in his capacity to use that description in such a way that the moments that are his subject are at once fleeting instances of his own experience and universally human. Despite his humanist longings, however, Baldwin refuses to ignore the countervailing evidence of the particular, which constantly undermines the claims of the universal.

That having been said, the aspiration to "render the transient eternal" by giving it form in social-critical writing is a treacherous one. Foremost among the dangers of making broader claims about the meaning of any individual experience of suffering or oppression is that of believing that this experience exceeds all others in depth or intensity. This is particularly so when that experience has been denied a public voice. Once having gotten the attention of a wide readership, Baldwin sometimes falls prey to such a temptation: either he loses sight of the plight of other oppressed Americans, or despite his rejection of the violent reduction of African Americans, male and female, old and young, into some category called "the Negro," his writing implies that what is most condemnable about such reductionism is what it takes from black men.[48] Although such inferences reinforce what Stuart Hall calls "the innocent notion of the essential Black subject," the sum of Baldwin's writing undermines the idea that such a subject exists.[49]

Conversely, Baldwin's best writing also refuses to reduce white women and men to a single, homogeneous group. The tension inherent in this undertaking is clear from the way that Baldwin takes "Americans" to task. His primary target, clearly, is those who profit from racial hierarchy and have the most to lose from admitting its existence. So "Americans" means, first and foremost, white Americans. And Baldwin is rightly regarded today as a pioneer in the investigation of whiteness, a forerunner of contemporary critiques of white supremacy.[50] Yet he also maintains that not all white Americans are deaf to claims of racial injustice, and not all black Americans can hear. Furthermore, he rejects attributions of racial guilt as fruitless. By making *Americans* his target, Baldwin attempts to undermine white supremacy without denying the humanity of either white or black people. What Baldwin conveys, in other words, is the significance of racial injustice "in all its endless variety and monotonous similarity."[51]

Eschewing dreams of transcendence, Baldwin aims to dissect and to expose the social anguish of his time.[52] "Penetrating," a recurring word in the book reviews that Baldwin wrote early in his career, connotes insight and intimates violence and pain. It also describes the kind of operation required to overcome a tradition of denial. By penetrating his own and his fellow citizens' attachments, anxieties, and fears, Baldwin discredits the idea that racial injustice grows out of a kind of backwardness that needs only to be exposed to right thinking in order to be overcome. He offers instead a moral psychology of the color line, an unflinching portrait of the men and women, white and black, whose lives are circumscribed by that line. And he looks to his own history and the larger story of the United States as a critical tool, "since it is to history that we owe our frames of reference, our identities, and our aspirations."[53]

His is a vocation animated by principle and frustrated by practice. Convinced that the persistence of the color line cannot simply be eliminated by its exposure as a violation of democratic principles, Baldwin's essays inhabit the space between principle and practice. Thus when, as a young writer, Baldwin allows that "the finest principles may have to be modified, or may even be pulverized by the demands of life," he is not advocating the abandonment of principles at all.[54] Instead, he shifts attention away from the principles themselves to their significance in the context of his life. The dual conviction that principles cannot be conceived or elaborated apart from human experiences and that those experiences repeatedly undermine the possibility that the principles will be realized lends an indispensable ambivalence to Baldwin's writing. The ferocity of his moralizing stems from an acute awareness of the distance between principles and practice, and yet his appreciation of human finitude makes him suspicious of the meanings of the principles themselves. Responsibility, being fully human, follows from the recognition of that limitation. Further, it points to what he would see as the greatest obstacle to thinking beyond race consciousness:

> It is exceedingly difficult for most of us to discard the assumptions of the society in which we were born, in which we live, to which we owe our identities; very difficult to defeat the trap of circumstance, which is, also, the web of safety; *virtually impossible, if not completely impossible, to envision the future, except in those terms which we think we already know.*[55]

When the inherited terms are political or moral and the setting in which they are elaborated is a racially hierarchical one, he argues, the project of articulating their meanings must balance an interest in their achievement with a suspicion of the ways in "which we think we already know" them. Baldwin's job as a social critic is to show

how the meanings of those inherited terms are deliberately unknown and to call attention to the experiences that are excluded from consideration when the content of the terms is taken for granted.

One term to which Baldwin dedicates a great deal of his energy is "democracy." Although he does not offer a concise definition, Baldwin fashions one indirectly. His narrative recreation of his own and others' American experiences intimates that, beyond guarantees of formal equality and the rights of citizens embodied in the Constitution and the civil rights legislation of the nineteenth and twentieth centuries, democracy requires the provision of the basic conditions of individual flourishing. And individual flourishing precludes substantial disparities in power and resources. Like Tocqueville, Baldwin understands that institutions alone are not definitive, that mores, traditions, "habits of the heart" shape the polity in critical ways. Like Tocqueville, he also warns against mistaking conformity for equality and giving up too easily the possibility of freedom. Baldwin goes beyond Tocqueville, however, in putting injustice at the center of the story he tells.[56] Considering democracy in America through the lens of black experiences, Baldwin demonstrates how far the United States is from the point at which each citizen can reasonably anticipate an opportunity to fulfill her or his own possibility. A genuinely democratic society, he avers, is one in which no citizen can be said to be free until every citizen is.

Over and over, Baldwin reminds his readers that participating in a democracy requires staking one's life on the good faith of others. For members of a society who know its underside all too well, he points out how appeals to principle mean nothing without explicit attention to the principle's relation to practice. Among Baldwin's great accomplishments is his capacity to give voice to the sense of justified distrust experienced by the more vulnerable members of society and to unsettle the assumptions that protect the less vulnerable from assessing honestly the accomplishments of American democracy.[57] Not noticing how much trust—in the good will of one's neighbors, in the efficacy of political participation, in the fairness of the justice system—serves as an underpinning of democratic conviction is a privilege of inclusion. Like racial privilege and other forms of inherited power, it is often invisible to those who enjoy it. As Annette Baier notes, "We inhabit a climate of trust as we inhabit an atmosphere and notice it as we notice air, only when it becomes scarce or polluted."[58] Putting his own experience of public dishonor and the alienation it engenders to the service of social change, Baldwin makes "watchful distrust" a democratic virtue.[59]

By reading his experiences as those of all African Americans, of all Americans, of all human beings, Baldwin offers African Americans' American history as a basis for assessing the demands of democracy. His account of African Americans' ambivalent relationship to the promises of American democracy reverberates in Patricia Williams's reflection on the meaning of "rights": "To say that blacks never fully believed in rights is true. Yet it is also true that blacks believed in them so much and so hard that we gave them life where there was none before; we held onto them, put the hope of them into our wombs, mothered them and not the notion of them."[60] Baldwin rarely speaks of rights, yet one might substitute the word "democracy" for "rights" and have a truly Baldwinian statement. Williams's words are particularly apt, for she sees the distance between rights as a concept and as a tangible, spiritual, emotional reality, and she uses language to bring the two sides into relation. In rendering that relationship as one of mothering, moreover, Williams shares Baldwin's preoccupation with the fate of the children—all children—who are endangered by the denial of the humanity of some. The purpose of such a comparison is not to suggest that Williams deliberately follows Baldwin's example or that the power of her writing should be judged by its affinity with Baldwin's. Instead, I mention this point of similarity to show how poetic economy can give voice to the most complex relationships between principle and practice. And I argue that democratic theorists—and all democratic citizens—need to attend to the witness of those citizens who have confronted the untrustworthiness of democratic ideals and who know that those ideals can only be realized through the active effort to make them worthy of trust.

James Baldwin's Democracy

If the conceptual tools that inspired and supported the fight against racial slavery and legal segregation are indeed inadequate antidotes to persistent racial injustice, what new or newly interpreted tools are available? And how does Baldwin assist in the effort to imagine alternative discourses of politics? My answer to these questions proceeds at two levels: I contend that Baldwin's essays enhance the capacity of political theories to rise to the challenges of race consciousness by inhabiting and illuminating the spaces between democratic ideals and American practices; and I argue that Baldwin, by simultaneously exposing race as a dangerous illusion and as a feature of American life too central to be eliminated by fiat, contributes to an emancipatory politics as well.[61]

Despite Baldwin's declaration that "all theories are suspect," his essays speak directly to the concerns of political theory.[62] The power of political theory resides in its capacity to serve as a bridge between philosophical principles and historical practices while providing a critical perspective on both. Theoretical consideration of the persistence of the color line is thus crucial to moving beyond the assertion that American citizens are by definition free and equal to the investigation of why, in fact, they are not. Although political theories take many forms, many of which contain vital resources for understanding the connections between racial injustice and democracy in America, a concentration of intellectual energies on elaborating political principles has muted the voices that speak to their violation. For political theorists, particularly those concerned with the conditions of democracy, who aspire to answer Judith Shklar's call to "give injustice its due," Baldwin's essays provide invaluable guidance.[63] They do so by reorienting the focus from the level of principle to the murky region between principle and practice.

Baldwin's ability to discern the resonances of political principles in everyday life illuminates the meanings of the principles and evokes what Stuart Hampshire calls "the tension of unrealised possibilities."[64] Directing his readers' attention to lived experiences Baldwin refutes claims to race-blind individualism without taking up the banner of an identity politics that itself forces the heterogeneity of individual experiences into narrow categories. He exposes the power and the ambiguity of racial identity, thereby promising to breathe life into often sterile debates about individual rights and the import of group membership. And he shows that taking stock of the specificity of African American experiences—not merely as an aspect of "difference" or an ascriptive category like any other, but as a basis by which the achievements of American democracy should be judged—is essential to the examination of racial injustice.

The simple-minded premise underlying this argument is that political theorists, no less than other human beings, are shaped by history and tradition. The kinds of deafness that stymie public debates about racial injustice can also inhibit theoretical inquiry. Baldwin shows how the presumption that political theoretical reflection can transcend race consciousness, "the prejudice against prejudice itself,"[65] disables theorists from differentiating between prejudices worthy of celebration and those that deserve rejection. And it stifles the imagination in ways that prevent contemporary theorists from addressing the limitations of formal equality as a means of redress for racial injustice. "We take our shape . . . within and against that cage of reality bequeathed us at our birth," Baldwin advises his readers, "and yet it is precisely through our dependence on this reality that we are most endlessly betrayed."[66] Baldwin discerns the degree to which Americans rely on racial markers as guideposts in their efforts to locate themselves and make sense of a volatile world. Race serves as a kind of crutch, according to Baldwin, propping up a sense of confidence in American democratic achievements. Such confidence is particularly misplaced at a time when the need for new accounts of multiracial democracy—accounts that take seriously the degree to which American experiences are shaped by reliance on racial markers—presents an opportunity for democratic theory to demonstrate its relevance to political life.

One way to understand Baldwin's contribution to democratic theory and practice is to view his work as witness as a form of situated social criticism. Situated social critics, according to Michael Walzer, are those members of society who expose "the false civility, the polite conventions, that hide the injuries of class or race or gender and that turn values into ideologies."[67] There are limitations to the comparison, for Walzer's conception of social criticism is itself susceptible to the charge of hiding or overlooking injuries of race.[68] Yet the extent of agreement between Walzer and Baldwin is evident in both Baldwin's practice and his reflections on his responsibilities as a witness. Demanding the realization of American democratic promises, Baldwin invokes the shared values of freedom and equality when he takes his fellow citizens to task. And in his ruminations on the responsibilities of the writer, Baldwin makes the sort of connections between embeddedness, moral commitment, and opposition that animate Walzer's accounts of social criticism. Baldwin notes that

> even the most incorrigible maverick has to be born somewhere. He may leave the group that produced him—he may be forced to—but nothing will efface his origins, the marks of which he carries with him everywhere. I think it is important to know this and even to find it a matter for rejoicing, as the strongest people do, regardless of their station. On this acceptance, literally, the life of a writer depends.[69]

Acceptance, as Baldwin uses it, is a heavy word.[70] It captures both his sense of human limitations and his insistence that they not engender despair. For the writer, acceptance involves seeing and reminding others of the gulf between "the myth of America"[71] and how Americans actually live. Like Walzer's critics, Baldwin's artist or writer "must never cease warring with [his society], for its sake and for his own."[72] Like Walzer, Baldwin sees this warring as a necessary outgrowth of love.

Although the tasks of criticism and those of theorizing are different, Walzer's account of their interrelation sheds light on the ways Baldwin's essays can enrich theoretical inquiry. Walzer explains that the work of social critics can both inform and be informed by philosophical disputes about the substance of moral or political principles. Because the principles are not immediately knowable, the work proceeds through interpretation. In both cases, the grounds of the analysis are provided by the society from which the theorist or critic comes.[73] But this is not to say that the meaning of the principles is unvarying, uncontested. Indeed, Baldwin's relentless inquiry into the causes and effects of racial injustice suggests that interpretation is always linked to struggle.[74]

If Baldwin's essays are always political, however, they are not always obviously so. Even those pieces that do provide straightforward political commentary may interweave assessments of the Algerian war for independence, the assassinations of Malcolm X and Martin Luther King, Jr., and the Omnibus Crime Control and Safe Streets Act with childhood memories of his mother holding a piece of velvet.[75] Furthermore, Baldwin's fluency in the theological language of sin and love, mystery and communion, suggest that his essays inhabit a purely private world. Preoccupied with personal transformation, Baldwin constructs no theory of the just society. Worse still, he has relatively little to say about specific political institutions and offers no systematic analysis of the economic injustices he describes so vividly. As Harold Cruse notes, Baldwin even publicly asserts that his interest lies elsewhere, far from "all this sociology and economics jazz."[76] But no reader of Baldwin's essays ought to miss the deliberate linkages of race and class in Baldwin's writing. While he frequently writes from the vantage point of individual experience, the experiences whereof he speaks are clearly shaped by systemic forms of inequality. When he describes the isolation of women and men confined to urban ghettoes in the language of damnation, for example, he is also speaking eloquently to the public consequences of unequal distributions of power and wealth.

For this reason, I reject as unhelpful attempts to draw lines between Baldwin's "political" essays (especially where "political" is meant to be derogatory) and his nonpolitical works, or claims that "his voice broke" when he got drawn into the civil rights struggle.[77] Rather, I draw from the entirety of Baldwin's corpus, and I focus most of my analysis on Baldwin's early essays, for there one perceives most clearly the radicalism of his project. By radicalism, I do not mean allegiance with any particular political platform. Instead, I use the term as it is articulated by civil rights activist Ella Baker: "We are going to have to learn to think in *radical* terms. I use the term radical in its original meaning: *getting down to and understanding the root cause.* It means facing a system that does not lend itself to your needs and devising means by which you change that system."[78]

The means that Baldwin devises are literary. His facility with language, his acuity in articulating the interrelation between matters generally considered private or personal and larger systems of power explodes restricted conceptions of politics. The experiences he relates are too multilayered and his analysis too ambivalent to be reduced to a single political agenda. Yet Baldwin's accent on the moral crystallizes something of the deeper significance of events and conditions that are always also political and material. When, for example, Baldwin considers the meaning of freedom, he allows that "it can be objected that I am speaking of political freedom in spiritual terms." "But," he avers, "the political institutions of any nation are always menaced and are ultimately controlled by the spiritual state of that nation."[79] What emerges from this jumble of observations is a strong, if not always clearly defined, sense of the interrelation of race and politics and morality, of current events and "the spiritual state" of the nation.

Consideration of one of Baldwin's least overtly political essays, "Stranger in the Village," attests to his significance as a democratic thinker. Written for *Harper's* magazine in 1953, the essay relates Baldwin's sense of radical dislocation in the "white wilderness" of alpine Switzerland, where he went to write in the early 1950s. "From all available evidence," Baldwin begins, "no black man had ever set foot in this tiny Swiss village before I came."[80] Not only is he a black man in a place where the villagers proudly report to him the number of Africans whose souls have been "bought" through their donations at church, but he is also a writer in a town where the only typewriter is his own. If "Stranger in the Village" dwells on personal details, however, it is not content to remain there; if it presents itself as a chronicle of life in Europe, the essay quickly disrupts the comfort of its American readers. "Stranger in the Village" is a meditation on American democracy and a condemnation of white supremacy. In it, Baldwin rings changes on the themes that preoccupy him throughout his career and that mark him as a distinctively democratic writer. He displays a passionate individualism, a belief in the value of every human life that is linked to a deep sense of the harms of exclusion and powerlessness; he offers an account of how individuals are formed by their history and how American history has given rise to twin dangers of rage and innocence, twin threats to the health of the polity; and, finally, he makes a plea for the kind of transformation necessary for the realization of democratic possibility in the United States.

Because Baldwin is so aware of his own status, not only in

Switzerland but also in Harlem and Paris and elsewhere, as an odd-
ity, his celebration of individuality often takes a negative form. His
praise of human singularity is linked to an account of the painful-
ness of exclusion and to the denial of humanity that is at its root.
Hence, in "Stranger in the Village," Baldwin presages the titles of
his later books, *Nobody Knows My Name* and *No Name in the
Street*, remarking: "Everyone in the village knows my name, though
they scarcely ever use it" ("Stranger," 161). In lieu of elaborate arguments for individual recognition or respect, he provides a phenomenology of exclusion, a phenomenology, moreover, of the experience
of excluding as well as that of being excluded. He shows how
anonymity harms and how the enforcement of others' anonymity
reassures. The essay is both funny and angry as it recounts how the
villagers greet Baldwin as "a living wonder" without any sense that
he might be a human being like themselves. While their desire to
touch his hair and their speculations about his smile or about
whether his skin color could rub off on them are not meant to hurt,
they deny Baldwin status as a person: "No one, after all, can be liked
whose human weight and complexity cannot be, or has not been,
admitted" (161).[81] A slight sentence, much shorter than so many
Baldwin writes, and buried in the center of a paragraph, this statement captures the basic ontological imbalance that is fundamental
to white supremacy. As Baldwin goes on to say, "What is crucial
here is that, since white men represent in the black man's world so
heavy a weight, white men have for black men a reality which is far
from being reciprocal" (166).[82]

The reaction of the villagers to this black stranger is importantly
unlike American racism. Still, Baldwin's recollections of his experiences in Switzerland provide the occasion for reflection on the ways
in which his individuality is deliberately denied in the United
States. The children of the village who greet him with cries of
"Neger! Neger!" ("Stranger," 161) obviously do not grasp how the
words resonate for Baldwin. Knowing too well the sting of their English equivalent, however, he uses the experience to introduce a discussion of the availability of the word *"Nigger!"* in the United
States and a diagnosis of what that availability reveals about the
state of American democracy. Not only does the word deny him
recognition as a human being and a citizen, he contends, it suggests

the effect that the denial of his individuality has had on American society as a whole. It is an indicator of "the war [his] presence has occasioned in the American soul" (168).

Baldwin's celebration of the individual and his understanding of the impact of exclusion and powerlessness on an individual's sense of identity are connected to an unsentimental appraisal of the human weaknesses that make democracy such a risky undertaking. Chief among the weaknesses he detects is a desire to exclude. When, for example, Baldwin describes the other visitors to the village—invalids who come for the curing qualities of the waters and create in the village the atmosphere of "a lesser Lourdes"—he notes how even the most decrepit among them is capable of reminding him of his status as an outsider, a freak:

> There is often something beautiful, there is always something awful, in the spectacle of a person who has lost one of his faculties, a faculty he never questioned until it was gone, and who struggles to recover it. Yet people remain people, on crutches or indeed on deathbeds; and wherever I passed, the first summer I was here, among the native villagers or among the lame, a wind passed with me—of astonishment, curiosity, amusement, and outrage. ("Stranger," 160–61)

Notable in this passage is Baldwin's articulation of the idea of human equality. All human beings, according to Baldwin, are both beautiful and vulnerable; and they are vulnerable not only to illness and death but also to assumptions of superiority. Such equality, Baldwin intimates, is especially terrifying for white people, whose status in the world has gone unquestioned for generations. This dimension of Baldwin's writing enables him to discern and describe the forces undergirding American exclusions and to offer an account of why declarations of formal equality are inadequate to eliminate everyday racial injustices in the American context. Also worth noting in this passage is Baldwin's unwillingness to demonize people who thoughtlessly cause him great pain. Baldwin's appreciation of his own weakness secures him from entertaining fantasies of revenge and supports his refusal of separatist solutions.

Baldwin's individualism is not abstract. Indeed, it is unintelligible apart from an acknowledgment of the historical circumstances from

which each individual develops. Citing James Joyce, Baldwin proclaims that history is "a nightmare" ("Stranger," 162–63), and he rejects as illusory attempts to define individual identity apart from
those circumstances. Chief among the circumstances he identifies
as constituting the foundation of American identities is the legacy
of racial slavery and Americans' troubled relationship to a past they
cannot admit. It is the nature of American slavery, he maintains,
that accounts for the centrality of the question of black humanity
for Americans ever since. The effect of this anxiety is not purely internal. Baldwin notes that the troubled constitution of American
identities, black and white, engendered the bloody sequence of
"lynch law and law, segregation and legal acceptance, terrorization
and concession" (173) that defines American racial history.

"Stranger in the Village" identifies two responses to this history,
two themes that recur throughout Baldwin's essays. One response is
what Baldwin calls "the rage of the disesteemed." The essay thus
gives voice to the justified anger engendered by the experience of ha-
bitual disrespect. And it illustrates how such rage hobbles some citizens, thereby preventing interracial understanding and warping society as a whole. No matter how deeply felt, this rage must be
dissembled if the "disesteemed" hope to survive. Baldwin's comment that such rage "is one of the things that makes history" indicates the nuance of his thinking. Neither does he accept the idea
that the oppressed are completely powerless victims. Nor is he lured
by the romance of a revolution in which the oppressed simply turn
the tables on their oppressors ("Stranger," 165). The relationship between "the disesteemed" and those who humiliate them is, as Baldwin presents it, always more complicated.

Far more devastating for the prospects of democracy is the second
response to American racial history: innocence. By innocence Baldwin means a willful ignorance, a resistance to facing the horrors of
the American past and present and their implications for the future.
This unwillingness to confront those horrors accounts for the resistance of racial injustices to remedy by formal, legal measures. For
innocence sustains a mind-set that can accommodate *both* an
earnest commitment to the principles of equal rights and freedom
regardless of race *and* a tacit acceptance of racial division and inequality as normal. "Stranger in the Village" provides an account of

the effort required to enable white Americans, in particular, to sustain the kind of double-think that justifies a racially unjust status quo. "There is," Baldwin asserts, "a great deal of will power involved in the white man's naïveté ("Stranger," 166). According to Baldwin, the product of that will power is the lumping together of African Americans into an undifferentiated mass represented as "the Negro." But such efforts are never sufficient to eliminate the anxieties engendered by the unspoken awareness that racial injustice is commonplace and that its victims are human beings with feelings and aspirations of their own. Thus he writes that "Americans attempt until today to make an abstraction of the Negro, but the very nature of these abstractions reveals the tremendous effects the presence of the Negro has had on the American character" (170–71).

"Stranger in the Village" extends the critique of racial innocence, showing how the refusal to acknowledge injustices regularly done to African Americans fosters a skewed sense of right and wrong more generally. Baldwin argues that, although Americans consider themselves to be free of European aristocratic traditions, they also project onto Europe an Edenic past in which blacks did not exist.[83] One result of this longing is a redoubled desire to divide the world into good and evil and to banish any evidence that Americans are anything but good. Using the first-person plural that implicates himself in the critique, Baldwin writes:

> The American vision of the world—which allows so little reality, generally speaking, for any of the darker forces in human life, which tends . . . to paint moral issues in glaring black and white— owes a great deal to the battle waged by Americans to maintain between themselves and black men a human separation which could not be bridged. It is only now beginning to be borne in on us . . . that this vision of the world is dangerously inaccurate, and perfectly useless. For it protects our moral high-mindedness at the terrible expense of weakening our grasp of reality. People who shut their eyes to reality simply invite their own destruction, and anyone who remains in a state of innocence long after that innocence is dead turns himself into a monster. ("Stranger," 174–75)

Baldwin thus investigates the monstrosity or moral sickness that overtakes society as a whole when the humanity of some of its members is denied. And he warns that the cure will be painful, for "the establishment of democracy on the American continent was scarcely as radical a break with the past as was the necessity, which Americans faced, of broadening this concept to include black men" (171). The lesson Baldwin derives from his reflections is that sustaining the dream of democracy entails appreciation of the fact that it has never been attempted, much less realized, in this country.

Still, Baldwin is a democratic believer. Although he shares Tocqueville's worry about the susceptibility of democracies to the worst prejudices of their members, Baldwin nonetheless shares his fellow citizens' hope that "when life has done its worst they will be enabled to rise above themselves and to triumph over life" ("Stranger," 171). And he believes that the inclusion of African Americans as full citizens, in fact and not only in the law, is central to the possibility of that triumph. The black American "is not a visitor to the West," Baldwin reminds his readers, "but a citizen there, an American; as American as are the Americans who despise him, the Americans who fear him, the Americans who love him—*the Americans who became less than themselves, or rose to be greater than themselves by virtue of the fact that the challenge he represented was inescapable*" (173).[84] Without making the exclusion of African Americans a model to which all other American exclusions are reducible or advancing the claim that African Americans exceed all others in the suffering they have endured at the hands of their fellow citizens, Baldwin offers black experiences as a test of the accomplishments of the American democratic experiment.

Thus, he concludes "Stranger in the Village," as he concludes so many of his essays, on a note of hope tinged with portent. The hope resides in the idea that the race "problem" presents an opportunity for Americans to plumb their own lives to understand what is at stake in the perpetuation of racial divisions; the portent stems from his conviction that the status quo is bound to change whether or not Americans are ready for it. What remains to be seen, he cautions, is what kind of change that will be. Baldwin insists that it is up to all Americans to fight for a more democratic way of life, finishing the essay with a statement that expresses simultaneously the facts as he sees them, his highest aspirations, and a dire warning about the folly of racial innocence: "This world is white no longer, and it will never be white again" ("Stranger," 175).

"A New Consciousness"

If Baldwin is right, then the primary significance of race is not that it is the deepest or most painful fault line in American lives but that "it is a symptom of all the problems in this country."[85] Lani Guinier's suggestion that race functions in American society much like a canary in a coal mine helpfully illustrates Baldwin's point: when the canary ails it signals that the air in the mine is unsafe; when African Americans live shorter lives, in poorer neighborhoods, with less access to economic or political power than white Americans, it indicates the unhealth of the polity.[86] Baldwin would agree with Guinier that Americans have too frequently responded by finding fault with the canary, seeking ways to fix the bird rather than clear the mine of its toxic atmosphere. And his essays probe further. They demand a direct confrontation with the complex of fears and interests that prevent Americans from admitting that the mine is poisoned.

Baldwin's appreciation of the habits of the heart that have allowed racial injustices to thrive even after legal barriers to equality have been destroyed has yet to be adequately recognized. The chapters that follow constitute a first step toward that recognition, an examination of Baldwin's contribution to democratic theory and practice. What joins the chapters is an interest in the ways race consciousness tests the limits of fundamental political or moral principles. Animating this interest is an intuition that matters of race are suppressed precisely where the commitment to those principles is called into question by the countervailing evidence of practice.

In the second chapter, I consider Baldwin's contribution to recent debates about democracy and difference. Baldwin's essays, I argue, expose flaws in presumptions of race blindness, on the one hand, and attempts to define an authoritative racial identity, on the other. Not content simply to reject the former as naive and the latter as divisive, Baldwin provides a probing account of why those claims are so powerful. One way to understand how Baldwin negotiates a path between the two alternatives is to consider race consciousness as a kind of double consciousness. Although he never uses the term made famous by W. E. B. Du Bois in *The Souls of Black Folk*, Baldwin goes beyond Du Bois in showing double consciousness to be an apt metaphor not only for black experience but also for American experience more broadly. He explores the kinds of twoness that are engendered in both white and black imaginations as a result of living with the color line. Written from the perspective of a racially ambiguous *we*, Baldwin's essay "Many Thousands Gone" intimates how the constitution of an "American" identity has been connected to the degradation of black Americans. Baldwin asks how the American "we" is constituted and how far "we" have really traveled from "our forebears, whose assumption it was that the black man, to become truly human and acceptable, must first become like us."[87] Furthermore, because *race* consciousness does not exhaust the meanings of double consciousness, this chapter also investigates other doublenesses in Baldwin's essays. In particular, I examine Baldwin's treatment of the interrelation of racial and sexual identity. And I conclude that the subtlety of Baldwin's exploration and refutation of the attempt to reduce identity to positive and negative poles exposes the limitations, as a way of realizing democratic ideals, of "the politics of recognition."

The third chapter probes the racial images that sustain American double consciousness and hinder the recognition of African Americans as individuals and as citizens. Baldwin's deft exposure of the ways racial images render black Americans generally visible and individually invisible shows how these images perpetuate the sense that African Americans are somehow different from "normal" citizens. Because disputes about the dangers of emphasizing victimization in making claims of injustice—racial and otherwise—have become so central in contemporary public discourse, this chapter focuses on Baldwin's rejection of the image of black Americans as victims. Here I read Baldwin against the grain. In contrast to critics who argue that Baldwin's career was dedicated to reinforcing the idea of black victimhood, I argue that the subtle stories rendered in the essay "Notes of a Native Son" demonstrate how Baldwin manages to decry victimization without either reducing the victims to their oppression or allowing their experiences to be eclipsed by systemic injustices. "Notes of a Native Son" not only demonstrates the humanity of the individuals whose lives are obscured by racial images but also raises questions about what the images reveal about the society that refuses to relinquish them. Baldwin's narratives convey beautifully what Judith Shklar calls the "sense of injustice." That is, they call attention to the experience of injustice and demand that any claim to democratic achievement be evaluated in light of that experience. Baldwin thereby reveals the urgency and the difficulty of apprehending the political import of black suffering: he exposes the fragility of the line between personal or private hurts and matters of public concern. And, in doing so, he provides a powerful response to Shklar's appeal to take injustice seriously.

How do racial images survive after overt racism has been publicly discredited? The fourth chapter provides one answer by looking more closely at Baldwin's critique of American innocence. Innocence, according to Baldwin, is a kind of deliberate blindness or deafness, a refusal to acknowledge uncomfortable truths. What makes Baldwin's critique so powerful is that it simultaneously alerts his readers to the connections between innocence and white privilege and refutes simplistic attributions of guilt to white people. Instead, he exposes the damage done by anyone who refuses to abandon the dream that race can be painlessly transcended—what he calls the "dream of all liberal men"—and suggests how the temptation to assert racial innocence hobbles both democratic practice and democratic theory in the American context. Contrasting Baldwin's social-critical essays with Michael Walzer's account of the practice of social criticism, this chapter explores how a theorist whose work equips him to grapple with issues of racial injustice nonetheless evades these issues. Baldwin's example, I argue, supports Walzer's claims about the importance of social criticism to political theory. But it also cautions that the work of social criticism is no guarantee of immunity to racial innocence. Hence, Baldwin demands that the critique of American democracy be more thoroughly situated in the experiences of citizens whose membership has historically been marginal or incomplete. The implication of Baldwin's critique of innocence is that theorists, no less than other citizens, need to become more actively race conscious and to accept the uncertainties that such a stance entails.

Returning to the questions raised about the possibility of "a broad, public conversation about issues of racial justice," the fifth chapter focuses on problems of language. It reads Baldwin's essays as a guide to the delicate work of making space for the stories that have been left out of public discourse without doing violence to the stories themselves. Baldwin's feelings about the English language he commands so remarkably are ambivalent, yet his essays represent an attempt to create an English language that will give voice to a history that has largely been denied. He redeploys the words of his inheritance to lay bare their meanings in the lives of the people who use them—and, in so doing, suggests that democratic principles cannot be substantially known until they have been considered from the perspective of individuals who have been largely excluded from their enjoyment. By following Baldwin's elaboration on equality and freedom in *The Fire Next Time*, this chapter essays to convey how these most familiar of democratic ideas are experienced by Americans who have no reason to take their meaning for granted.

The afterword extends the discussion of the preceding chapters, asking what they imply about democratic possibility in the post–civil rights era. What is the practical import of essays that speak so magnificently about "America" and the effects of the color line in an era marked by accelerating globalization and the multiplication of racial distinctions? If attempts to transcend race are simply exercises in racial innocence, then what is to be done? Despite his abiding distrust of programmatic solutions, I maintain that Baldwin's call to consciousness provides a powerful model for contemporary critics of white supremacy. Old-fashioned though his moralism may appear, and responsive to the particular political needs of another era though it may be, Baldwin's political thought is nevertheless still vibrant. And it still has a great deal to teach about how revolutionary the effort to overcome racial injustices must be.

"A Most Disagreeable Mirror"

Reflections of a Stranger

When Swiss children shout *"Neger! Neger!"* at a young Baldwin
on his first day in their remote village, they unintentionally evoke
in him a keen recollection of how it feels to be reduced to a name, a
racial epithet, in the United States. They remind him not only of his
painful ambivalence about his identity as an American but also of
the discomfort his American identity engenders among white
Americans, "the war [his] presence has occasioned in the American
soul."[1] Marveling at the ease with which the Swiss villagers inhabit
the world, he observes: "They move with an authority which I shall
never have." "And," he continues, "they regard me, quite rightly,
not only as a stranger in their village but as a suspect latecomer,
bearing no credentials, to everything they have—however uncon-
sciously—inherited."[2] Whether or not Baldwin's assessment of the
villagers' relationship to their European heritage is accurate, his reflections on what it means to be "a suspect latecomer" to the West
and what it means, for white Americans, to look at him as a heritor

of a common culture, provide the basis for a penetrating assessment of race consciousness and the dilemmas of inclusion.

Baldwin's report from Switzerland emphasizes the treacherousness of any claim to speak for "us" without examining the unacknowledged assumptions that undermine the acceptance of African Americans as unproblematically free and equal members of American society. While the point is not originally or exclusively Baldwin's, he provides a forceful reminder of why it merits close attention. Consider the contrast between Baldwin's writing and Richard Rorty's essay "Solidarity." Rorty argues that any sense of who "we" are requires that someone be beyond the pale: "I claim that the force of 'us' is, typically, contrastive in the sense that it contrasts with a 'they' which is also made up of human beings—the wrong sort of human beings."[3] Baldwin would not quarrel with Rorty's account of how "we" are defined. But his intimate understanding of what it means to be among "the wrong sort of human beings" prevents him from sharing Rorty's vision of moral progress as an ever-expanding circle of insiders. Understood in this way, the inclusion of formerly excluded individuals in "our" club requires no interrogation of the composition of those of "us" who profit from presumptive inclusion. Rorty's lack of interest in "*which* similarities and dissimilarities strike us as salient" and *why* leaves too much unsaid.[4] As a consequence, Rorty's vision of a growing solidarity is too sanguine about overcoming deep-rooted barriers to inclusion.[5] Furthermore, it leaves the burden on the outsiders to show how they are like "us" or to start a club of their own. And the costs of exclusion are not merely psychological. Because decisions about how public resources are allocated, which individuals deserve promotion, and whose claims for redress against injustice are compelling belong to those of "us" already on the inside, the price of solidarity in Rorty's world is an unchallenged status quo.

Rorty's claims, while controversial, are also exemplary insofar as they echo a relatively commonplace story about how democracy has been, progressively, realized in the United States, and they lay bare something political theorists of many stripes implicitly accept when they talk about "us." Baldwin's account of race consciousness challenges this story. Unsurprisingly, among the rhetorical weapons Baldwin wields most effectively is his use of the first-person plural.

Although he welcomes his inclusion in the expanded circle of insiders, he carries with him the memory of being one of "the wrong sort of human beings." And he demands an honest assessment of the forces that have prevented his inclusion. By embracing his white readers in a racially ambiguous "we," he forces them to ask themselves how able they are to regard him, unself-consciously, as one of "us." This embrace also distances Baldwin from other African Americans, thereby unsettling fixed notions of black identity. Understanding how white and black identities are predicated on each other, Baldwin contends, is a necessary precondition for the definition of a multiracial "we" that neither clings to an assimilationist ideal nor exaggerates the extent of racial separation.

Baldwin's attention to the constitution of the American "we" harks back to the work of W. E. B. Du Bois. In offering a "forethought," a preface to *The Souls of Black Folk*, Du Bois proposes that understanding "the strange meaning of being black here in the dawning of the Twentieth Century" is of importance even to white Americans, "for the problem of the Twentieth Century is the problem of the color-line."[6] Understanding "the strange meaning of being black," moreover, involves reckoning with what Du Bois calls "double-consciousness." Although the term is generally interpreted, and sometimes dismissed, as the classic expression of a psychological wound afflicting a black male elite, it remains a powerful resource for exploring the dimensions of race consciousness among black and white Americans more broadly.[7] My aim in revisiting Du Bois's 1903 text in conjunction with Baldwin's essays is to shift the interpretive emphasis away from the reading of double consciousness as a peculiarly black "problem." Instead, this chapter mines *The Souls of Black Folk* for clues about how Du Bois uses double consciousness to convey the struggles of a whole society haunted by a history of racial oppression. It then turns to Baldwin for an expanded account of this American "problem." While he never uses the term made famous by Du Bois, Baldwin puts the notion of double consciousness to critical use, complicating discussions about who "we" are and raising questions about the relationship between racial identity and full inclusion in that "we." The moral psychology developed in Baldwin's essays, especially "Many Thousands Gone," discredits dreams of race blindness. At the same time,

Baldwin undermines claims to racial authenticity by exploring the multiple doublenesses of his own identity. His understanding of the complexity of racial identity and the intricacies of the interrelation of identity and injustice thus indicates the limitations of "the politics of recognition."

Behind the Color Line

Although the connections between Baldwin and Du Bois are many and deep, my concern here is not to trace Du Bois's influence on the younger writer or to invite larger comparisons of their work. Rather, I look specifically at how each conjoins the details of his life, through powerful prose, with the experiences of all African Americans and appeals, at the same time, to a white readership to serve a double end. The first aim of *The Souls of Black Folk* and of Baldwin's essays is to make a case for the humanity of black Americans, for neither Du Bois nor Baldwin sees evidence that white Americans have absorbed this simple point. The second aim is captured by Du Bois's conclusion in the essay entitled "Of Our Spiritual Strivings":

> Merely a concrete test of the underlying principles of the great republic is the Negro Problem, and the spiritual striving of the freedmen's sons is the travail of souls whose burden is almost beyond the measure of their strength, but who bear it in the name of an historic race, in the name of this the land of their fathers' fathers, and in the name of human opportunity. (*Souls*, 12)

In the move from "an historic race" to the "fathers' fathers" (who may well be white) to all of human opportunity, Du Bois, like Baldwin after him, places African Americans at the center of an account of American history and indicates that the realization of democratic principles in the United States stands or falls with the fate of its black citizens.

For Du Bois, double consciousness is both a gift and a burden.[8] It is second sight, a way of seeing that which escapes notice by the white majority. Endowed with an enlarged vision, Du Bois endeavors to take a myopic white readership "behind the veil" that divides black from white so that they might see the beauty of the humanity that lives there. Du Bois's project is political: *The Souls of Black Folk* makes demands for black suffrage, "civic equality," and equal access to higher education (*Souls*, 45). But his political claims are rooted in a conviction about the equal value of the culture of white Americans and that of their slaves. A heritor, by education, of European intellectual traditions and, at the same time, "bone of the bone and flesh of the flesh of them that live within the Veil," Du Bois uses his own double consciousness as the foundation upon which he constructs his social criticism and his vision of racial justice (2).

As second sight, double consciousness allows Du Bois to observe the distance between the American ideals he cherishes and American practices of systematic racial degradation. Hence, he contends that the experiences of slavery and exclusion allow African Americans to understand the promise of freedom in a way that white Americans cannot. "Actively we have woven ourselves with the very warp and woof of this nation," he reminds white Americans. "We fought their battles, shared their sorrow, mingled our blood with theirs, and generation after generation have pleaded with a headstrong, careless people to despise not Justice, Mercy, and Truth, lest the nation be smitten with a curse" (*Souls*, 215). Double consciousness thus provides insight into the content of American promises as they are not understood by those who have the luxury of taking those promises for granted.

But double consciousness is a menacing insight. In "a world which yields [the Negro] no true self-consciousness," it compounds the misery inflicted on African Americans from without by providing an internal echo of white Americans' judgment of them (*Souls*, 5). Double consciousness thus involves participating in an "American" culture that sees his African heritage as degraded. From this dilemma arises "a painful self-consciousness, an almost morbid sense of personality and a moral hesitancy which is fatal to self-confidence" (164). Too often the result of this consciousness of dishonor, Du Bois remarks, is the resort to rebellion or hypocrisy.

Du Bois's efforts to reach out to a white audience reveal the price of inclusion. In decrying the economic barriers to African American freedom, he argues that the wretched are human, "even as you and

I," thereby identifying himself with an "us" that is set apart from most African Americans (*Souls*, 118). The conviction with which Du Bois makes his appeal to the reasonable among his fellows belies the ambivalence engendered by double consciousness. While Du Bois does hold fast to a universal humanism, he also acknowledges that a strategy of dissemblance is a crucial component of making humanist claims; indeed, he indicates that it may be African Americans' only effective way of gaining access to a racist mainstream. Thus he seeks inclusion in a catholic culture, knowing that "the price of culture is a Lie." The price of culture, furthermore, is the substitution of deception for the cultivation of the very virtues—"impulse, manliness and courage"—that he believes American society prizes most highly (*Souls*, 166–67). From this requirement of deception for the purpose of inclusion arises "such a double life, with double thoughts, double duties, and double social classes, [which itself] must give rise to double words and double ideals, and tempt the mind to pretence or to revolt, to hypocrisy or to radicalism" (165).

Accompanying this account of double consciousness in African American lives there is another, less developed story of double consciousness in *The Souls of Black Folk*. This second story is that of the impact on white conciousness of "the swarthy spectre [that] sits in its accustomed seat at the Nation's feast" (*Souls*, 7).[9] For white Americans, whose place at the table is unquestioned, the ghostly presence serves as a constant reminder of hands that will never be clean. Implied in Du Bois's observation that white Americans always approach him haltingly—wondering "How does it feel to be a problem?"—is the suggestion that the omnipresence of the color line in American life effects a sort of double consciousness in white Americans as well (3). Du Bois notices how the plight of African Americans inhabits the imaginations of their white fellow citizens, despite white refusal to acknowledge or take responsibility for that plight. The ubiquity of the unasked question raises another question: "Whose problem?"

The place of the "problem" in white lives emerges clearly in Du Bois's depiction of the eerie order of life in the segregated South. By looking South, Du Bois does not absolve northern whites from censure. His elaboration of "the unasked question"—and its spoken counterparts, including: "Do not these Southern outrages make your blood boil?"—highlights northerners' insistent distancing of themselves from racial injustice (*Souls*, 4). Thus Du Bois turns to the South of the late nineteenth and early twentieth centuries as the region in which there is the most extensive contact between black and white Americans, and he offers his analysis of relations there as a template for understanding the psychological ramifications of in-terracial contact more generally. What he finds is that southern women and men assiduously govern their lives by unspoken racial-ized rules. Like participants in some complicated dance, black and white come together and part on cue, never unaware of their rela-tive positions, never needing to articulate the threat posed by trans-gression of the racial code.[10] Vividly, Du Bois describes the un-healthiness of this society that inhales "tainted air," that still breathes the "foul breath of slavery" (35, 71). From this physically unhealthy situation comes emotional distress. The very existence of free blacks, Du Bois observes, incites "as deep a storm and stress of human souls, as intense a ferment of feeling, as intricate a writhing of spirit, as ever a people experienced" (147–48).[11]

This "storm and stress" assaults white southerners' most deeply felt commitments. On the one hand, Du Bois writes, the belief in equality of all humanity and the Christian disavowal of caste divi-sion defeat attempts to justify the degrading effects of the color line. On the other hand, he relates that southerners nonetheless respond to their uneasiness by pointing out that the African Americans they know live in ignorance and are prone to laziness and crime. "Can a self-respecting group hold anything but the least possible fellowship with such persons and survive?" they ask (*Souls*, 152). Du Bois re-jects their protest on two grounds: it ignores the examples of African Americans who rise above the condition of the "masses," and it obscures the ways in which social, economic, and political structures serve to create the very masses it despises. Du Bois not only undermines white Americans' defenses against recognizing the humanity of black citizens, but he also intimates how the presence of the color line forces the unacceptable choice between hypocrisy and rebellion on *all* Americans. When he writes about the double trap laid for black Americans, Du Bois asks: "Is not this simply the writhing of the age translated into black,—the triumph of the Lie?" (165).

Writing in the context of the segregation of mid-century, Baldwin similarly takes his mostly white readership behind the veil of color. Without using the term "double consciousness," he too considers the psychological impact of racial division on black and white Americans. Where Du Bois offers his portrait of life in the post-Reconstruction South as a key to understanding racial interaction in the United States, Baldwin plumbs his own experiences for insights into a broader racial order. When he writes that "to be a Negro meant, precisely, that one was never looked at but was simply at the mercy of the reflexes the color of one's skin caused in other people," Baldwin nearly echoes Du Bois's description of double consciousness.[12] He conveys the depth of the color line's imprint on American psyches by recalling how it feels to grow up circumscribed by unspoken rules:

> Long before the Negro child perceives this difference [between white and black Americans], and even longer before he understands it, he has begun to react to it, he has begun to be controlled by it. Every effort made by the child's elders to prepare him for a fate from which they cannot protect him causes him secretly, in terror, to begin to await, without knowing that he is doing so, his mysterious and inexorable punishment. He must be "good" not only in order to please his parents and not only to avoid being punished by them; behind their authority stands another, nameless and impersonal, infinitely harder to please, and bottomlessly cruel. And this filters into the child's consciousness through his parents' tone of voice as he is being exhorted, punished, or loved; in the sudden, uncontrollable note of fear heard in his mother's or his father's voice when he has strayed beyond a particular boundary.[13]

Learning to recognize his transgression of that boundary in the reflexes of his parents, Baldwin begins to intuit what it means to measure his worth by the reactions of a hostile society.

In spite of the hurts inflicted by this coming to consciousness, Baldwin does not reduce black double consciousness to a reactionary moment. When he states that "in every aspect of his living [the Negro] betrays the memory of the auction block and the impact of the happy ending," Baldwin reiterates Du Bois's view that with affliction comes the gift of insight.[14] He maintains that by preventing black Americans from taking democratic values for granted, the memory of the auction block makes possible a more mature aspiration toward freedom and equality. That is, he attributes to black Americans a view of the future that is grounded in a realistic appraisal of the past.

Baldwin's assessment of the companionship of the ideals and the horrors of democracy in America represents a shift from Du Bois's account of double consciousness. The sting of Du Bois's double consciousness comes from an awareness that white Americans may never acknowledge the beauty of "the souls of black folk" and participate with their black neighbors in the merging of the two great streams of American culture. Baldwin echoes Du Bois in arguing for the essential role of African Americans in creating the United States, both literally and culturally. Yet he contends that even as white and black Americans live apart, the streams have long been irrevocably merged.[15] Whereas Du Bois reminds his readers that he is "bone of the bone and flesh of the flesh of them that live within the Veil (*Souls*, 2)," Baldwin writes that to recognize the heritage of the auction block and the happy ending is to grapple with the fact that, with respect to white Americans, black Americans are "bone of their bone, flesh of their flesh."[16]

But there is another, more important difference in Baldwin's account of the mutual implication of black and white Americans' fates and identities. When Baldwin writes that the land and institutions of the oppressor belong at least equally to those whose blood was spilled involuntarily, he adds a new spin to the story:

> The land of our forefathers' exile had been made, by that travail, our home. It may have been the popular impulse to keep us at the bottom of the perpetually shifting and bewildered populace; but we were, on the other hand, almost personally indispensable to each of them, simply because, *without us, they could never have been certain, in such a confusion, where the bottom was*; and nothing, in any case, could take away our title to the land which we, too, had purchased with our blood. This results in a psychology very different—at its best and at its worst—from the psychology which is produced by a sense of having been invaded and over-

run, the sense of having no recourse whatever against oppression other than overthrowing the machinery of the oppressor. We had been dealing with, had been made and mangled by, another machinery altogether. It had never been in our interest to overthrow it. It had been necessary to make the machinery work for our benefit and the possibility of its doing so had been, so to speak, built in.[17]

Whereas *The Souls of Black Folk* offers a heroic portrait of African American participation in a history that is threatened, indeed from within, by racism, Baldwin's story pushes Americans to consider how the glory of that history is related to the maintenance of the color line. Baldwin would second Du Bois's claim that "actively we have woven ourselves with the very warp and woof of this nation," but he would expose as "the very warp and woof of the heritage of the West, the idea of white supremacy."[18] Lacking confidence that white Americans are prepared to give up the security of knowing "where the bottom [is]," Baldwin's response to his own doubleness is even more ambivalent than Du Bois's endeavor to celebrate the cultural gifts of black and white Americans.

One clue to that difference lies in Baldwin's account of the reach of double consciousness. Baldwin's version of double consciousness provides a critical metaphor for the experiences of white Americans as well as those of blacks, although it manifests itself differently in the two cases. Thus, when Baldwin notes that the color of his skin functions "as a most disagreeable mirror," he demands that white readers look not only in the mirror but at it.[19] For in order to see the humanity of their black neighbors, Baldwin believes that whites must inquire how black degradation affirms their confidence in the value of being "American."

Crossing the Color Line: "Many Thousands Gone"

Perhaps Baldwin limns the interrelation of blackness and whiteness and the tensions that inhere in American identity most vividly in the essay "Many Thousands Gone." There he deploys a rhetorical strategy that deliberately uncouples the narrator's "we" from any stable point of reference. By dividing "the Negro" from "Americans," the essay accepts the color line as fundamental to American society. But throughout the piece, Baldwin slips back and forth across the line—now aligning himself with African Americans, now looking at them from a distance, now obscuring the difference. With the economy of a simple juxtaposition, he accomplishes in this essay what he strives for in a long career as a fiction writer whose stories might foreground the perspective of a white bisexual American man in Europe or a pregnant, black nineteen-year-old New Yorker.

Baldwin's foray across the color line in "Many Thousands Gone" is different from the "we" employed by Du Bois to gain the sympathy of an educated white audience. While Du Bois defines double consciousness as a struggle with "two warring ideals" that are both worthy of celebration, Baldwin's maneuvering casts doubt on the reader's commitment to the ideals themselves. By the end of the essay, the number of possible "we's" has multiplied beyond accurate accounting (although the essay is most severe when the "we" in question refers to white northern liberals). The only sure thing left to say about white and black American identities at the conclusion of "Many Thousands Gone" is that "we" know too little about who "we" are and how "we" are related to American democratic promises.[20]

It is worth pausing to try to follow Baldwin's trail as he moves back and forth across the color line, playing with the identity of his intended audience as deftly as he confounds readers' expectations about his own. Baldwin undermines the stable location of the color line from the very beginning of "Many Thousands Gone." He opens the essay as a distant commentator, noting that music is the only avenue through which "the Negro in America" can speak to "Americans." The narrator then observes that "Americans['] selective interpretation of the tales told in this medium only confirms their assumptions about the order of the world, and black and white places within it. It is in the third sentence that he offers the warning which serves as an epigraph to this book: "We find ourselves until today oppressed with a dangerous and reverberating silence." Who is the "we" that is oppressed? Clearly, one of the themes of "Many Thousands Gone" is that African Americans have historically had no public language to make their suffering audible to white ears. But

Baldwin also uses the "we" to indicate what whites lose by their inability to hear these voices and by their unwillingness to wrestle with what that deafness reveals about their own values. As he nears the end of the paragraph, the ambiguous "we" appears again. "The ways in which the Negro has affected the American psychology are betrayed in our popular culture and in our morality," he notes. And, finally: "We cannot ask: what do we *really* feel about him—such a question merely opens the gates on chaos. What we really feel about him is involved with all that we feel about everything, about everyone, about ourselves."[21]

The short paragraph that follows declares that "the story of the Negro in America . . . is the story of Americans." Read in this way, "the story of Americans" is not heroic. And "the Negro in America, gloomily referred to as that shadow which lies athwart our national life, is far more than that. He is a series of shadows, self-created, intertwining, which now we helplessly battle" ("Many," 24).[22] "The story of America" is thus, in important respects, a story of double consciousness. The shadows against which "we" battle are the memory of slavery and the knowledge that a coincidence of birth still condemns millions of Americans to life outside the promises of freedom and equality which "we" are all guaranteed. That these shadows are "self-created" casts doubt on the possibility of a stable selfhood, an American identity untroubled by racial oppression.

Already, Baldwin is prodding a white readership, particularly readers who thoughtlessly trust in the possibility that racism and racial identity can be effortlessly transcended, to look upon their beliefs about racial equality, and their beliefs about those beliefs, with mistrust. Above all, what Baldwin aims to undermine is the conviction that the present is divisible from the past. Until a real accounting of what was at stake in racial slavery and what that says about American democracy has been accomplished, Baldwin contends, white Americans will continue to be haunted by unasked questions. "In our image of the Negro breathes the past we deny, not dead but living yet and powerful, the beast in our jungle of statistics," he cautions. Like "the swarthy spectre" of Du Bois's imagination, Baldwin's beast never fully retreats from the consciousnesses of white Americans who aim to achieve racial equality by putting the past behind them without examining its traces in the present. According to Baldwin, "It is this [past] . . . which continues to defeat us, which lends to interracial cocktail parties their rattling, genteel, nervously smiling air: in any drawing room at such a gathering the beast may spring, filling the air with flying things and unenlightened wailing. . . . Wherever the Negro face appears a tension is created, the tension of a silence filled with things unutterable" ("Many," 28–29). To avoid dealing with the historical dehumanization of black Americans is thus to allow the beast to roam in white imaginations and the fear of the chaos brought on by true racial equality to rage unchecked.

If the "we" with whom Baldwin identifies as the essay opens is not white but black, then the question of what "we" feel about "the Negro" lends itself to another reading. Referring at once to all black Americans and to no one in particular, the term makes an abstraction of the lives subsumed by it. In many places in the essay, "the Negro" might just as easily be written as "the problem." The definite article and singular noun reinforce the sense that "we" understand to whom it refers. By leaving the racial identity of the "we" ambiguous, and by locating himself across the line from "the Negro," Baldwin asks whether his African American readers are the victims of Du Boisian double consciousness. He dares them to ask how much they have internalized the examples of successful assimilation or disastrous revolt, how much they measure their own lives "by the tape of a world that looks on in amused contempt and pity" (*Souls*, 5). And he observes that the consequences of having one's identity and experiences compressed into "the Negro" are written indelibly on the consciousnesses of black Americans: "One must travel very far, among saints with nothing to gain or outcasts with nothing to lose, to find a place where [being a Negro] does not matter—and perhaps a word or a gesture or simply a silence will testify that it matters even there" ("Many," 26–27).

In order to expose what "we" might really think about "the Negro," Baldwin considers white and black Americans' relationship to Bigger Thomas. Baldwin's choice of the main character from Richard Wright's *Native Son* is complicated by his difficult relationship with Wright. But the most obvious reason for this focus is the novel's enormous influence in the postwar United States. Irving Howe, for example, goes so far as to state that "the day *Native Son* appeared, American culture was changed forever."²³ When Baldwin comments that Bigger "is the monster created by the American republic," he means that Wright's novel captures an American fantasy about the people it imported as slaves and eventually abandoned to a debased freedom ("Many," 41). The purpose of this essay, and of so much of Baldwin's writing, is to expose the myths perpetuated about African Americans and to explore what those myths reveal about the people who cling to them. But knowing where the bottom is, Baldwin admonishes, exacts a terrible price from both white and black Americans. By assuring "us" that the fear of the black other who was thereby created is justified, Bigger Thomas's violent passage from tenement to death row assuages "our" consciences. Baldwin's version of Bigger Thomas thus serves as a definitive marker of where the bottom is—in American society and in a broader moral order.

When he locates himself on the white side of the line between "us" and "the Negro," Baldwin argues that "our" image of Bigger serves as a barrier to real interracial communion. The remoteness of Chicago's black tenements insulates most of "us" from meeting Bigger himself. Nonetheless, his image is so ingrained in "our" consciousnesses that it prevents "us" (here he means, most pointedly, white liberals) from looking at African Americans simply as other human beings. "He stands at our shoulders when we give our maid her wages," Baldwin notes. "It is his hand which we fear we are taking when struggling to communicate with the current 'intelligent' Negro, his stench, as it were, which fills our mouths with salt as the monument is unveiled in honor of the latest Negro leader" ("Many," 37). Baldwin's point is that the resonance of the image of Bigger Thomas (or Willie Horton?) in American culture exposes white discomfort just below the surface of an avowedly interracial "we."

When Baldwin situates himself on the black side of the color line, the significance of Bigger Thomas is terrifying. For those whose lives are hidden in the formulation "the Negro," the force of the image may be especially destructive. "No American Negro exists," he avers, "who does not have his private Bigger Thomas living in the skull." Although Bigger's story flattens the variety of black lives into the monster represented by "the Negro," Baldwin contends that blacks are "compelled to accept the fact that this dark and dan-

gerous and unloved stranger is part of [themselves] forever"
("Many," 42). Baldwin dwells on the image of Bigger Thomas because prevailing racial images have a material bearing on the ways
white and black Americans treat themselves and each other. But
they do not exhaust the possibilities for African American identity.
Part of Baldwin's challenge here is to make real the weight of racial
oppression without reducing African Americans to that experience
of oppression. This, then, is the "savage paradox" of African Americans' relationship to their own American culture. The culture that
created Bigger Thomas and denies the humanity of African Americans inhabits the very skulls of black citizens. It is a culture, un-
avoidably, to which African Americans belong.

The conclusion "Many Thousands Gone" builds toward is one
that demonstrates how Baldwin's incursions across the color line
discredit the idea that it is possible—or desirable—to transcend
racial identity without confronting the sources of its centrality in
American life:

> Though there are whites and blacks among us who hate each
> other, we will not; there are those who are betrayed by greed, by
> guilt, by blood lust, but not we; we will set our faces against them
> and join hands and walk together into that dazzling future when
> there will be no white or black. This is the dream of all liberal
> men, a dream not at all dishonorable, but, nevertheless, a dream.
> For, let us join hands on this mountain as we may, the battle is
> elsewhere. It proceeds far from us in the heat and horror and pain
> of life itself where all men are betrayed by greed and guilt and
> blood-lust and where no one's hands are clean. Our good will, from
> which we yet expect such power to transform us, is thin, passion-
> less, strident: its roots, examined, lead us back to our forebears,
> whose assumption it was that *the black man, to become truly hu-*
> *man and acceptable, must first become like us.* ("Many," 44–45)[24]

However earnestly racial justice is desired, appeals to race blindness
disguise the degree to which the assumption that black Americans
need to prove themselves "truly human and acceptable" still resonates and obscures the price of inclusion in the American "we."
"This assumption once accepted," Baldwin warns, "the Negro in

America can only acquiesce in the obliteration of his own personality, the distortion and debasement of his own experience" ("Many," 45).

If the suppleness of language exhibited in "Many Thousands Gone" is among Baldwin's greatest rhetorical achievements, it is an achievement that could not be sustained in all political contexts. As the critiques of black nationalists, who saw in Baldwin's experimental embrace of a white persona "the obliteration of *his* own personality, the distortion and debasement of *his* own experience," mounted in the 1960s, and as white intransigence confirmed Baldwin's own suspicions that patient appeals to white consciences were merely abject, Baldwin discards the racially ambiguous "we." Even as he locates himself on the black side of the color line, however, Baldwin retains his commitment to an interracial "we." And even when he strains to refashion the ambivalences of his writing into more righteous pronouncements or declarations befitting the anger of the time, his essays provide moments of keen insight into the psychological burdens and the moral and political implications—for all citizens—of living with the color line.

Baldwin's Double Consciousnesses

To claim that Baldwin's account of double consciousness provides a moral psychology of the color line is to demand a place for his writing in contemporary debates about race and identity. But is this notion of doubleness sufficiently flexible to accommodate the range of experiences contained by racial categories? Or does Baldwin's emphasis on race consciousness require a certain degree of blindness to the differences *among* blacks or whites? Consideration of the multiple doublenesses of Baldwin's work indicates that while Baldwin does sometimes fall prey to the temptation of making claims for a singular black experience, his public explorations of the tensions that inhere in his own identity make vivid the shortcomings of claims to racial authenticity.[25]

One sort of doubleness, the double existence Baldwin led as a "commuter" to the United States, simultaneously provides him the necessary distance to write about Americans' racial predicament and raises questions about Baldwin's qualifications as a commentator on black experience. Yet part of the value of Baldwin's contribution resides in the fact that he is at once conscious of how far he lives from the Harlem of his childhood and able to see how much Harlem lives in him. The move to Europe teaches Baldwin that there is no running away from his history, that the indelibility of experience precludes the attempt to drop out and find a new "us" to join or a new home in which to settle. If his flight reinforces Baldwin's sense of his American identity, however, his periodic moves back to the United States also remind him of the singularity of his own experience. This sort of double consciousness emerges poignantly in Baldwin's reports on trips he made to the South in the late 1950s and early 1960s.[26] By discovering how ill equipped he is to abide by the rules of Jim Crow, Baldwin comes to see how little he shares with the experiences of rural African Americans of the South, and how much.

In addition to this double identity as a commuter, Baldwin's notion of himself as an artist divides him from other Americans. Artistic consciousness, for Baldwin, involves the cultivation of a unique form of alienation. This alienation in turn enables him to hold a mirror to an unwitting society, for being an artist is as much about the courage to face what is ugly as the ability to create something beautiful.[27] Dwelling as he does on ugly truths, Baldwin wrestles constantly with a despair not apparent to his more insouciant fellow citizens. Although Baldwin's views about the vocation of the artist or writer sometimes suffer from undue romanticization,[28] his exploration of the double-edgedness of his talents still usefully complicates his understanding of racial identity. The particular burdens that artistic estrangement places on black artists are a recurrent topic of Baldwin's essays, as is the kind of distance that accompanies celebrity. Not only do the pressures of acting as a spokesman threaten to alienate Baldwin from the very experiences that animate his art, but material success and acceptance by a largely white readership also divide him from the people whose lives inspire his art in the first place.[29]

Of the many doublenesses in Baldwin's work, the intertwined twonesses of gender and sexuality shed the most light on his conception of double consciousness. They illuminate, first, insofar as they reveal the complexity of Baldwin's conception of racial identity: he understands that human beings are never *only* identified as black or white but are always also classified male or female. Further, the persistence of the color line is always related to issues of sexuality in Baldwin's estimation. Beneath white resistance to integration and fears of black power, Baldwin discerns a tangle of sexual fears projected onto black Americans by whites. And he discerns how those sexual fears are bound up with a hierarchy not only of race but also of gender. Moreover, Baldwin's treatment of the divide between "normal" and "perverse" sexualities, like the divide between men and women, proceeds from same premise as his arguments against white supremacy. By showing how the exclusion of a degraded or subordinated group reassures members of the dominant group of their insulation from the fragility of human existence, Baldwin discloses what is at stake in asserting the fixity of identity.

That the author of "Many Thousands Gone" would refuse to adhere to sexual rules of order is not surprising. That he did so in the postwar period, when links between homosexuality and communism were used to legitimize the persecution of gay men and lesbians as a threat to American society, indicates Baldwin's courage.[30] Making no secret of his own homosexuality, Baldwin crossed the color line artistically and jeopardized a fragile reputation as a "Negro writer," when he published his second novel in 1956. Not only does the novel, *Giovanni's Room*, feature no African American characters but it explicitly details a sexual relationship between two men. Despite his openness about his own attractions and his fictional explorations of homosexual love, however, Baldwin devotes little space in his essays to the question of what it means to be "gay."[31] Does this reticence indicate a submission to the requirements of racial authenticity? Although this question cannot be answered definitively, Baldwin's own response is instructive.[32]

"Homosexual, bisexual, heterosexual are 20th-century terms which, for me, really have very little meaning," Baldwin explains.[33] Or, as the protagonist of his novel *Tell Me How Long the Train's Been Gone* declares in exasperation, the word "gay" represents for him "the incomprehensible vernacular."[34] Such comments may be attributed, in part, to Baldwin's generation. Not only did he leave New York more than twenty years before the Stonewall uprising and the beginning of a national gay rights movement, but he came of age in a period in which the hetero-homosexual line had not yet been so starkly defined.[35] Thus, the preoccupation with labels may have appeared to Baldwin as the sexual equivalent of the "one-drop rule"—a single sexual encounter of the "wrong" type marking one's position, permanently, on the degraded side of the line.

But there is, for Baldwin, a deeper reason for saying that the terms carry no meaning. Sexual labels and slogans, no less than racial labels and slogans, dehumanize insofar as they deny the complexity of human lives.[36] Baldwin implies that embracing a "gay" identity requires an unacceptable choice. It takes no account of the complications of his own experience, as someone who nearly married early in life and whose intimate relationships with other men did not always conform to settled sexual categories. A believer in the redemptive possibilities of genuine human communion, Baldwin views the quality of an individual's attachments as the measure of that individual's integrity.[37] He is thus most suspicious of any political stance that reduces human relationships to a formula. Hence, when he complains that André Gide's homosexuality "was his own affair which he ought to have kept hidden from us,"[38] or when he declares to an interviewer that the question of sexuality is "absolutely personal,"[39] Baldwin is not suggesting that there is anything shameful in homosexuality. Instead his aim is to protect the dimension of life most valuable to him. To make a political identity of sexuality, he fears, is to accept the reality of the line between normal and abnormal and therefore to acquiesce to a society that would make certain attachments shameful.[40]

Where Baldwin's essays do address "the homosexual problem," they shift attention away from finding solutions and turn instead to the investigation of what is invested in the idea that homosexuality is a problem. On the question of whether homosexuality is "natural," Baldwin remarks, "I really do not see what difference the answer makes. It seems clear, in any case, at least in the world we know, that no matter what encyclopedias of physiological and scientific knowledge are brought to bear the answer can never be Yes." The answer cannot be "Yes," Baldwin reasons, because "it would rob the normal—who are simply the many—of their very necessary sense of security and order, of their sense, perhaps, that the [human] race is and should be devoted to outwitting oblivion—and will surely manage to do so."[41] The persecution of gays and lesbians here resembles racial persecution: both tell more about the fears that haunt the majority than about the minority they fear.

Baldwin develops his suspicions about the sources of homophobia by interrogating the naturalness of gender divisions and attacking swaggering ideals of masculinity. Of the homosexual, he writes, "His present debasement and our obsession with him corresponds to the debasement of the relationship between the sexes."[42] And in "Preservation of Innocence," an essay published before Baldwin's twenty-fifth birthday, he proposes an answer to the riddle of the natural relation between the sexes:

> Men and women seem to function as imperfect and sometimes unwilling mirrors for one another; a falsification or distortion of the nature of the one is immediately reflected in the nature of the other. . . . Matters are not helped if we thereupon decide that men must recapture their status as men and that women must embrace their function as women; not only does the resulting rigidity of attitude put to death any possible communion, but, having once listed the bald physical facts, no one is prepared to go further and decide, of our multiple human attributes, which are masculine and which are feminine.[43]

As soon as the decision of which attributes belong to which sex is made, he adds, one finds counter-examples everywhere, and the impulse behind the rigid division is felt even more keenly. The only way out of this paradox is to accept the fluidity of gender, or, as Baldwin argues at the very end of his career, androgyny: "We are, for the most part, visibly male or female, our social roles defined by our sexual equipment. But we are all androgynous, not only because we are all born of a woman impregnated by the seed of a man but because each of us, helplessly and forever, contains the other—male in female, female in male, white in black and black in white."[44] In dismissing fixed notions of male and female identity, Baldwin attacks the impulse to naturalize the divisions his society has created.[45] He urges his readers instead to see how racial identity must also be fluid.

Despite these gestures toward an account of the complicated interrelation of racial and sexual identity, Baldwin's essays do not go so far as to address how "blindness" to differences of sexual orientation and gender among African Americans compounds the injuries of race blindness. Part of the explanation resides in Baldwin's desire to remain relevant to a changing struggle for black freedom. Of the nationalist attacks on Baldwin's authority, Eldridge Cleaver's "Notes on a Native Son" may be the most famous. Cleaver reviews Baldwin's fiction and nonfiction through *The Fire Next Time* and finds that "Baldwin's antipathy toward the black race is shockingly clear."[46] What becomes shockingly clear in Cleaver's assessment, however, is that Cleaver's outrage is inseparable from his loathing of Baldwin's open homosexuality. By equating Baldwin's sexuality with "acquiescing in [a] racial death-wish,"[47] Cleaver emphasizes the policing that occurs when claims of racial authenticity are on the table. Cleaver thus dismisses Baldwin's critique of the leaders of the *négritude* movement as the *ressentiment* of an unmanly intruder: "Baldwin felt called upon to pop his cap pistol in a duel with Aimé Césaire, the big gun from Martinique."[48]

The effects of this policing on Baldwin's writing become apparent not in any denial of the varieties of sexual attachment in his fiction or of his sexual orientation, but in the increasingly masculinist language of Baldwin's essays of the 1960s and 1970s. Even Baldwin's early essays generalize about racial oppression from the emasculation of black men.[49] (He never considers what it might mean, for a woman, to have a "private Bigger Thomas living in the skull.") But his later writing goes further. A disjuncture emerges, in Cora Kaplan's words, between "the poetics of homosexuality and the politics of masculinity" in Baldwin's work.[50] *No Name in the Street* provides an example of how this masculinism reduces interracial struggles to the conflicts between white and black men. There, Baldwin asserts that "in the case of American slavery, the black man's right to his women, as well as to his children, was simply taken from him, and whatever bastards the white man begat on the bodies of black women took their condition from the condition of their mother: blacks were not the only stallions on the slave-breeding farms!"[51] Where Baldwin takes notice of the particular horrors slavery visited on black women, he folds them into a larger claim about emasculation. Unsurprisingly, this kind of rhetoric deafens Baldwin to claims about the gendered structure of power among African Americans. In a public dialogue with poet Audre Lorde, for example, the subtlety of Baldwin's understanding of how men and women mirror each other is lost in his reiteration that the great harm of American racism is that it takes from black men the capacity to support and protect their women and children. And it makes it difficult for him to hear Lorde's rejoinder that the inability to protect one's family is no less painful for a black woman than for her father, brothers, and sons.[52]

Insofar as Baldwin capitulates to a traditional understanding of manhood, he misses his own insights into the doublenesses of identity and, indirectly, repudiates his own experiences. But Baldwin's conception of double consciousness provides the tools to criticize such blindness. For insofar as he investigates what it means to be, in this society, a commuter, an artist, a homosexual, and a man, he contributes substantially to his readers' understanding of the complexity of being race conscious. "Princes and Powers" sums up as well as any essay Baldwin's attempt to mediate the conflicts that divide him from white Americans and from other blacks. The critical power of Baldwin's ambivalence, his double consciousness, is suggested by this approving account of writer George Lamming's comments at the international conference of Negro-African writers and artists that convened in Paris in 1956:

> It seemed to me that Lamming was suggesting to the conference a subtle and difficult idea, the idea that *part of the great wealth of the Negro experience lay precisely in its double-edgedness.* He was suggesting that all Negroes were held in a state of supreme tension between the difficult, dangerous relationship in which they stood to the white world and the relationship, not a whit less painful or dangerous, in which they stood to each other. He was suggesting that in the acceptance of this duality lay their strength, that in this, precisely, lay their means of defining and controlling the world in which they lived.[53]

Baldwin's Mirror and the Limits of Recognition

A writer who insists that the pretense of race blindness allows racial injustice to persist, Baldwin might be an identified as a proponent of what Charles Taylor calls "the politics of difference."[54] A writer, on the other hand, whose refusal to flatten the variety of individual experience for the sake of group identity leads to the conclusion that "a coalition has to be based on the grounds of human dignity,"[55] he seems a forceful advocate for what Taylor calls "the politics of equal respect." Yet Baldwin's double consciousness conforms to neither model. Taylor's rich story about the development of modern selfhood has contributed too much to contemporary thinking about identity and difference to be treated adequately here. But a brief consideration of "The Politics of Recognition," Taylor's answer to the challenge of escalating claims for more than "difference-blind" inclusion in contemporary liberal societies, provides a fitting conclusion to this discussion of Baldwin and double consciousness. For reading Baldwin against Taylor reveals two blind spots in Taylor's essay, blind spots that remind political theorists why Americans' racial dilemmas have proved so intransigent. Hidden in the first blind spot are the ways that the historical misrecognition of black Americans relate to whites' sense of themselves as American citizens; lost in the second are the paradoxes of racial group membership. Without advancing an alternative "politics" of his own, Baldwin suggests the kinds of questions that still must be addressed for the promise of freedom and equality to be extended in fact to black Americans.

Taylor's sensitivity to the harms inflicted by misrecognition exposes connections between the psychological and political. Given that degrading images can deeply damage the psyches of blacks, or women, or other disfavored groups, Taylor observes that "due recognition is not just a courtesy we owe people. It is a vital human need."[56] Recognition in this sense is certainly part of what Baldwin's exposition of doubleness demands. One aim of Baldwin's essays is to force an unwilling readership to acknowledge, truly, the humanity of African Americans. Yet recognition of black Americans by whites does not alone suffice. Baldwin contends that white Americans will not have accepted the equal humanity of blacks until they are able to admit the racial construction of their own identities and ask how that construction affects their commitments. And the ramifications of such an inquiry is not only psychological; it is intimately tied to matters of relative material comfort and power.[57] For example, Baldwin would demand that white Americans extolling the ideal that all citizens should be free to live where they choose ask how many black Americans they would welcome into their neighborhoods.[58] Despite earnest claims to the contrary, the vulnerability of white Americans' egalitarian commitments surfaces when they perceive that the order of their lives is threatened, or, tellingly, that their race blindness is being called into question (as is indicated by the prevalence, in American conversations, of sentences that begin "I'm not a racist, but . . ."). Without the interrogation of the play of prejudices on "our" sense of what is normal, "race blind" appeals to equal human dignity may thus appear hollow. According to Baldwin, white Americans refuse to see the degree to which the value of whiteness has depended, historically, on its distinction from a degraded sense of blackness. This will to innocence, rather than expressions of overt racism, prevents his fellow citizens from acknowledging that democracy has not yet been truly tried, much less realized in this country.

If it aims to speak to the specificity of African Americans' experiences, then "the politics of recognition" needs to be reconceived to take account of the pathos of the color line—of the damage wrought not only by misrecognition but also by an inflated sense of self-worth. To the extent that unspoken assumptions about African Americans retain their currency, Baldwin's double consciousness provides a basis for critical reflection. While Baldwin welcomes the end of legal segregation and celebrates improvements in African Americans' status, he greets every change with a question: How far have "we" come from "our forebears, whose assumption it was that the black man, to become truly human and acceptable, must first become like us" ("Many," 45)?

The second blind spot relates to the first. Beyond pointing out that any "politics of recognition" needs to attend to the unacknowledged identity politics of the privileged, Baldwin warns against eliding tensions within the groups demanding recognition. Taylor's essay, which devotes the most attention to Canadian struggles over cultural identity, suggests that minority groups seeking recognition are distinct from one another and unified internally. The end of the "politics of recognition," according to this view, is to sustain a group's distinctness in the face of the homogenizing forces of the majority culture. The challenge posed by race consciousness is not just to acknowledge that the "distinctness" of African American experience "has been ignored, glossed over, assimilated to a dominant or majority identity," although it certainly has.[59] Nor is the challenge adequately characterized by Taylor's account of the situation of "diasporic" peoples. For Taylor's assumption that every diaspora has a center, a center that lies elsewhere, misdescribes the experiences of that North American portion of the African diaspora that is older than the United States.[60] Rather, the entrenchment of race consciousness requires that Americans confront their deep alienation from and attachment to each other. The root of "the Negro problem," Baldwin proposes, is that "it is not simply the relationship of oppressed to oppressor, of master to slave, nor is it motivated merely by hatred; it is also, literally and morally, a *blood* relationship" ("Many," 42).[61]

Hence, when Baldwin alerts his readers to "the savage paradox of the American Negro's situation," he warns that race consciousness, in the normative sense, can be understood neither as a demand for the annihilation of difference nor as pure opposition. As his misgivings about *négritude* indicate, blackness holds no intrinsic value for Baldwin.[62] Yet he insists on the acknowledgment of the particular contributions of African American men and women. The difficulty consists in the impossibility of dividing, finally, the positive elements of black heritage from the negative, the black from the white. Commenting on "the relentless tension of the black condition," Baldwin writes: "Being black affected one's life span, insurance rates, blood pressure, lovers, children, every dangerous hour of every dangerous day. There was absolutely no way *not* to be black without ceasing to exist. But it frequently seemed that there was no way to be black, either, without ceasing to exist."[63]

Attempts to overcome "the relentless tension of the black condition" may manifest themselves internally in battles for the mantle of authenticity. As Cleaver's assessment of Baldwin indicates, struggles over "the right of authoritative description" can serve to dehumanize members of the very group in whose name the struggle is undertaken.[64] Baldwin's appreciation of both the impact and the contradictions of his black identity enables him to distinguish between what Ross Posnock helpfully calls "the rhetorical effect of authenticity" and "the ideology of authenticity."[65] No "politics of

recognition" is acceptable to Baldwin that oversimplifies the workings of race consciousness. No politics is acceptable that, by allowing him to affirm his humanity as an African American, requires
that he deny his worth as "an aging, lonely, sexually dubious, politically outrageous, unspeakably erratic freak."[66]

"Whatever may be their use in civilised societies, mirrors are essential to all violent and heroic action."[67] Virginia Woolf's observation intimates the force of Baldwin's double vision. Where would
the British Empire be, she asks, without the reflective power of the
stable of adoring women whose weakness serves to puff up the confidence of the nation's leading men? What would the American experiment in democracy be, Baldwin demands, without slavery and
the continued degradation of African Americans to confirm, by contrast, the value of the American "we"? By holding up his "most disagreeable mirror," Baldwin exhorts his readers, white and black, to
ask this question and inquire how their lives are reflected in the answer. Although he believes such scrutiny is necessary to make the
promise of equality real, Baldwin knows that his attack on American democratic pretensions is not without its risks. For mirrors are
double devices: they reflect and, as glass, they cut.

Blessed Are the Victims?

Speaking as a Victim

To extend the inquiry into how race consciousness is sustained and how it affects the recognition of African Americans as free and equal citizens, I return to a point made in chapter 2 about the power of racial images. There, the discussion focused on "Many Thousands Gone" and on Baldwin's treatment of Bigger Thomas as "the dark and dangerous stranger" haunting American imaginations. The point was a simple one: racial images have a significant bearing on the ways black and white Americans perceive themselves and each other. As long as the sources and the effects of those images remain unexamined, Baldwin argues, they perpetuate the power of the color line. Thus, he writes of Bigger Thomas: "To tell his story is to begin to liberate us from his image and it is, for the first time, to clothe this phantom with flesh and blood, to deepen, by our understanding of him and his relationship to us, our understanding of ourselves and of all men."[1]

Relentlessly, therefore, Baldwin probes the images that compress the variety of black experiences into the abstract formulation "the Negro," and that then set "the Negro" apart from "Americans." He dissects the assumptions that effect the curious arithmetic in which one person becomes many, and many are represented by an individual actor. And he specifies the ways in which this arithmetic, though implausible, distinguishes black Americans from "normal" citizens, whose individuality is unquestioned. Part of Baldwin's lasting power resides in his deft exposure of how, in a race-conscious society, racial identity renders African Americans generally visible and individually invisible. If Vincent Descombes is correct in positing that "the citizen of a modern Western society is asked to display both social conformity *and* individuality,"[2] then Baldwin shows how racial images doubly mark black Americans as outsiders.

Baldwin's critique of the deindividualizing effects of racial images contributes to a more general argument about the possibility of achieving a broadly inclusive democracy without looking squarely at the barriers to inclusion. And where he excels is in his perceptive descriptions of those barriers that are cultural and psychological. What drives Baldwin, in other words, is not merely unmasking the untruth of racial images but revealing what they have to say about the society that clings to them. Seeing by image is a way of not seeing, Baldwin maintains, and the freedom of those who think they can choose not to see is always compromised. "That image one is compelled to hold of another person—in order . . . to retain one's image of oneself—may become that person's trial, his cross, his death," Baldwin observes. However, he continues, "It may or may not become his prison: but it inevitably becomes one's own."[3] As long as racial images are deployed to contain the untidiness of human lives, those images will prove as nightmarish for the society that sustains them as they are for those who are always imperfectly defined by them.

Alternately denying and overstating African Americans' agency, the images perpetuate the racial exclusivity of the polity. They do so by suggesting that the presence of black citizens strikes an inharmonious note in a society that aims to unite diverse peoples as individuals and members of a common citizenry. The images make it appear reasonable, furthermore, to discount black claims and, at the same time, to hold individual black Americans accountable for all members of the group. This is not to say that the phenomenon is an exclusively American one. Frantz Fanon's meditation on being viewed as an object of fear by a white child in the colonial world of the Caribbean beautifully makes the same point: "I was responsible at the same time for my body, for my race, for my ancestors. I subjected myself to an objective examination, I discovered my blackness, my ethnic characteristics; and I was battered down by tom-toms, cannibalism, intellectual deficiency, fetichism, racial defects, slave-ships, and above all else, above all: 'Sho' good eatin'."[4] Baldwin's contribution to a broader understanding of the force of racial images is an account of how those images work in the context of the American polity. He exposes the links between degrading assumptions about black Americans and the depreciation of their claims to the fruits of citizenship.

In this chapter, I explore the political implications of Baldwin's effort to convey the substance of the lives obscured behind racial images and his analysis of the forces that perpetuate those images. If the specter of Bigger Thomas continues to resonate in the American public imagination—as the furor over Willie Horton attests—images of black victimhood are equally pernicious. For public discussions of injustice, racial and otherwise, are so frequently dominated by a kind of either/or logic, either denying the agency of the victim in pressing claims of racial injustice or downplaying the degree of the harm in order to make the case for the agency of the victim. Thus, an exploration of the ways that black Americans have been misrepresented as victims is essential to understanding the persistence of racial injustice. But such an exploration must also proceed with caution: it is crucial to uncover the distorting power of the images without sacrificing the capacity to identify victimization when and where it occurs. It is crucial, in other words, that the critique of images of victimhood not undermine the critique of racial injustice.

The delicacy of undertaking to discredit images of black victimhood arises from the political usefulness of these images as a means of pressing claims of racial injustice. According to historian Daryl Michael Scott, liberal social scientists have, in the latter half of the twentieth century, deployed images of black Americans as damaged products of a racist society to justify public policy measures aimed at achieving racial equality.[5] The arguments made on behalf of black schoolchildren in *Brown v. Board of Education* provide a pointed example of how effective this strategy can be. Patricia Williams reinforces this point, noting that the most successful plaintiffs seeking redress of racial injustice are those seen as the most defenseless or nonthreatening. "The best way to give voice to those whose voice had been suppressed," she recalls, "was to argue that they had no voice."[6] And economist Glenn Loury similarly indicates the effectiveness of victim imagery when he criticizes black leaders and intellectuals for "adopt[ing] the posture of the aggrieved claimant, the historical victim who, in his helplessness, is nothing more than the creation of his oppressor."[7] Each of these examples indicates the double-edged character of victim imagery: it can work to group and individual advantage even as it reestablishes the relationship between the relatively powerful and the relatively powerless.

A forceful, recent example of the currency of victim imagery—and its pitfalls—emerges from the concluding sessions of the Anita Hill–Clarence Thomas hearings. If the most vivid moment in the hearings occurred when Thomas asserted that he had been subjected to a "high-tech lynching" and rejected the sexual stereotyping of black men that is associated with lynching's history, his assertion that he was "a victim of the process" was at least as significant.[8] For by making that claim Thomas traded one racial image for another. Up to that point, he had stood by a narrative of self-reliance and denied that race was at all relevant to his nomination. The white senators, who judged him and who were intent on proving themselves innocent of racism, had cooperated, largely avoiding questions on any topic that directly involved race. (For instance, they did not ask Thomas to elaborate on his views about affirmative action, nor did they did substantially challenge his record on civil rights.) Nevertheless, once the charges of sexual harassment had been, in Thomas's words, "painted on [him]" and left their "indelible mark,"[9] the judge replaced his earlier account of himself as an exemplar of individual initiative, which now threatened to call up Bigger's ghost, with one of passivity and victimization. What is telling about this story is the speed with which the same senators who had earlier congratulated Thomas on his ability to overcome obstacles joined him in proclaiming Thomas "a victim of the process." The availability of the image of black Americans as victims allowed Thomas to disavow his earlier claims to agency, thereby demonstrating that his nomination posed no threat to the status quo. And it enabled the senators to disown their own responsibilities for the proceedings.

Beyond its effectiveness as a tool for exacting demands for redress or enabling the advancement of individual black Americans, victim imagery serves a further political purpose. It unites the victims and distinguishes them from a common enemy. The images provide fuel for the righteous indictment of injustice and simplify the project of identifying one's comrades in struggle. Calling this reactionary mobilization "the politics of *ressentiment*," Wendy Brown warns that it fixes the contested identities more firmly.[10] Not only does such a politics reduce the members of a group to their victimhood, it enshrines the status of the victimizers as an unattainable ideal. As Brown notes, identities based primarily upon a common exclusion from a universalist "we" are compromised by their dependence upon that ideal and their exclusion from it.[11] Hence, attachment to one's victimhood may provide a sense of moral superiority and may even provide the energy for political action, but it does so at the price of assuring that the victimhood be permanent.

Fully aware of the dilemmas of embracing/rejecting images of African Americans as victims, Baldwin puts forth his own story. By showing what it feels like to be a victim, he aims to remind his readers of the humanity and the complexity of the people whose lives are invisible behind the images. Baldwin's essays thus complement structural analyses of racial subjugation, providing a phenomenological account of the many ways oppression is experienced at an individual level. By connecting his victimization to claims about the achievements of American democracy, moreover, he shows that individual suffering from victimization is not simply a "personal problem" but a symptom of larger shortcomings in American democratic achievements. Despite the dangers of constructing a politics of victimhood and Baldwin's keen appraisal of a variety of racial images, I concentrate on images of African Americans as victims for three reasons.

The first reason is that Baldwin has been misread on this point. He has been categorized as someone whose career was dedicated to reinforcing the idea of black victimhood and white guilt. Perhaps the most damning assessment is that of Stanley Crouch, who maintains Baldwin created a race "industry" dedicated to beatifying black Americans as victims.[12] More worrisome is Jerry Watts's identification of Baldwin as a "quintessential black victim status intellectual."[13] This reading is more worrisome than Crouch's because it identifies so precisely the pitfalls Baldwin aims to avoid. Watts uses the term "victim status" to describe the relationship between victim and victimizer that Baldwin rejects: in exchange for the acknowledgement that a wrong has been done and the granting of some form of redress, the victim reaffirms both the good will and the relative power of the victimizer. A "victim status intellectual," furthermore, is someone who attributes to suffering a claim to moral superiority.[14] There is some truth to the claim that Baldwin's popularity reflects, in part, his capacity to appeal to the guilt of his white readers. And there are examples of moments, particularly later in his career, when he asserts a special moral authority as a descendant of slaves and a victim of racial injustice.[15] Yet even if it is true that Baldwin's success as a writer indicates a desire on the part of his white readers to be, in Albert Murray's words, "insulted, accused, bullied or baldwinized from time to time," Baldwin is wary of indulging his readers thus.[16] He understands his purpose to be undermining the persuasiveness of the idea that black Americans are essentially or first and foremost victims. "I refuse, absolutely, to speak from the point of view of the victim," he declares. "The victim can have no point of view for precisely so long as he thinks of himself as a victim. The testimony of the victim, as victim, corroborates, simply, the reality of the claims that bind him—confirms, and, as it were, consoles the jailer, the keeper of the keys."[17] To dismiss Baldwin as a "victim status intellectual," therefore, is to neglect the subtlety of Baldwin's best writing, writing that assaults racial injustice without diminishing the humanity of its victims or falling prey to comparative claims about who has suffered most and at whose hands.

It follows, then, that the second reason for the focus of this chapter is to reveal how Baldwin unpacks the images of African American victimhood. I investigate Baldwin's use of his gifts as a personal essayist to convey how it feels to be victimized without reducing his experience to a catalogue of the ways he has suffered unjustly.

Baldwin's understanding of the multiples sources of his identity precludes his embrace of a politics that depends on representing black Americans only as victims. He apprehends, furthermore, the inadequacy of a shared victimhood as the basis for imagining emancipatory alternatives to the status quo. Writing about Aimé Césaire and the attempt to forge a new black identity from the colonial experience, Baldwin notes: "The anatomizing of the great injustice which is the irreducible fact of colonialism was not yet enough to give the victims of that injustice a new sense of themselves."[18]

Baldwin shows that seeing black experiences solely through the lens of victimization is simply another way of seeing African Americans as a "problem." To be first and foremost a victim is to be less than a fully human agent, someone capable of taking responsibility for oneself. Because the images implicitly reinforce the idea that there is something about African Americans themselves that accounts for their victimization, there appears to be no victimizer. Accepting these images relieves Americans, particularly white Americans, from assessing their participation in the perpetuation of racial inequalities or asking how racial privilege continues to benefit those Americans whose race does not get noticed. Images of black victimhood forestall change, for the images comfort an anxious white majority with the promise of black Americans who pose no challenge to the social order. At the same time, the images enlarge the agency of the privileged, for the capacity to improve the situation, provide redress, still resides entirely with the powerful to whom the victim pleads.[19] And they help sustain a public discourse that frames redress as assistance to the needy, rather than recompense for past and present crimes. Although quite aware of these risks of reinforcing assumptions about black willessness, Baldwin nonetheless argues that examining the images and what lies behind them is the only way to defeat them.

The third reason for focusing on images of African American victimhood concerns what I take to be the best aspirations of political theory. For women and men who understand political theory to be a vocation, reflection on the conditions of democratic life requires engagement with the dilemmas that test the limits of our theories.[20] Such reflection demands that theorists investigate the gaps between principle and practice rather than ignoring them or explaining them away. This claim owes a great deal to Judith Shklar's contention that political theorists' preoccupation with the conditions of justice neglects the distinctive character of injustice. Shklar maintains that attending only to questions of justice reinforces the presumption that injustices are aberrant or exceptional. She notes that paying attention to the words of individuals who have been marked as victims reveals how difficult it is to draw a line between wrongs that are of public concern, that is, injustices, and wrongs that are merely instances of personal misfortune. Laying bare private details of his life in the service of public remonstrance, Baldwin illuminates the connection between individual hurts and the state of American democracy. Baldwin thus retains his appreciation for the individuality of the men and women marked as victims even as he rails against the damage of racial oppression. He provides an instructive response to Shklar's demand that theory "give injustice its due."

Three Stories

Nowhere does Baldwin open up, question, and, ultimately, undermine the one-dimensional character of images of black victimhood more penetratingly than in the essay "Notes of a Native Son." First published in *Harper's* magazine in 1955, this essay, provides an intimate glimpse into the experience of victimization. By marrying moments of Baldwin's life to observations about racial exclusion in American society, it "utilize[s] the particular in order to reveal something much larger and heavier than any particular can be."[21] Without resorting to didacticism, Baldwin's narrative surveys key moments in African American history during the first half of the twentieth century—the Great Migration out of the South, segregation and discrimination in northern war production industries during World War II, the Detroit and Harlem riots of 1943—and raises pointed questions about the political achievements of a nominally democratic society in which so many citizens are forced to live as he, his family, and their neighbors have.

"Notes of a Native Son" proceeds through the telling of several interwoven stories, of which I concentrate on three: the story of Baldwin's father, who lost his mind to bitterness long before he died

in the summer of 1943; the story of Baldwin's coming to consciousness of the power of race to affect not only his life prospects but also
his possibilities of escaping his father's fate; and the story of the race
riot that tore Harlem apart as Baldwin's father was dying. Each narrative relates how racial injustice constrains the agency of its victims. Each clarifies how it feels to believe that, in a hostile society,
the only alternative to a fatalist acceptance of one's victimhood is
self-destruction. Yet, in the narration of the stories, Baldwin refuses
to diminish the humanity of the men and women he describes or to
make their suffering into a political virtue. He impresses on the
readers that the great crime of racial injustice is not that its victims
are peculiarly helpless but that they are as beautiful and as loath-
some, as dignified and as flawed, as any other human beings.

The essay begins simply: "On the 29th of July, in 1943, my father
died."[22] Baldwin then proceeds to relate that his father was born in
New Orleans, the son of a slave, and joined the generation of men
and women moving north after World War I. Baldwin reports that he
managed to learn little else about his father's background; David
Baldwin was preoccupied with weightier matters than entertaining
an inquisitive son with stories about Louis Armstrong's New Orleans. Struggling to support his family and to protect nine children
from the temptations of the streets, the elder Baldwin ruled his
household with a stern authority that terrified his children. And he
related to the outside world with an uneasiness that diminished the
demand for his services as a minister and alienated him from his
friends. "We went from church to smaller and more improbable
church," Baldwin recalls ("Notes," 88). By the time of his death,
alone in a hospital on Long Island, David Baldwin was so thoroughly
beaten that he appeared to his son "all shriveled and still, like a
little black monkey," his voice reduced to a whistle in his throat
and his body nearly overwhelmed by the tubes and other equipment
keeping him alive (102).

Unquestionably, David Baldwin's story is that of a victim of a
racist society. He is portrayed as both deeply distrustful of white
Americans and so abject in his relations with them that, when a
white teacher sought permission to take James to the theater, to a
world the elder Baldwin believed to be damned, he was unable to
refuse it. Seeing this capitulation, his son remembers, only added to

the contempt he already felt toward his father. The portrait of David Baldwin's isolation is so complete that he appears incapable of any human contact, even with his own children:

> He claimed to be proud of his blackness but it had also been the cause of much humiliation and it had fixed bleak boundaries to his life. He was not a young man when we were growing up and he already suffered many kinds of ruin; in his outrageously demanding and protective way he loved his children, who were black like him and menaced, like him; and all these things sometimes showed in his face when he tried, never to my knowledge with any success, to establish contact with any of us. When he took one of his children on his knee to play, the child always became fretful and began to cry; when he tried to help one of us with our homework the absolutely unabating tension which emanated from him caused our minds and our tongues to become paralyzed, so that he, scarcely knowing why, flew into a rage and the child, not knowing why, was punished. ("Notes," 87–88)

If genuine human communication is difficult under the most auspicious circumstances, Baldwin shows, it becomes virtually impossible under conditions of perpetual constraint and humiliation. By exposing the costs of his father's degradation, he conveys how a lifetime of racial injustice can produce, among other things, a particularly terrifying variety of silence.

"Notes of a Native Son" relates a second story about the unraveling of Baldwin's conviction that he could remain unaffected by the kind of poison that corroded his father's life. The essay fleshes out the development within Baldwin's own consciousness of what he elsewhere calls "the rage of the disesteemed."[23] Baldwin shows how that rage impinges on an individual's freedom and makes mute, self-destructive action seem unavoidable. He recalls:

> The year which preceded my father's death had made a great change in my life. I had been living in New Jersey, working in defense plants, working and living among southerners, white and black. I knew about the south, of course, and about how southerners treated Negroes and how they expected them to behave, but it

had never entered my mind that anyone would look at me and expect *me* to behave that way. *I learned in New Jersey that to be a Negro meant, precisely, that one was never looked at but was simply at the mercy of the reflexes the color of one's skin caused in other people.* . . . In the beginning, to make matters worse, I simply did not know what was happening. . . . I knew about jim-crow but I had never experienced it. I went to the same self-service restaurant three times and stood with all the Princeton boys before the counter, waiting for a hamburger and coffee; it was always an extraordinarily long time before anything was set before me; but it was not until the fourth visit that I learned that, in fact, nothing had ever been set before me: I had simply picked something up. Negroes were not served there, I was told, and they had been waiting for me to realize that I was always the only Negro present. ("Notes," 93)[24]

Once Baldwin realized this, he waged a campaign to enter as many places as possible where he knew he was likely to be "the only Negro present." This behavior earned him a reputation as a madman, and that reputation eventually cost him his job.

On the last night before his return to New York, Baldwin fulfilled the expectations of white New Jerseyans, proving that he was, perhaps after all, insane. Having endured a year of humiliation, Baldwin once again found himself refused service at a diner. With uncanny clarity he describes how, under the "browned-out" lights of wartime Trenton, the stream of white faces in the streets overpowered him. "People were moving in every direction," he recalls, "but it seemed to me, in that instant, that all of the people I could see, and many more than that were moving toward me, against me, and that everyone was white. I remember how their faces gleamed" ("Notes," 95). The effect was overwhelming, and Baldwin snapped. Next, he tells his readers, he walked into a restaurant knowing he would not be served. When the waitress repeated the phrase "We don't serve Negroes here," Baldwin picked up the only available weapon, a mug of water, and hurled it, with murderous purpose, at her head. The mug missed and smashed against a mirror behind the bar. Waking from his trance, Baldwin realized that he had nearly killed a white woman and that his act had transformed a roomful of diners into an angry mob. He barely escaped alive. Years after his escape, Baldwin wonders what kind of a person he has become. In the murderousness of his intentions, he sees himself as the victim of "some dread, chronic disease, the unfailing symptom of which is a kind of blind fever, a pounding in the skull and fire in the bowels." "Once this disease is contracted," Baldwin declares, "one can never really be carefree again, for the fever, without an instant's warning, can recur at any moment" (94).

The third narrative is the story of the riot of 1943, during which Harlem's residents turned neighborhood shops inside out and left the remains to waste on city streets. Baldwin recollects how overcrowded conditions and economic frustrations and, especially, anger over the training of black soldiers, in the South, to die abroad for someone else's freedom filled everyone with a tense apprehension that made the destruction that followed seem almost inevitable. Describing the period before the revolt, Baldwin reveals a remarkable ear for the unsaid: "The situation in Harlem had grown bad enough for clergymen, policemen, educators, politicians, and social workers to assert in one breath that there was no 'crime wave' and to offer, in the very next breath, suggestions as to how to combat it." Baldwin continues, "These suggestions always seemed to involve playgrounds, despite the fact that racial skirmishes were occurring in the playgrounds, too" ("Notes," 99). Tellingly, the solutions for this crime-wave-that-does-not-exist bear little relation to the question of *why* the situation was so volatile. Furthermore, Baldwin shows how this faith in the redeeming power of playgrounds, located of course within the confines of the ghetto, represents an attempt to confine the concerns of the men and women who live in Harlem within ghetto boundaries as well. Baldwin's assessment of this containment policy is, typically, poetic: "Perhaps the most revealing news item, out of the steady parade of reports of muggings, stabbings, shootings, assaults, gang wars, and accusations of police brutality, is the item concerning six Negro girls who set upon a white girl in the subway because, as they all too accurately put it, she was stepping on their toes." "Indeed she was," Baldwin notes, "all over the nation" (99).

What is so remarkable about that summer, according to Baldwin, is how it united people who otherwise avoided one another. The barriers of religion and respectability and race pride that normally divided Harlem broke down; "everybody felt a directionless, hopeless bitterness, as well as that panic that can scarcely be suppressed when one knows that a human being one loves is beyond one's reach, and in danger" ("Notes," 101). The depth of feeling proved profound enough that when a black soldier was shot, the story was spread and enlarged, and Harlem erupted. With dreadful detail, Baldwin maps the route of destruction that ensued—a route that never left the confines of the ghetto—and marvels at the "waste" of the outburst ("cans of beans and soup and dog food, along with toilet paper, corn flakes, sardines and milk tumbled every which way, and abandoned cash registers and cases of beer leaned crazily out of the splintered windows and were strewn along the avenues") (111). The actions of the mob served little purpose; they appear reactionary, senseless. As Baldwin admits, "It would have been better" if the contents of stores had been left where they were and windows had remained unbroken. Yet that was not an option for those men and women at that time, Baldwin explains. "It would have been better, but it would also have been intolerable, for Harlem had needed something to smash. To smash something is the ghetto's chronic need" (111).

What might a reader make of these three stories? Do they affirm the idea that African Americans are, first and foremost, victims? Does Baldwin's emphasis on voicelessness, rage, and impotence in a white world or his use of such racially charged images as that of a "monkey" reinforce the unspoken assumption that for reasons of biology or culture or environment, black Americans simply cannot make a place for themselves in American society? Or do the stories accomplish something else? Consider, again, David Baldwin's story. If David Baldwin is a victim of society, he is not *only* a victim. In the same passage that describes the "bleak boundaries" that fix David Baldwin's life, his son also notes that "there was something else in him, buried in him, which lent him his tremendous power and, even, a rather crushing charm" ("Notes," 87).

The force of "Notes of a Native Son" emerges from the ways Baldwin teases out the more complicated story from what might otherwise be a straightforward narrative about how a susceptible individual is destroyed through the conspiracy of oppression and mental illness. Baldwin thus transforms his father's funeral into an occasion to plumb the experiences hidden behind David Baldwin's bitter encounter with life. Whereas Baldwin hated his father's tyranny over the family and despised his impotence against rest of the world, he understands later that the extremity of the elder Baldwin's sickness reflects a suffering that might as easily be his own—might as easily belong to anyone confronted by psychologically and materially oppressive conditions. "In my mind's eye I could see him," Baldwin remembers, "sitting at the window, locked up in his terrors; hating and fearing every living soul including his children who had betrayed him, too, by reaching towards the world which had despised him. There were nine of us. I began to wonder what it could have felt like for such a man to have had nine children whom he could barely feed" ("Notes," 90).

Hearing the funeral sermon and watching the reactions of the other mourners in the room, Baldwin wonders further. Although the man described by the minister—the generous, loving man—bears no relation to the father Baldwin had struggled against, the sermon also suggests to Baldwin how little he knows about his father. "The real man, whoever he had been, had suffered and now he was dead," Baldwin observes. "This was all that was sure and all that mattered now" ("Notes," 105). But he pushes further still, speculating about the private world of David Baldwin, a world obscured by the elder Baldwin's madness and the younger Baldwin's contempt. He discerns in his father's story a larger human experience of despair:

> Only the Lord saw the midnight tears, only He was present when one of His children, moaning and wringing hands, paced up and down the room. When one slapped one's child in anger the recoil in the heart reverberated through heaven and became part of the pain of the universe. And when the children were hungry and sullen and distrustful and one watched them, daily, growing wilder, and further away, and running headlong into danger, it was the Lord who knew what the charged heart endured as the strap was laid to the backside; the Lord alone who knew what one *would* have said if one had had, like the Lord, the gift of the living word. It was the Lord who knew of the impossibility every parent in that room faced: how to prepare the child for the day when the child would be

despised and how to *create* in the child—by what means?—a
stronger antidote to this poison than one had found for oneself.

Baldwin concludes this meditation with a reminder to himself and
to the reader: *"Thou knowest this man's fall; but thou knowest not
his wrassling"* ("Notes, 105–6).[25]

The effect of this passage is not to diminish the difficulty of living
with David Baldwin or the terrors his children associated with his
presence. Nor does the religious language suggest that Baldwin, who
left the church as a teenager, is interested in making claims for the
omniscience of "the Lord." The force of Baldwin's imagination is
put to a different use. The pictorial power of his prose enables the
reader to see herself or himself also alone, at midnight, pacing, helpless. It conveys a sense of what it might feel like to find oneself unable to communicate with one's children or to assure somehow that
the condition of their lives would be not be defined by the "bleak
boundaries" that had circumscribed one's own. By painting such a
portrait, Baldwin does not make victimization beautiful or suffering
virtuous. And he does not reveal the wasted lives of his neighborhood as evidence of the "pathologies" of the ghetto, calling on his
readers to pity the damaged creatures who live there. He is not simply declaring, "My father has been victimized, and he is human just
like you."

Rather, Baldwin deploys his father's experiences and his own and
those of the men and women of his neighborhood, in order to deny
his readers their innocence, their capacity not to see the lives and
the griefs and the motivations of the men and women hidden behind ghetto walls and racial images. And his narratives serve a further purpose as well. They indicate the broader, societal implications of racial injustice. By denying his readers the luxury of reading
the events he describes as a "black problem," Baldwin pushes them
to reappraise their own responsibilities in a situation that confines
the public expression of some citizens to reactionary acts of rage
and traps others in a web of dishonesty and fear.

Fittingly, the end of "Notes of a Native Son" transforms the inte-
riority of Baldwin's thoughts at his father's funeral into a call for action. As Baldwin reflects on his heritage, he discovers that understanding his relationship to the past entails a new attitude toward

his future. "All of my father's texts and songs, which I had decided were meaningless, were arranged before me at his death like empty bottles," he recalls, "waiting to hold the meaning which life would give them for me" ("Notes," 113). The meaning that they intimate to him is personal but not only personal. For Baldwin's call for action does not discriminate between the responsibilities of those who have been marked as victims and those who have been insulated from such demarcation. It reaffirms both the fact of the victimization and the limits of that fact. The lesson Baldwin derives, finally, from his meditation on his father's death is what it means to be a democrat:

> to hold in the mind forever two ideas which [seem] to be in opposition. The first idea [is] acceptance, the acceptance, totally without rancor, of life as it is, and men as they are: in the light of this idea, it goes without saying that injustice is a commonplace. But this [does] not mean that one could be complacent, for the second idea [is] of equal power: that one must never, in one's own life, accept these injustices as commonplace but must fight them with all one's strength. ("Notes," 113–14)

The Private Life of Racial Injustice

Among the strengths of "Notes of a Native Son" is Baldwin's keen appreciation of the relationship between intensely private pain and matters of public concern. His account of being refused service at a restaurant, by exposing the impact of such exclusion, reveals not only that racial segregation is wrong but also *how* it is wrong. Not all personal hurts are instances of injustice, surely, yet Baldwin challenges the idea that a line can be definitively drawn between matters of justice—or injustice—and personal problems. He conveys why outlawing segregation, while allowing him to purchase a hamburger and a cup of coffee, cannot undo the experience of powerlessness and the rage it engenders. Like "Many Thousands Gone," "Notes of a Native Son" tells a double story: it links its account of the suffering of black Americans to an account of willful obliviousness on the part of white Americans. And it anticipates the inadequacy of the declaration of formal equality as an antidote to the poison of exclusion. For Baldwin's narrative demonstrates that declaring all citizens equal before the law is neither sufficient redress for his pain, nor adequate to transform the white diners who silently witnessed Baldwin's humiliation into men and woman capable of seeing Baldwin as someone unquestionably entitled to the kind of respectful treatment they take as their due.

Baldwin's attention to the links between hurts that merit public response and those that do not goes to the heart of democratic theories' claims to relevance in a race-conscious society. And it complements Judith Shklar's argument for the development of richer accounts of the experience of injustice. The narratives in "Notes of a Native Son" capture powerfully what Shklar calls the "sense of injustice." According to Shklar, "No democratic political theory can ignore the sense of injustice that smolders in the psyche of the victim of injustice." She continues: "If democracy means anything morally, it signifies that the lives of all citizens matter, and that their sense of their rights must prevail."[26] Shklar offers her account of the sense of injustice as a corrective for political theories that focus exclusively or primarily on the conditions of justice. Such work, by treating injustices as an aberration and restricting claims of injustice to cases that meet narrowly defined criteria, "misdefine[s]" the victim's experience.[27]

Shklar extends her objection from the realm of theoretical debate to the realm of political practice, where an impoverished theoretical imagination, one consumed with matters of justice, deflects attention from the pervasiveness of "passive injustice." And she discerns the transformative possibilities inherent in the effort to give priority to the voices of citizens who have been victimized, arguing that such an effort allows for the development of more genuinely equal rules.[28] Shklar does not suggest that the victims are always right about the moral significance of their experiences. Rather, she maintains that they are owed what Laurence Thomas calls "moral deference," the acknowledgment that justice requires a willingness to honor the claims of the oppressed for which imaginative identification alone is no substitute.[29] Tellingly, Shklar takes the experiences of African Americans as "the most obvious example" of the difficulty of sorting out the difference between suffering that results from personal misfortune and suffering caused by injustice. She intimates that one obstacle to the formulation of more adequate responses to racial injustice is that it accentuates the tenuousness of any line between misfortune and injustice and undermines confidence in the possibility that such a line can be drawn at all.[30] As one of only a few political theorists who have located the "ineradicable curse" of racial slavery at the heart of her account of American democracy, Shklar indicates how stories such as Baldwin's are essential to contemporary American democratic theory.[31]

While Baldwin's attempts to put his private hurts to public use reinforce Shklar's arguments, one of the hazards of discussing the relationship between "public" and "private" in his writing is that he uses the terms in so many different registers. The private may be personal, spiritual, emotional; the public may be political, spiritual, cultural. Indeed, Baldwin seems undecided at times about the possibility of describing the workings of the private world at all. He asserts that "experience is a private, and a very largely speechless affair," thereby undercutting his project as a writer who probes his own and others' inner lives.[32] Privacy, as a barrier to communication, is a recurring theme of his fiction.[33] Further, as the discussion of sexuality in chapter two indicated, Baldwin is fiercely protective of the privacy of those dimensions of life he prizes most. And he recognizes the particular importance, for marginalized members of society, of the kind of privacy that takes advantage of the turned backs and closed eyes of the powerful to create an uninvaded space and a source of strength.

In spite of his convictions about the necessity and the desirability of insulating some portion of human lives from public view, Baldwin believes equally forcefully that the connections between private and public must be reckoned with. "The interior life is a real life," he observes, "and the intangible dreams of people have a tangible effect on the world."[34] Baldwin's treatment of the relationship between personal hurts and public wrongs invites comparison with feminist theorists whose work is similarly concerned with the ways that a line between public and private is drawn. Whereas many feminist theorists take issue with a division of social life that relegates women's traditional functions to the private or domestic sphere, Baldwin asks how the distinction between black and white has been naturalized and why it persists after biological notions of racial difference have been discredited. Like feminist critics, furthermore, Baldwin displays a keen ear for what is silenced and an attentiveness to what is "forgotten" when the division of public and private is treated as though its meaning does not vary with the circumstances of different citizens' lives.[35] He resembles them in his interest in disclosing how power relations become taken for granted and how the demarcation of public concerns from personal ones reinforces those relations of power by denying the political import of many sexual or racial injuries. While Baldwin's essays are of little help to the theorist concerned with providing a general account of the proper relationship between public and private realms, the blurs and tangles that define his prose are precisely right. Such confusion is evocative of the intricate relationships that constitute human identities. And in a race-conscious context, Baldwin's musings about the public and the private provide clues to the boundary-effacing character of the racial degradation of formally free and equal citizens.

My purpose in raising these issues of publicity and privacy, injustice and misfortune, is to gain a better understanding of how they collide with the issue of racial imagery. Whereas the publicity of racial images defies relegation to the private sphere, the images, by concealing the individuality of victims of injustice, relegate racial crimes into a remote privacy. In other words, the authority of the images often outweighs the testimony of the individual they purport to describe. Hortense Spillers captures this dynamic in her reflection on her own reception in public venues: "Let's face it. I am a marked woman, but not everybody knows my name." Even to people she has not met, she explains, she is "'Peaches' and 'Brown Sugar,' 'Sapphire' and 'Earth Mother,' 'Aunty,' 'Granny,' God's 'Holy Fool,' a 'Miss Ebony First,' or 'Black Woman at the Podium.'"[36] Her voice hidden in the din of competing identities, Spillers is wholly anonymous and thoroughly exposed. Liberal conceptions of selfhood are clearly of little assistance in protecting Spillers in a race-conscious context. Her status as an individual or a citizen with immediately recognizable rights retreats behind her identification with a complex of assumptions about black women. By obscuring the person, the images hide the injuries. They stifle any probing inquiry into the meaning of individual experiences of racial injustice and enable instead the thoughtless repetition of what Baldwin calls "perhaps the most asinine and perhaps the most insulting" question he knows: "What does the Negro want?"[37]

The partner of the deindividualizing effect of racial images is hyperindividualization, a refusal to consider individual experience in light of larger social dynamics. This reverse effect emerges poignantly in Baldwin's reflections on his best friend, who threw himself into the Hudson River at twenty-four. "I will be told that he had 'personal' problems," writes Baldwin. And, Baldwin remarks, he did. His personal problems included joblessness, homelessness, and the fact that "there was not, then, nor is there, now, a single American institution which is not a racist institution."[38] Baldwin puts the point strongly. But is it so far-fetched? Baldwin's career is an effort to do more than simply answer, "No." Part of that answer consists in Baldwin's effort to unpack the contention that white Americans cannot hear the political and moral meanings of black suffering. By fleshing out the stories of the persons compressed into the abstract formulation of "the Negro," Baldwin examines how racial images either perpetuate the location of individual African Americans' experiences outside the realm of public concern or misdescribe those experiences as symptoms of the race "problem."

The kinds of links that Baldwin discerns between racial images and the dislocation of African American claims of injustice have received a great deal of attention in the work of critical race theorists and others who study the relationship between race and law. Williams writes, for example, that stories of black experiences in the United States have been accommodated by American culture as literature or entertainment, but they are denied recognition as *political* expression.[39] According to Cheryl Harris, American law has been defined by a "studied ignorance" about the significance of group identity for members of disadvantaged groups.[40] And Mari Matsuda echoes Baldwin's concern about the distinction between "personal" problems and society-wide injustices, noting that "the kinds of injuries historically left to private individuals to absorb and resist through private means are no accident." In a tone reminiscent of Baldwin, she continues: "The places where the law does not go to redress harm have tended to be the places where women, children, people of color, and poor people live."[41] Among the dangers of such privatization is that it contains the scope of redress without containing the harm of racial injustice. Images of black victimhood are of particular importance in supporting private discrimination and perpetuating the exclusion of African American concerns from public consideration, according to Kimberlé Crenshaw. She argues that assumptions about black docility are central to the construction of black otherness, which allows the persistence and subterranean normative valorization of racial domination.[42] What all of these writers share with Baldwin is an appreciation that race blindness—or deafness—is not an appropriate response. Whereas racial images affect black citizens' efforts to gain recognition as individuals, the disavowal of the relevance of race to political identity hampers attempts to show that individual grievances are connected to broader injustices.

Baldwin's essays illuminate how the unwillingness to hear African Americans' claims of injury as political claims is evidence of a political discourse which brackets those experiences that fundamentally challenge its premises. That discourse, he believes, protects white Americans from facing the truth about African Americans' American history. Speaking of the popularity of *Native Son* and the availability of Bigger Thomas to a "mainstream" American audience, Baldwin observes: "The privacy or obscurity of Negro life makes that life capable, in our imaginations, of producing anything at all; and thus the idea of Bigger's monstrosity can be presented without fear of contradiction, since no American has the knowledge or authority to contest it and no Negro has the voice."[43] Privacy here does not mean a domestic sphere that is immune to political interference from without. Rather, it denotes a dead-letter office where claims of racial oppression that are deemed not recognizably political collect. Hence, Baldwin takes little satisfaction in the claim that popular images of African Americans have been replaced by images of young, upwardly mobile black women and men. "Before . . . our joy at the demise of Aunt Jemima and Uncle Tom approaches the indecent," Baldwin cautions, "we had better ask whence they sprang, how they lived? Into what limbo have they vanished?"[44] Before we celebrate the end of racial images, he might have added, we need to inquire how traces of those images live on in the public imagination.

"Notes of a Native Son" provides one reply to such questions in its exploration of the causes and consequences of the Harlem riot of 1943. Baldwin views the assault on stores and restaurants in Harlem, like his own attack on the waitress in Trenton, as self-destructive and purposeless. Yet he also relates how these actions spring from a justified sense of outrage. In the case of the riot, such outrage was the product of letters from the South describing the abuse and killing of black soldiers training there, of newspaper articles and posters describing the enemy ("yellow-bellied Japs") in overtly racial terms, of exclusion from all but the most menial and dangerous positions in both the war industries and the armed forces, of residential segregation and disproportionately high prices in black neighborhoods.[45] In light of such concerns, Baldwin's sardonic commentary on the inefficacy of playgrounds as a solution to unrest in the ghettoes exposes a public policy of evasion. His vivid description of the weird congregations that gathered in the weeks before the riot—"Seventh Day Adventists and Methodists and Spiritualists seemed to be hobnobbing with Holyrollers and they were all, alike, entangled with the most flagrant disbelievers" ("Notes," 100)—provides a powerful counter-narrative to declarations by both white and black leaders in New York that the riot was simply the work of "hoodlums."[46] And his observation that the violence was not random, that the participants explicitly targeted white-owned businesses as symbols of "white power," discredits any simple division of Harlem's residents between criminals, on the one hand, and upstanding, passive citizens, on the other. Baldwin's account of how a broad cross-section of Harlem's black population joined together in common cause redescribes what officials characterized as an outburst of criminal activity. The riot thus appears to be the protest of angry citizens to whom other avenues of public self-expression had been denied.

Of course, one might accept the foregoing account of the events of 1943 and still ask what relevance they have for contemporary political life. One response is provided by the uprising in Los Angeles following the acquittal of four police officers for beating Rodney King in 1992. Analysts of those events similarly remark on the deafness

of policymakers, journalists, and the larger public to its possible political or moral meanings. For example, Robert Gooding-Williams
notes that television coverage of the event could be roughly divided
into a "conservative" perspective, which reinforced assumptions
about black lawlessness, and a "liberal" perspective, which blamed
poverty, unemployment, and other social ills for the violence and
looting. What neither the blacks-as-hoodlums nor the blacks-as-vic-
tims theses admitted, according to Gooding-Williams, was the possibility that the uprising revealed a sense of moral outrage about the
acquittal of King's attackers. By appealing to racial images (of hoodlums or victims), both perspectives implicitly endorse the idea that
it is black citizens, rather than the circumstances they frequently
must endure, that need repair. My point here is not to endorse
Gooding-Williams's characterization of the events but to ask what
it reveals about the currency of racial images when the claims of
black citizens are at issue. That these images were even considered
appropriate to such a complex set of events involving members of so
many different racial and ethnic groups, moreover, suggests their
continuing grip on the American political imagination.[47]

How Can the American Negro Past Be Used?

Racial images have public effects. Yet the images are extremely
difficult to oppose politically. Unlike a sign on a water fountain or
an exclusionary practice like red-lining, images do their work in private, at the level of consciousness where they are not subject to ex-
ternal scrutiny. The relationship between the public availability of
the images and their power to obscure both individual experiences
and systemic injustices fosters a cycle in which the devaluation of
claims about the experiences of racial subjugation contributes to the
persistence of the images, and the images perpetuate the accep-
tances of a certain degree of racial subjugation as normal. Baldwin's
perception that the sources of this cycle are rooted in American history harks back to one of Tocqueville's most trenchant warnings:
"Memories of slavery disgrace the race, and race perpetuates memories of slavery."[48] Baldwin examines how racial images preserve that
intricate interrelation of race, memory, and disgrace and shows that

the power of the images resides in their capacity to help manage "memories of slavery" and to forestall the admission of black grievances as real.

By providing a way of not seeing African Americans as individuals, racial images can sustain the kind of forgetting that prevents direct confrontation with questions about what the United States owes its black citizens. This point is not solely Baldwin's. Sheldon Wolin, for example, reminds readers how the selectivity of collective memory sustains the coexistence of injustices and democratic pretensions. Writing about Americans' desire to forget the Civil War that racial slavery eventuated, Wolin comments, "Society will be reluctant henceforth to want to confront radically the grievances of those who still carry the marks of the original wrong."[49] Neither free from anxiety about "the original wrong" nor willing to accept responsibility for its aftermath, Americans continue to invest meanings in blackness, meanings that speak with more authority than the individuals who carry them on their skin.

The impulse to privatize African Americans' grievances thus reflects a desire to deflect the claims of citizens whose inclusion is perpetually questioned. Seen in this light, the assumption that African Americans seek recognition as whites' equals appears tantamount to expecting that this brutal treatment will be forgotten. Remembering the everyday pain and the history of struggle against it presents an obstacle to the realization of the promise of formal equality. Wolin notices the dilemma when he writes that "the trade-off is equality for remembrance, or rather a certain kind of equality—not equality as an ideal that is necessarily at war with power (because power presupposes inequality) but equality as a fiction that serves to legitimate power."[50] Like Wolin, Baldwin appreciates that, unless equality is reconceived, its expansion may bring with it the suppression of the memories of citizens who feel inequality's sting.

Racial images insulate Americans from facing the kinds of questions that Wolin and Baldwin raise. Yet these images are intertwined with the idea that the line can be definitively drawn between misfortune and injustice in ways that render the asking of such questions both difficult and necessary. As the discussion of double consciousness in chapter two indicated, Baldwin shows how Americans' interior lives are permeated by racial assumptions. For black Americans, looking squarely at those assumptions means asking to what degree negative racial images are inherent in their own self-images. For white Americans, it means asking to what degree a raceless self-image is predicated on an assurance of privileged status in a racial hierarchy. On this latter point, Baldwin advances the idea that

> segregation has worked brilliantly in the South, and, in fact, in the nation, to this extent: it has allowed white people, with scarcely any pangs of conscience whatever, to *create*, in every generation, only the Negro they wished to see. As the walls come down they will be forced to take another, harder look at the shiftless and the menial and will be forced into a wonder concerning them which cannot fail to be agonizing. It is not an easy thing to be forced to re-examine a way of life and to speculate, in a personal way, on the general injustice.[51]

Among the lessons of Baldwin's understanding of double consciousness is that coping with one's feelings about the individuals unseen and unheard behind racial images requires taking stock, for the first time, of what Wolin calls "the presence of the past."

"How can the American Negro past be used?" Baldwin repeats this question in so many of his essays because he believes that the availability of degrading images of black Americans signals a denial, by all Americans, of the continuing significance of American racial history. The coexistence of racial slavery and legal segregation with declared commitments to freedom and equality posed and poses a radical challenge to Americans' sense of their own democratic possibilities. Concealing behind images the experiences of women and men who have suffered as a result of this coexistence provides a way out. Whether the images reinforce unspoken assumptions about African American sexuality or criminality or passivity, they suggest unfitness for full participation in American public life. And by hiding the individuals whose very presence reminds an unwitting society of its deepest flaws, these images protect Americans from coming to terms with a terrifying fact: the vulnerability of democratic societies to the worst prejudices of their members.

The inclination to see by images suggests a more personal kind of vulnerability as well. By making vivid the hurts inflicted by racial injustice, Baldwin not only criticizes the injustice but also relates it to a general claim about human fears in the face of uncertainty and death. Thus, he writes that "in the same way that to become a social human being one modifies and suppresses and, ultimately, without great courage, lies to oneself about all one's interior, uncharted chaos, so have we, as a nation, modified and suppressed and lied about all the darker forces in our history."[52] Racial images thus serve to protect Americans from that "interior, uncharted chaos" by providing an explanation and a tacit justification for the reigning racial order.[53] "The black man has functioned in the white man's world as a fixed star, as an immovable pillar," Baldwin writes, "and as he moves out of his place, heaven and earth are shaken to their foundations."[54] By calling on his readers to evaluate their own investment in the reduction of African Americans to images of victimhood, Baldwin requires them to examine their own susceptibility to despair. In so doing, "Notes of a Native Son" exposes as illusory the reassurance provided by the racial images that set David and James Baldwin and their neighbors apart from the rest of *us*.

Baldwin's focus on "the American Negro past" is thus not merely an angry reminder that African Americans have been victimized throughout American history. First, he recognizes that there are other histories that have, likewise, been suppressed and for analogous reasons. Commenting on the popularity of the image of "the good Indian," he concludes that the ubiquity of cowboy-and-Indian stories in American culture is "designed to reassure us that no crime was committed."[55] Second, whether describing history as a "force"[56] that operates within and through every person or as a "nightmare," Baldwin fights the notion that it is all-determining. "The Negro is forced to say 'Yes' to many a difficult question," Baldwin notes, "and yet to deny the conclusion to which his answers seem to point. His past . . . has not been simply a series of ropes and bonfires and humiliations, but something vastly more complex, which, as he thinks painfully, 'It was much worse than that,' was also, he irrationally feels, something much better."[57] Baldwin is explicit about the horrors of African Americans' experiences—he maintains that they surpass human expression—but he asserts equally explicitly that the lives of black Americans cannot be reduced to those horrors. Baldwin is interested, finally, in the purposes for which history is used. Instead of supplying a catalogue of the unspeakable, he understands that an investigation of "the history of the present"[58] is necessary to imagine a different future.

By making an offering of his own "American Negro past," Baldwin thus puts forward a critical reminder of the fallacy of two myths. The first myth, which is sustained by racial images, is the myth of African Americans as damaged products of centuries of oppression. Baldwin counters this form of social determinism through narratives that intimate the complexity and variety of lives obscured by those images. He further dismisses the denial of agency that accompanies this view with the warning, "That victim who is able to articulate the situation of the victim has ceased to be a victim: he, or she, has become a threat."[59] The second myth Baldwin debunks is equally troubling. This is the myth that, to put an end to images of black victimhood, Americans need to stop talking about how African Americans have been and continue to be victims of racial injustice. No adequate account of justice is possible, Baldwin shows, that fails to listen for the distinctive experiences of injustice.

Baldwin decries images of black victimhood, finally, in order to make possible a public discourse that takes the victimization of African Americans seriously. In lieu of both myths of victimhood, he exhorts his fellow citizens to question their own freedom from moral implication in the lives of the most vulnerable members of society. Implicitly he also calls on political theorists to interrogate the racial innocence that is protected in the determination to draw clear boundaries between injustices and personal misfortunes. By taking his readers into the homes and the hearts of men and women in Harlem, Baldwin demands that his readers interrogate those boundaries and omissions that insulate them from a direct confrontation with "the presence of the past." "It is a terrible, an inexorable, law that one cannot deny the humanity of another without diminishing one's own," Baldwin concludes. "In the face of one's victim, one sees oneself. Walk through the streets of Harlem and see what we, this nation, have become."[60]

Presumptions of Innocence

Beyond Innocence and Guilt

Summing up the complex sources of violent eruptions in American ghettoes, Baldwin offers a simple explanation: *"Negroes want to be treated like men."* But is it too simple? Insofar as Baldwin's claim presumes that the meaning of what it means to "be treated like men" is unproblematic or that all black Americans, regardless of gender, want to be treated that way, it clearly falls short. Although these are serious matters, however, to dismiss Baldwin's point too quickly on the grounds of its universalist language is to miss the larger point: that "people who have mastered Kant, Hegel, Shakespeare, Marx, Freud, and the Bible find this statement utterly impenetrable."[1] Perhaps Baldwin's claim will strike readers as exaggerated, outdated, or merely wrong. But this chapter aims to explore the implications of Baldwin's assessment and his basis for believing that it is true:

> The idea seems to threaten profound, barely conscious assumptions. A kind of panic paralyzes their features, as though they

found themselves trapped on the edge of a steep place. I once tried to describe to a very well-known American intellectual the conditions among Negroes in the South. My recital disturbed him and made him indignant; and he asked me in perfect innocence, "Why don't all the Negroes in the South move North?"[2]

More troubling even than the naivete of the assumption of complete mobility implied by the question is the idea that black life in the North is acceptable as long as Jim Crow lives somewhere else. It is this second element, born of the confidence that the North was on the right side of the Civil War and the fight for civil rights, that inflames Baldwin. In locating racism somewhere else, it deflects responsibility and blocks any probing consideration of the obstacles to acknowledging African Americans' claims on American society. Whether the asker's "perfect innocence" is feigned—in which case, he deliberately ignores the confinement of black Americans in northern ghettoes—or genuine—which reveals a glaring ignorance—it effaces the idea that African Americans, like other human beings, do not want to be trapped in substandard living conditions, of either the southern or northern variety.

To be innocent in the manner Baldwin decries is to be "protected against reality, or experience, or change" and to succeed in "placing beyond the reach of corruption values [one] prefers not to examine."[3] Innocence, in other words, is a kind of disconnection. Embodied in the dream of clean hands and clean breaks, innocence impedes engagement with the difficulties of living. The destructiveness of such disconnection is one of the great themes of all of Baldwin's writing: his fiction traces the effects of innocence on personal relationships; the essays appraise its social costs.[4]

Baldwin uses his essays to redraw the maps by which his readers see their world. His critical geographic sensibility undermines the force of American innocence by showing that the somewhere else of racial injustice is always here.[5] To that end, many of Baldwin's essays consider the meaning of Harlem to the American landscape, and Fifth Avenue provides one of his most effective metaphors for the state of American democracy. In the essay, "Fifth Avenue, Uptown," Baldwin revisits the "wide, filthy, hostile Fifth Avenue" of his childhood as an occasion for reflecting on the costs of maintaining "the renowned and elegant Fifth." Describing his old neighborhood, Baldwin deploys a string of penal images: colorless buildings, barbed wire, a hostile police force. Everywhere, he identifies the "human gaps," the absences created by lives lost to violence or fanaticism or exhaustion or even an anguished success.[6] Reminding his readers that the qualification, "uptown," insinuates the existence of its pair, Baldwin denies his readers the illusion that their lives are unconnected to those of the women and men of Harlem. Even changes, like the erection of a middle-class housing complex on "the rehabilitated side of the avenue," indicate white New Yorkers' desire to ensure that black New Yorkers remain uptown.[7] The effect of this incarceration is to divide the citizens who frequent Fifth Avenue, downtown, from a population of beleaguered men and women "whose only crime is color."[8] And if the women and men who frequent Fifth Avenue's shops and museums are oblivious to the suffering in the blocks to the north, the two ends of the avenue are linked nonetheless. So when Baldwin describes the subjection of Harlem's citizens to the often brutal whims of the armed guards who patrol their neighborhoods, he reminds his readers that "it is hard . . . to blame the policeman, blank, good-natured, thoughtless, and insuperably innocent, for being such a perfect representative of the people he serves."[9]

Building on Baldwin's observations about racial geography, this chapter expands the treatment of the relationship between innocence and American democracy sketched briefly in chapter 1. Offering a more extended discussion of the specific challenges race consciousness poses for political theory than I have in the preceding chapters, I elaborate on Baldwin's definition of innocence and then use that definition as the basis for an examination of the dangers of innocence for theoretical reflection. To do so, I revisit Michael Walzer's conception of social criticism, highlighting the ways in which many of Baldwin's concerns go unaddressed by a political theorist whose work equips him to recognize and respond to them. My aim here is not to show that Baldwin's essays do or should influence Walzer's account of social criticism. Rather, I read the moments of disconnection in Walzer's work as an indicator of larger concerns. That Walzer succumbs to the appeal of innocence both demonstrates the difficulty of race-conscious theorizing and reaffirms his arguments about the kinship of social criticism and the practice of political theory.

Before proceeding to an examination of the implications for theory, it is critical to say more precisely what Baldwin means by innocence. Who, for example, is innocent? The first, obvious answer is white Americans. Indeed, Baldwin has been heralded as a prophetic figure, someone who interrogated whiteness long before interrogating whiteness was fashionable. Still, the intricate ambivalence of Baldwin's conception of racial identity precludes reductionism when speaking of white people, as it does in the case of black people. Rather than simply defining whiteness as a quality naturally inherited by people with white skin, Baldwin characterizes it as a kind of delusion. To be sure, this delusion afflicts most Americans who are identified as "white," endowing them with a false confidence that comes from believing that they deserve their history. "People who imagine that history flatters them . . . are impaled on their history like a butterfly on a pin," Baldwin warns. They "become incapable of seeing or changing themselves or the world."[10] They become indifferent, furthermore, to the suffering of others who must, likewise, have done something to deserve *their* history.

Contending that "habits of thought reinforce and sustain the habits of power," Baldwin alerts his readers to the political and material tolls of white innocence.[11] Baldwin's assessment is borne out in various ways by recent scholarship. Cheryl Harris's trenchant analysis of "whiteness as property," David Roediger's account of the "wages of whiteness," and George Lipsitz's investigation of the "cash value" of whiteness, reinforce Baldwin's contention that whiteness involves a privileged access to a variety of benefits.[12] These benefits, in turn, are perceived as entitlements, settled expectations that are recognized as legitimate by American society and that disguise the domination that inheres in the status quo. Recent debates about affirmative action provide just one example of the connections between whiteness and innocence. The effectiveness with which opponents of affirmative action have emphasized the punishment "innocent" white men must bear for racial inequalities they did not create indicates a continuing presumption of white innocence.[13] Angry protestations that "I did not own slaves" or "I did not endorse segregation" or "My ancestors were poorer than a lot of black Americans" signal a disconnection between past and present circumstances. Not only do they deflect questions about the origins of the speakers' expectations but they also reaffirm the guilt of black Americans, who are presumed to require special treatment in order to succeed.

Baldwin's assault on American innocence is primarily directed at white Americans, who have the most to lose from the abolition of white privilege, yet he understands that deafness and blindness are human traits. He would not be surprised, for example, by the writings of cultural critic Shelby Steele on the subject of innocence. Like Baldwin, Steele discerns in white Americans' presumption of innocence an unwillingness to come to terms with troubling truths, and he explores the meanings of white guilt. However, Steele undercuts the critical effects of his investigation of the psychological dimensions of American innocence by reducing all claims—black and white alike—to morally equivalent plays for power. Among the effects of such an interpretation is Steele's simultaneous rejection of Ronald Reagan's appeal to innocence and celebration of Reagan's invocation of "American values" ("individual initiative, self-sufficiency, and strong families") as the solution to racial inequalities.[14] While Baldwin would reject the idea that there is an equivalence of power between black and white Americans, he would nevertheless insist that the equal humanity of all Americans means that black Americans, too, are susceptible to the temptation to turn away from a bitter history.

A second question arises: Who is guilty? To this question Baldwin has a different kind of answer. Although fierce in his assault on American innocence, attributions of racial guilt are not part of Baldwin's project. "Guilt," he maintains, "is a luxury that we can no longer afford."[15] This formulation is a bit misleading, for Baldwin never views guilt as a resource worth its price. Indeed, one mark of his moral subtlety is Baldwin's conviction that the attack on racial innocence must be part of a larger refutation of moral schemes which presume that it is possible to divide the innocent cleanly from the guilty.

The first reason is that focusing on the guilt of the relatively privileged often leaves privilege intact. Baldwin believes that white Americans already suffer enough from "an anguished inability to come to terms" with the horrors of American history and "the guilty fear and shame" engendered by the knowledge of those horrors.[16] He also believes that the anguish and the fear and the shame do nothing to generate the kind of will required to oppose racial injustices. To concentrate on assigning guilt is to divert attention away from the racial injustice itself and to refocus it on the guilty agent seeking reassurance that he or she is really not a racist after all. In "Many Thousands Gone," Baldwin illustrates how racial guilt operates as an impediment to recognizing African Americans as human beings, simply:

> Nothing has succeeded in making [the Negro face] exactly like our own, though the general desire seems to be to make it blank if one cannot make it white. When it has become blank, the past as thoroughly washed from the black face as it has been from ours, our guilt will be finished—at least it will have ceased to be visible, which we imagine to be much the same thing. But, paradoxically, it is we who prevent this from happening; since it is we, who, every hour that we live, reinvest the black face with our guilt; and we do this—by a further paradox, no less ferocious—helplessly, passionately, out of an unrealized need to suffer absolution.[17]

Thus, Baldwin argues that a preoccupation with white guilt demands a heavier price from the black citizens, who are expected to forgive, than from white citizens, who yearn to forget. As long as they function as "a most disagreeable mirror," black Americans will be expected to absolve and console their white neighbors. Genuine dialogue about racial injustices becomes impossible under such circumstances. Further, the attempt at dialogue may foster white resentment of African Americans, who hold the key to an absolution perpetually undercut by the fact that their blackness will not disappear. For black Americans on the other hand, it may foster another kind of resentment, a feeling of contempt for the person who looks at them, guiltily, as a "moral problem."[18]

A second and related reason to be wary of focusing on white guilt is that the reductionism required to proclaim the guilt of one race and, thereby, to insinuate the innocence of another, circumscribes too narrowly the range of possible black and white identities and experiences. As the discussion in chapter 3 indicated, the assignment of black Americans to the role of victim does nothing to undermine the idea that the victim is simply the creation of the victimizer. Em-

bracing the idea of white guilt—and, by extension, black innocence—is to advance the cause of black moral purity at the cost of
disclaiming black agency. Baldwin, I argued in chapter 2, provides a
complex and highly ambivalent account of racial identity, and he is
resistant to the kinds of claims for racial authenticity that diminish
his singularity as a human being. This is not to say that he never falls
prey to the temptation to make sweeping generalizations. But Baldwin at his most eloquent and most complicated evades the pitfalls of
assigning moral weight to racial categories.

Consider again the narratives from "Notes of a Native Son." Even
as he catalogues various kinds of damage done to African Americans
by life in a racist society, he does not conclude that black Americans
are, by virtue of their suffering, peculiarly virtuous. For example, his
recollection of how he obtained permission to go the theater by pit-
ting his father against a white teacher—"suspect[ing] that the color
of this woman's skin would carry the day"—suggests his own capacity to manipulate racial power relations cruelly.[19] And his loving descriptions of the same teacher (who remained an important figure in
Baldwin's life until he died) indicates the uselessness of blanket condemnation of white Americans. Moreover, Baldwin's exploration of
his own guilty feelings as a lucky survivor—both of the kind of violence that left Medgar Evers, Malcolm X, and Martin Luther King,
Jr. dead within a five-year period and of the conditions he left behind
in Harlem—intimates that racial guilt does not only operate *across*
the color line. Baldwin's point is neither to blame whites nor to be-
atify blacks for an accident of birth. To do either, he avers, is to neglect the humanity of black and white Americans alike and to glo-
rify oppression itself.

Baldwin also shows how appeals to racial guilt mislead. The emphasis on guilt, insofar as it directs attention to the wickedness of
racism, diverts attention from the everydayness of the racial injuries that are tacitly accepted even as deliberate racism is con-
demned. Denouncing this kind of racial guilt can perpetuate innocence. Because the ills Baldwin attacks are often imperceptible to
the privileged, identifying intentional wrongdoing is inadequate. As
Laurence Thomas notices, "Except for the blatant bigot or sexist,
participating in the downward social constitution of another rarely
has any special phenomenological feel to it."[20] Baldwin's focus,

therefore, is not so much on sins of commission as on the sins of ignorance and apathy, Shklar's "passive injustice." Worse still, this ignorance can breed self-satisfaction. "A civilization is not destroyed by wicked people," he advises his readers. "It is not necessary that a people be wicked but only that they be spineless."[21] Thus, although Baldwin's contention that he is more comfortable with southern segregationists than with northern liberals rings untrue—it certainly does not reflect any genuine desire to live in the South—it reinforces the point that open racism may be less dangerous than racial carelessness. This warning against the temptations of insulation from wrestling with racial injustice becomes all the more acute today, in a time when the signs of racial subjugation are less obvious to the people who participate in and benefit from it.

The emphasis on racial guilt misleads, finally, because the concept of guilt is best suited for individual crimes, and the absence of an individual miscreant can be too easily understood as evidence that no harm has been done. Systemic patterns of subordination disappear in this formulation, as do the effects of race consciousness. In this regard, Baldwin anticipates one of critical race theorists' central disputes with anti-discrimination law. Although he does not reject the idea that an individual may be innocent or guilty of discrete, racially motivated crimes, he sees how, in the case of racial injustice, a preoccupation with such claims often also functions as a diversion. Baldwin counters this misdescription by painting vivid portraits of American innocents. He shows how the comfort taken from the knowledge that one is nothing like a *real* racist—a George Wallace or Mark Fuhrman or David Duke—is linked to a larger evasion. The focus on questions of innocence and guilt fosters an expectation that there is a responsible individual for every individual harm and relieves the rest of *us* from facing the ways in which *we* too are responsible for maintaining the conditions in which racial injustices flourish. It is another way of locating racial injustice somewhere else.

The View from Uptown

When Baldwin chastises "people who have mastered Kant, Hegel, Shakespeare, Marx, Freud, and the Bible" for failing to recognize the humanity of black Americans, he reiterates the idea that race consciousness is not merely a form of backwardness or irrationality. As a consequence, scholarly rigor is insufficient to inoculate against racial innocence. The challenge that Baldwin's essays implicitly put to political theorists, therefore, is to ask whether the elaboration of democratic principles can be done without locating racial injustice somewhere else. Meeting Baldwin's challenge requires an attempt to understand the distance between the declaration of racial equality as a matter of law and the persistence of racial inequalities as a matter of fact. It involves attending to the specificity of African American experiences and reorienting theoretical inquiry from the level of principle to the spaces between principle and practice and accepting the messiness that inheres there. And it exposes the vulnerability of theories—both abstract and situated—to the appeal of racial innocence.

First, Baldwin's challenge exposes the limits of abstract conceptual analysis. By removing to the level of principle, theorists can sort out and evaluate conflicting viewpoints and devise a rational basis for mediating among them.[22] This approach offers clarification. One of the most powerful tools of theoretical inquiry, it establishes uniform moral priorities in a world defined by contestation and change. Yet, such an approach can also obscure insofar as it risks leaving out significant matters that may defy clarification. Theoretical arguments at the level of principle, where race is not relevant, may serve to protect the sort of racial innocence Baldwin attacks. Operating on many levels and undergirding racial hierarchy in ways that are difficult to detect, race consciousness is thoroughly interwoven into the fabric of Americans' experience. Hence, denying the import of assumptions about racial identity and difference disables theorists' capacity to address racial injustice. This possibility ought to be of particular concern to democratic theorists: it suggests that "race-blind" theorizing may exclude from consideration the specific insights of men and women most acquainted with racial injustice.

Within recent philosophy and political theory, there is a substantial literature that identifies innocence as an intellectual position of which to be wary. An unwillingness to acknowledge the virtues (and vicissitudes) of experience, including the experience of race consciousness, accounts for what Stuart Hampshire calls the "fairy-tale quality" of so much contemporary Anglo-American moral theory.[23] Such an enterprise is a fairy tale, Baldwin might add, because, rather than inspiring imaginative responses to life's most difficult conundrums, it falls prey to the dream of racial transcendence. In addition to Hampshire's work on the subject, feminist philosopher Jane Flax advances an argument that liberal theory from Locke to Rawls attempts to acquire "innocent knowledge" by dividing the pure sound of reason from the din of human prejudices and attachments. Such an aspiration, she shows, protects the theorist's innocence by locating knowledge in an objective realm that stands apart from the theorist her- or himself.[24] Theorists who attend to the normalizing forces of democratic order issue a similar warning. For example, Thomas Dumm takes on the denial of the cruelties of American history, interrogating the blindnesses protected by the "celebration of the present." When Dumm writes that "our complex innocence, our Americanness, is rooted in an impulse to keep fear outside our souls," his language and his message are positively Baldwinian.[25] What each of these critiques suggests is that theories of politics that abstract from racial identity may move too quickly into the raceless future without struggling with the significance of a race-conscious present. By breaking from experience, such theories fail to supply the resources needed to evaluate the possibility of multiracial democracy in America.

In chapter one, I suggested an alternative approach, a kind of theorizing that acknowledges the context of its production. But the perils of seeking moral resources in the uneven record of human societies are no less serious than those of aspiring to transcend it. It may be, as Seyla Benhabib suggests, that contextualist theories lack the resources to contribute an emancipatory vision of the future. It may be, furthermore, that they represent instead a longing "for the certitudes of one's own culture and society in a world in which no tradition, no culture, and no society can exist any more without interaction and collaboration, confrontation and exchange."[26] Certainly, it is on this second road that wishful histories make their entrances, that theorists may find themselves "in the grip of a weird nostalgia, dreaming of a vanished state of security and order."[27]

The sheer difficulty of hewing to history and maintaining a critical stance can be read in the ways in which the appeal of innocence seduces even the most historically conscious theorists to bracket troubling questions about the possibilities of democracy in a race-conscious society with an ugly racial history. Michael Walzer's work on social criticism provides an example of just this sort of evasion. His arguments are self-consciously situated in the experiences of particular people and reveal a profound appreciation for the phenomenological dimension of political and moral commitments. Further, Walzer tackles both general issues of inclusion and matters that relate specifically to African Americans. Unwilling to succumb to "the very nearly unconscious assumption that it is possible to consider the person apart from all the forces which have produced him,"[28] Walzer rejects as escapist reflections on principles that take no account of their place in specific human societies.[29] He maintains instead that moral and political principles must be located somewhere, that they reflect the workings of history on human allegiances, values, and identities, and that they are to be used for the good of all people who live there. Yet I argue that reading Walzer's work on social criticism in conjunction with Baldwin's social-critical essays suggests that the difficult matter of grappling with race consciousness slips out of Walzer's account precisely where he loses sight of his own arguments for embedded criticism.

In *Interpretation and Social Criticism* and *The Company of Critics*, Walzer advances social criticism as a key to a contextualist political philosophy that is not simply celebratory of traditional authority and the status quo.[30] If his attunement to the beliefs of particular societies resonates with the arguments of traditionalists like Alasdair MacIntyre, Walzer eschews the language of loss and decay. His interest, by contrast, is in change. Hence Walzer extols the value of men and women who understand their vocation to be the chastisement of their neighbors, who shatter the pretense of innocence. Their work of revealing a society's flaws to itself provides the link between embedded principles and progressive action:

> Hopes and ideals have an actual location—in our "souls," in our everyday consciousness of the moral world. It is only the social order within which hopes are realized and ideals acted out that is located "nowhere." The point of holding up the mirror is to demon-

strate that the ideal order is not here, or that we're not there. The stories that we tell ourselves about the realization of freedom and equality are untrue: one has only to look in the glass and see.[31]

What Walzer rejects in the view from nowhere is that it allows men and women, even if not deliberately, to evade the horrific aspects of experience and to replace them with a vision that is itself nourished by the same experience.

Despite this commitment to social criticism, no matter how unpleasant the critique, Walzer's fluency in a language of "comfort" and "fit," "the natural" and "the familiar," contains the scope of change. "The moral world," Walzer writes, "has a lived-in quality, like a home occupied by a single family over many generations, with unplanned additions here and there, and all the available space filled with memory-laden objects and artifacts" (*Interpretation*, 20). From this account of the moral world it follows that "moral philosophy is . . . a reflection on the familiar, a reinvention of our own homes" (17). And social critics are the men and women who demonstrate that what our homes actually look like falls short of what we would like them to be. Walzer uses the imagery of home to vivid effect as a counterpoint to abstract theories that offer what he calls a "hotel room" solution to the problems of diversity and conflict (13–17).[32] Yet the ease with which an argument for embeddedness slides into moral confirmation suggests that Walzer finally shrinks from accepting the ramifications of situatedness. "Where we are . . . is always *someplace of value*, else we would never have settled there"(17),[33] Walzer writes. On the contrary, Baldwin would respond, to say that the place we call home is a place of value does not mean that it is the home we would have chosen.

Baldwin, also, would reject a "hotel room" morality as too sterile to capture anyone's imagination or allegiance. He spent enough of his adult life in hotel rooms to speak authoritatively to their inadequacy as a substitute for "home," and it would not be unreasonable to read, in the loneliness of so much of Baldwin's prose, a longing for precisely the lived-in, comfortable single-family home of Walzer's description. But the image of home he proffers, while less anonymous, is not cozy. That it is familiar does not mean that it is comforting. Baldwin's musings on how it must have felt to be a black soldier arriving in the United States after fighting, in a segregated unit, for European freedom indicate the term's double edge:

> *Home!* The very word begins to have a despairing and diabolical ring. You must consider what happens to this citizen, after all he has endured, when he returns—home: search, in his shoes, for a job, for a place to live; ride, in his skin, on segregated buses; see, with his eyes, the signs saying "White" and "Colored," and especially the signs that say "White Ladies" and "Colored Women"; look into the eyes of his wife; look into the eyes of his son; listen, with his ears, to political speeches, North and South; imagine yourself being told to "wait."[34]

Much has changed since soldiers returned from segregated units and since Baldwin wrote about their return. The signs of segregation in all of their crude frankness have long since been legally erased from the American landscape. But Baldwin's central point remains. The price of preserving the comfort of "home" is exacted in patience from those who rightfully demand change. Critical reflection, for Baldwin, not only begins at "home" but also ends there: "Any real change implies the breakup of the world as one has always known it, the loss of all that gave one an identity, the end of safety."[35]

Walzer and the Bounds of Social Criticism

As the picture of home as a nurturing enclave suggests, innocence, in Walzer's case, involves boundaries. And the drawing and erasure of the bounds of criticism insulate the critic from some of the least tractable issues of racial injustice. The comparison with Baldwin reveals how Walzer takes great care to situate social criticism in relation to the bounds of membership (critics are insiders), power (critics stand outside the realm of power), and history (critics reveal society's inner truth), and, in so doing, neglects racial meanings that have no respect for such boundaries. Against readers who criticize Walzer's work for its reliance on shared understandings rather than abstract principles, I will argue that Walzer's account of social criticism does not reveal a resistance to universal principles so much as a reluctance to follow his hermeneutical commitments to their conclusion and to accept the uncertainty that they entail. I contend that Walzer's work proves to be *insufficiently* situated in a racially saturated context. What is so telling about Walzer's work, finally, is that despite his keen ear for the moral cadences of his society, he finds comfort in the silence of things not said.

The contrast between Walzer's and Baldwin's observations on membership points out a first sort of innocence of which to beware. Critics, according to Walzer, stand inside the city walls or national borders that enclose the societies they criticize. They are members of the "political community."[36] Describing membership as "the primary good that we distribute to one another," Walzer makes a direct link between boundedness and a rich complex of obligations and rights.[37] The meaningfulness of these obligations and rights, moreover, derives from the fact that members of a society share a history. By this account, members of a society who profess an allegiance to values such as freedom and equality "have been worked on, so to speak, for many generations; and they inhabit a society that 'fits' their qualities and so supports, reinforces, and reproduces people very much like themselves."[38] Whether one is born into an ancient and largely homogeneous society or emigrates to a more frantic and heterogenous "immigrant society,"[39] to be an insider is to have a life in common with other members, to be like them in important respects.

From this account of membership it follows that critics must be acknowledged as fellows of the people they criticize. "Standing," which is the quality that strangers and enemies lack, is crucial to the reception of the critic's message,[40] and it is the first criterion by which the Hebrew prophet Amos emerges as Walzer's paradigmatic critic. Jonah, by contrast, is a stranger to the people he chastises and can only operate as a "minimalist critic," in Walzer's view (*Interpretation*, 90). Jonah's appeal is restricted to "thin" universal moral claims, for he is excluded from that richer moral life of the people to whom he speaks. "What makes the difference is Amos's membership," Walzer declares. "His criticism goes deeper than Jonah's because he knows the fundamental values of the men and women he criticizes (or because he tells them a plausible story about which of their values ought to be fundamental)" (90). The conversation of the critic and the people he or she criticizes "is parasitic upon a previ-

ously accepted and commonly understood morality," Walzer writes
(78). Despite the disagreements that may occupy them on a day-to-
day basis, the citizen-members of societies described by Walzer appear fundamentally alike. And while he alerts readers to questions
about the extent of commonality in Amos's own society, he dis-
poses of them with a disclaimer: "(For my present purposes I will ignore the political division between the rival kingdoms of Israel and
Judah; the two share a history and a law, and prophets like Amos go
back and forth between them)" (80). Walzer's reader might reasonably wish he would pause there to relate the content of the rivalry
that split the kingdoms and explain how a shared history and law
muted it.

Although Baldwin discusses belonging and citizenship in terms of
"identity" rather than "membership," he shares Walzer's interest in
the ways boundaries are drawn. Keenly aware of how it feels to be
regarded as a stranger or to enjoy no standing in the eyes of his fellow citizens, Baldwin attends to the boundaries that do not embrace
him. His descriptions of the experiences of those whose membership is fragile or incomplete illuminates those boundaries that are
invisible in Walzer's work and reveals the ways in which the very
bounds of membership are constructed in contrast to those who lie
outside.

First, he would point out how the emphasis on the bounds that
demarcate this society from that one understates the existence and
effects of internal boundaries.[41] "Fifth Avenue, Uptown" and Baldwin's other writings on Harlem serve to remind his audience that
the mere fact of citizenship does not suffice to erase the line between members and those perceived as strangers or enemies. Continuing resistance of white Americans to residential integration provides just one example of the acuity of Baldwin's assessment. In
spite of Walzer's conviction that democratic societies should be
broadly inclusive, he reinforces Baldwin's account of the contrast
between outside and in with an appropriately military image: "The
political community grows by *invasion* as previously excluded
groups, and one after another—plebians, slaves, women, minorities
of all sorts—demand their share of security and welfare."[42]

If the notion of "invasion" captures something about how excluded groups are perceived as strangers or enemies, it reflects only

partially the way Walzer distinguishes between members and their opposites. When talking about exclusion in the American context, Walzer suggests a third contrast—between members and victims. While the victimization is cause for outrage, an unwillingness to probe its sources causes Walzer difficulties when he looks specifically at the place of less privileged insiders. His evaluation of Simone de Beauvoir, for instance, understands her discomfort with her own, female, body as an instance of a more general phenomenon—the self-hatred of the oppressed. Thus he writes that "De Beauvoir joins the ranks of the assimilated Jew, Albert Memmi's 'colonized' man, the American black before the age of 'black is beautiful,' whose standards of physical attraction and cultural excellence are borrowed and derivative."[43] Even if the sentence is meant only to signal the harms of exclusion, it reduces the identities of members of excluded or oppressed groups to those harms and ignores the extent to which full-fledged members' "standards of physical attraction and cultural excellence" are themselves borrowed, derivative, hybrid.

Walzer presages the casting of members and victims as opposites in a courageous early essay. Written against the turbulent backdrop of the 1960s, "The Obligations of Oppressed Minorities" advances the idea that "the mere existence of an *oppressed* minority suggests forcefully that the [democratic] rules are being worked, twisted, and manipulated, often brutally so, in the interests of the majority or of its leaders."[44] It begins from the pivotal question of the meaning of membership of individuals who are both oppressed and citizens. Moreover, by describing black Americans as "victims of *popular* oppression," rather than political oppression simply, Walzer acknowledges white supremacy as a broader cultural phenomenon.[45] Despite the italicization, however, the essay represents black Americans as victims, rather than querying what could make oppression popular or how the "majority" participates in and benefits from the subjugation of minorities in its midst.

Deploying the language of "us" (Americans) and "them" (African Americans), Walzer ponders the effect of oppression on "their" consciousness and concludes that it is total. "Oppressed individuals," he notes, "rarely experience their oppression as individuals." And he adds that "it is the fate of the oppressed that the whole of their moral lives be mediated by their common situation."[46] No less than membership in the "majority," membership in an oppressed minority group is presented in all-or-nothing terms. Hence, Walzer's account of "oppressed individuals" makes the oppression seem like the only salient aspect of experience, thereby subordinating the "individuals" entirely to the modifier "oppressed." Walzer's essay is important, and it is rare, for it grapples seriously with the obligations of citizens who are free and equal in name only. Still, by overlooking the complexity of the experiences of the oppressed, the essay reinforces the division between members and victims.

Either to ignore or to overstate the boundaries that divide citizens from one another is to miss two of Baldwin's most insistent points: the experience of victimization does not exhaust the experience or identity of individuals who suffer systematic oppression; nor can it be disentangled from the experience or identity of individuals who are privileged by such oppression. Despite Walzer's appreciation for multiple memberships and allegiances, he fails to recognize the ways in which the identities of the groups themselves develop in relationship to others. And, in spite of his interest in all of the facets of "moral culture," Walzer draws an American landscape that appears as though it is dotted with bounded communities and held together by underlying principles.[47] This picture, as Baldwin's essays show, erases the evidence of race consciousness and racial domination in the construction of the boundaries and the interpretation of the principles.

Walzer signals a second kind of innocence with a quotation from a Jewish sage that appears in both books on social criticism: "Love work, do not domineer over others, and never seek the intimacy of public officials."[48] As a warning against the temptation to turn the power of critical eloquence into an unholy power over the people on whose behalf the critic speaks, this adage demonstrates Walzer's sensitivity to the distinction between official or state power and the power of exhortation. As a claim for the purity of social criticism, however, it confines the critique to certain realms presumed to be untainted by domination and leaves relations of power in those arenas unexamined.[49] It depends on a second kind of boundary that Baldwin would call into question.

If Walzer's view of membership discredits the idea that critics can operate at some Archimedean point above the fray, his account of social criticism nonetheless proposes that critics can remain aloof from the domination over others. "It is not connection but authority and domination from which we must distance ourselves," Walzer explains. And this distance requires abstinence from "certain sorts of power relationships within society" (*Interpretation*, 60). Walzer's insistence on avoiding the constraints of "governmental responsibility, religious authority, corporate power, [and] party discipline" reflects a keen appreciation of the moral compromises required in public life.[50] In understating the operations of power outside those special arenas, however, Walzer fails to ask what the pervasiveness of racial domination as a general feature of a society means for the work of social criticism.

One consequence of this kind of critical distance is that it severely restricts the possibilities for critical work within conventional social and political institutions—or at least at their upper echelons. Would a figure like Martin Luther King, Jr., one wonders, be excluded from the company of critics on account of his leadership positions in the Baptist church and the civil rights movement? Such questions become more pointed when one considers how Walzer uses the distinction between priest and prophet to portray the critic as isolated from traditional forms of political power. Here, the aptness of Amos as Walzer's model critic stems from his status as someone who is neither a priest nor even a professional prophet (Amos 7:14–15). Priests, according to Walzer, represent established power; prophets are hostile to it.[51]

The location of social critics beyond the reach of power's taint resonates with a broader strain in Walzer's work: the contrast between political and common morality. Explaining the dilemma of "dirty hands," Walzer argues that, too often, doing the right thing in politics requires doing something that is otherwise wrong. "I do not think I could govern innocently," Walzer admits. "Nor do most of us believe that those who govern us are innocent."[52] The complement to this expectation that politics is an inherently dirty game is an impulse to protect the innocence of social critics by removing them from the arena in which they are forced to make immoral choices. When, for example, he takes note of Gramsci's credentials as an "innocent communist," Walzer hints that Gramsci's appropriateness as a model social critic derives from the fact of imprisonment and his inability, as a result, to participate in actual political life.[53]

Here Walzer reveals the depth of his debt to Max Weber. Eschewing an ethic of ultimate ends, Walzer ponders the paradox of political life. Politics is about means. The right thing to do politically, Walzer writes, is mostly determined by a utilitarian calculus that can never measure up to the demands of an absolutist position. Nor should it measure up.[54] Although Walzer recognizes that the problem of dirty hands may arise in private life, he identifies it as a particular feature of politics for three reasons: politicians serve themselves while acting for others; they control others; and they use force against them.[55] It is the second reason, the rule over others, that is particularly problematic in a racially stratified society. By identifying the successful politician as "the visible architect of our restraint," Walzer confines the discussion of relations of power to the realm of the visible and his worries to people who intentionally dominate others.

The idea that the critic can stand in a place outside the realms of domination neglects, first of all, the multiple channels through which the authority of tradition invoked by the prophetic critic exerts power in shaping the identities and defining the roles of members of a community. In the American context, moreover, it neglects structures of power, white supremacy most notably, that less visibly or invisibly shape citizens' lives. It is not essential to embrace a Foucauldian notion of the omnipresence of power—which Walzer explicitly rejects—to see that this requirement of critical innocence may render the critique ineffective against the kinds of racial domination and privilege that have outlived the abolition of slavery and legal segregation.

Baldwin's arguments against the accommodationism of individuals recognized as "Negro leaders" suggest that he shares Walzer's concerns about the ramifications of wielding political power.[56] And his most famous experience of the "intimacy of public officials"—a 1963 meeting with Robert Kennedy that devolved into a bitter misunderstanding—reaffirms the wisdom of avoiding official power. But Baldwin's distrust of public officials has less to do with the failings of the individuals who exercise authority over others than it does with the expectation that a few can provide redress for problems that belong to all citizens. For Baldwin, it further misses the point to say that the writer "is a critic of the regime, not of the people."[57] The distinction between "the people" and "the regime" is always suspect in democracy. As Baldwin's disarming use of the first-person plural in many of his fiercest attacks indicates, critics, like their fellow citizens, are implicated in a vast network of relationships that sustain various forms of hierarchy. Their work entails exposing the deeper roots of allegiances and beliefs wherever they happen to find themselves. In disavowing critical innocence of the second kind—distance from structures of authority—it is *Baldwin* who reminds his readers of what it means for critics to be members of the society they criticize.

Unlike Baldwin's insistence on the relevance of "the American Negro past," Walzer's use of the past as the basis for critique discloses a third kind of innocence. Although Walzer makes it clear that social criticism is forward-looking, he argues that the critic gains his or her power either by looking backward, to a time when a people's beliefs were solidly reflected in their practices, or by appealing to principles that appear primordial insofar as they are taken to be defining for an entire society or nation. The temporal confusion engendered by this backward-looking/forward-looking vision is obvious when the claims of black Americans are at issue, and it indicates the perils of reclaiming a history in which the articulation of noble principles and the failure to imagine what their implementation requires are so inextricably intertwined.

Walzerian social criticism operates by waking a society up to its neglect for or disregard of values that once informed communal life. Nowhere is this appeal to the past more clearly illustrated than in Walzer's discussion of the criticism of the Hebrew prophets. "Prophecy aims to arouse remembrance, recognition, indignation, repentance," he argues. "In Hebrew, the last of these words derives from a root meaning 'to turn, to turn back, to return,' and so it implies that repentance is *parasitic upon a previously accepted and commonly understood morality*" (*Interpretation*, 75).[58] Again, Walzer chooses Amos as the prophet whose example best speaks to the demands of social criticism, this time because of Amos's alienation from the growing upper class of his day. From this vantage point, Amos demands a return to "what had been, and still was ideally, an association of freemen" (84). Although Walzer allows that inequalities probably existed in the ancient society that Amos recalls, he nonetheless holds that the excesses of Amos's present render the comparison with the past morally compelling. What is troubling is not the claim for the embeddedness of social criticism but that the claim is couched in language suggesting that some virtue inheres in the past.

Walzer's explanation of the basis of social criticism sits uneasily alongside his rejection of longings for an idealized past[59] and his interest in assuring a democratic future. The power of the principles of freedom and equality, Walzer might say, resides in their status as part of *our* American past. Yet the value of that legacy, forged as it was in a time of racial slavery and restricted suffrage, is ambiguous. Its creation was itself a moment of racial innocence that continues to bedevil its inheritors. Given the impossibility of dissociating, historically, the pure principles from their violation or perversion, an appeal to the past-ness of the principles suggests that the relevant past can be restricted to those elements untouched by racial oppression. Not only would Baldwin challenge the notion that such elements can be found, he would also add that the idea that democracy is something to be returned to, rather than something never genuinely tried, reinforces the idea that black Americans stand outside its promise.[60]

As if concerned about the conservatism implied by such language, Walzer contends that what the critic appeals to is not the past-ness of the principles but the way they are known to a society's members. These principles constitute what Walzer calls the "core" of a society (*Interpretation*, 87). To the extent that the discussion of the "core" enables Walzer to evade the nostalgia of traditionalists, it leads him to make the very sort of extrahistorical claims that he rejects as escapist. For example, Walzer's elaboration on the development of the notion of equality from a bourgeois to a critical concept glides over the question of African Americans' experience of equality. He explains how the work of criticism has enlarged the idea of human equality: what was once a middle-class political slogan can become the inspiration of the working class. The appeal of equality is unambiguous, by his account, for it is "a common idea." "How can [the workers] be wrong about the value and significance

of equality in their own lives?" Walzer asks (44). In reply, Baldwin
might ask, Where would a story about the racial exclusivity of these
workers' unions and jobs and neighborhoods fit into this tale?
If "the argument is about meaning and experience," and "its term
are set by its cultural as well as its socioeconomic setting" (44),
then overlooking the significance of racial meanings in this case
consigns African Americans to someplace outside the universe of
equals.[61]

The dispute turns on the uses of history. The defining features of
social criticism, according to Walzer, are "the identification of public pronouncements and respectable opinion as hypocritical, the attack upon actual behavior and institutional arrangements, the
search for core values (to which hypocrisy is always a clue), the demand for an everyday life in accordance with the core" (*Interpretation*, 87). Because this description begs the question of what constitutes the "core," Baldwin would detect in Walzer's description an
incomplete reading of the historical record. Despite Walzer's emphasis on cultural meanings, the account of how social critics draw
upon those meanings reveals a selective hermeneutics. The circle it
draws him into is a vicious one, for the critic's standards come from
a "core" in which equality and inclusion are prized. But insofar as
that "core" is connected to historical experience, then either the experiences of the excluded and degraded only count at those moments when the circle expands to include them, or the values of the
"core" are themselves vitiated. What is central in Walzer's story is
the act of inclusion; what remains unexamined are queries about
the appeal of exclusion to those on the inside and the price society's
outsiders must pay to join the society of equals.

Walzer might respond that this sort of selective remembering is
precisely what his work on social criticism is meant to oppose. He
might, further, remind his readers that "interpretation does not
commit us to a positivist reading of the actually existing morality, a
description of moral facts as if they were immediately available to
our understanding" (*Interpretation*, 29). Yet he suggests that the aspect of the past enabling a people to recognize its failings is clearly
divisible from the aspect supporting those same failings. The difficulty is not that Walzer underestimates the extent of moral conflict
but that, like the abstract theorists who understand moral philoso-

phy as a sort of "discovery" or "invention," he only acknowledges *some* of the cultural meanings of the moral principles invoked, thereby losing sight of his own arguments about embeddedness. Offering these meanings as "ours" without defending their selection, he too abandons history.

The alternative Baldwin offers is neither to wallow in history's miseries nor to relinquish the aspiration toward more democratic forms of life. Rather, Baldwin's social criticism aims for a fuller acknowledgment of the ways degrading racial meanings, even those no longer openly accepted, reverberate in the common ideas that undergird this democratic society. He discerns in most American appeals to the past a sense of panic about the present and proposes an alternative.[62] Writing about the courage of student civil rights demonstrators in the South, Baldwin notes that "it is because these students remain so closely related to their past that they are able to face with such authority a population ignorant of its history and enslaved by a myth."[63] The history to which they lay claim is that of the Declaration of Independence and southern lynchings, that of the Fourteenth Amendment and northern segregation. And even the meaning of the best moments—of the passage of the Bill of Rights and the Civil Rights Act of 1964, for example—is always susceptible to troubling questions about how the status quo is protected. The past thus serves not as a judgment on the present but as a key to understanding it. "The truth about that past is not that it is too brief, or too superficial," Baldwin contends, "but only that we, having turned our faces so resolutely away from it, have never demanded from it what it has to give."[64]

The critical distance between Walzer and Baldwin is expressed by their understandings of the bounds of social criticism. The boundaries that occupy Baldwin are those of human limitations, the finitude of imagination and absence of will that prevent so many Americans from considering what it would mean to absorb the significance of the "American Negro past." Distrustful of the comforts of home, he puts his critical imagination to the service of opposing racial injustices, knowing that there is no way to determine, definitively, the degree to which even his own thinking is informed by his race consciousness. If the ills of racial injustice are to be overcome, no bounds can be presumed innocent. No inside can be understood except in relation to an excluded outside. Thus, Baldwin takes pains to point out the view from the other side of borders erected to assure members of a humanity denied to victims. He questions borders that claim to circumscribe the realm of domination. And he demonstrates the permeability of borders that are supposed to preserve the moral core of history from contamination by rejoinders from people trampled in that history.

The Ambivalence of Home

William Faulkner's unwitting provocation of a national uproar in a 1956 interview provides a poignant illustration of the difficulty of grappling with all that history has to give. The subject of the interview was southern resistance to the desegregation of schools and the prospects of federal intervention.[65] In it, Faulkner laid bare his allegiances. He allowed that he would defend his fellow Mississippians against the intrusion of the federal government "even if it meant going into the street and shooting Negroes." "After all," he added, *"I'm not going out to shoot Mississippians."* When the interviewer inquired whether Faulkner meant white Mississippians, the writer replied: "No, I said Mississippians—in Mississippi the problem isn't racial. Ninety per cent of the Negroes are on one side with the whites, against a handful like me who believe that equality is important."[66] Were Faulkner an avowed segregationist or conservative, the remarks might have been, simply, appalling. But he was not. This is the same Mississippi writer whose novels Baldwin credits with penetrating the tragedy of American racial history. The same man who once commented that "to live anywhere in the world today and be against equality because of race or color is like living in Alaska and being against snow."[67]

Faulkner is neither a straw man nor simply a symbol of the tenacity of southern racism. Although his gradualism is representative of a particular time and place, its significance extends beyond the Mississippi of the 1950s. For Faulkner's inability to extricate himself from an interview without loading outrage upon outrage exposes a larger dilemma. The community and the history from which his identity is forged are intertwined with his egalitarian commitments in a way that defies separation. "It is easy enough to accuse [Faulkner] of hypocrisy when he speaks of man being 'indestructible because of his simple will to freedom,'" Baldwin reasons. "But he is not being hypocritical; he means it. It is only that Man is one thing— a rather unlucky abstraction in this case—and the Negroes he has always known, so fatally tied up in his mind with his grandfather's slaves, are quite another." The difficulty, Baldwin contends, is that "Faulkner means everything he says, means them all at once, and with very nearly the same intensity."[68] Echoing Du Bois's description of double consciousness, Baldwin observes that "the southerner clings to two entirely antithetical doctrines, two legends, two histories."[69] To insist that only one of those doctrines, legends, histories constitutes the core of Faulkner's community makes no sense.

What Baldwin condemns in the Mississippian is not his inability to reconcile the warring strands of his identity. Baldwin understands that reconciliation is not possible and that Faulkner must confront the deep terror that accompanies the end of what is most familiar to him. Baldwin censures Faulkner, however, for appealing to a "middle-of-the-road" politics that would sacrifice another generation of African Americans to the uncertain workings of progress. Such a politics accepts the need for change but asks that it take place without too much risk or bloodshed or loss—and, above all, not too soon. One is reminded of Martin Luther King, Jr.'s "Letter from Birmingham Jail," which counterposes a list of the injuries of living under segregation against the plea, by white Americans, to "wait."[70] Or of the caveat, "with all deliberate speed," that assured that the pace of school desegregation in the South would proceed with so little speed.[71] What Baldwin conveys so forcefully is that the demand for more time ignores the toll that generations of inequality have extracted from black Mississippians, the "human gaps" created by the status quo. He emphasizes the devastating losses that follow when the fears of the privileged overshadow the needs of those who have been excluded by that tradition of privilege.

Baldwin implores his readers to understand that Faulkner's struggle and his southern history cannot be detached from a broader American and, indeed, human story.[72] "Faulkner and Desegregation," like "Fifth Avenue, Uptown," uses geography to critical effect, undermining any attempt to disconnect part of the polity or its people from the whole. While the circumstances of northern segregation may be quite different from the world Faulkner knows, the color line there is no less entrenched or destructive; and even if it were not, northerners would still bear some responsibility for conditions elsewhere in the country. The implications of Faulkner's turmoil, moreover, reach beyond their context. Relating Faulkner's situation to a universal human encounter with the tragic, Baldwin begins the essay with a reflection on what it means to confront "the breakup of the world as one has always known it, the loss of all that gave one an identity, the end of safety."[73]

The radicalism of Baldwin's social criticism consists in his recognition that a commitment to social change means a willingness to give up the pretense that outcomes can be controlled or identities fixed, an openness to a new order whose parameters cannot be specified in advance. While Baldwin insists on the influence of values inculcated at home, he has little patience with the "certitudes of [his] own culture and society."[74] One risk of refusing the temptation of innocence is that the critic may fall prey to the temptation to give over, permanently, to hopelessness. And Baldwin battles this temptation throughout his life. Yet, late in his career, Baldwin makes it clear that he does not see, in the end of innocence, a cause for despair: "Human history reverberates with violent upheaval, uprooting, arriving and departure, hello and good-bye. Yet I am not certain that anyone ever leaves home. When 'home' drops below the horizon, it rises in one's breast and acquires the overwhelming power of menaced love."[75]

The Living Word

Baldwin's Art of Resistance

If social change requires "the end of safety," as Baldwin insists, then the practice of social criticism itself involves a willingness to work without a net. What are the implications of Baldwin's conception of change for democratic theory? For the possibility of a public dialogue about racial injustice? Although the context in which these questions are posed is remote from the period in which Baldwin produced his early essays, "Everybody's Protest Novel" provides an instructive response. First published in 1949, "Everybody's Protest Novel" lays out Baldwin's dispute with literature that aims for social improvement by galvanizing opposition to some moral outrage. In this case, the outrage in question is slavery and the racial oppression that succeeds it; the objects of Baldwin's attack are *Uncle Tom's Cabin* and, to a lesser extent, *Native Son*.[1] At the same time that Baldwin demolishes the literary value of the protest novel, he demands an alternative standard for moral and political critique. He aspires to find a language to express the wrongs of racial injustice without losing sight of the complicated workings of race consciousness in American society. I argue that this aspiration, and Baldwin's appreciation of the sheer difficulty of realizing it, offers valuable guidance for American democratic theory and practice today. For the ease with which the language of formal equality has been deployed against the purposes of the civil rights movement indicates the urgency of Baldwin's warnings about the dangers of disconnecting democratic principles from the lives of the women and men who are expected to abide by them and hold them dear.

The opening passage of "Everybody's Protest Novel" recreates a moment in *Uncle Tom's Cabin* in which Miss Ophelia, a proper northerner, conveys her horror at the uses to which southerners put their black slaves. Miss Ophelia's reaction, according to Baldwin, provides the novel's "moral, neatly framed, and incontestable like those improving mottoes sometimes found hanging on the walls of furnished rooms."[2] What Miss Ophelia responds to is indeed outrageous. Yet Baldwin contends that her declaration of moral horror, insofar as it distances her personally from the cause of the outrage, is no less incongruous in a world built upon racial hierarchy than the cheery order implied by the "improving mottoes" set against the anonymous setting of a furnished room. This incongruity makes a larger point about invoking moral principles without investigating the causes of suffering of those to whom counsel is offered; to them, the principles not only may appear unconnected to their experience but may even serve as an affront to it. Protest novels resemble Miss Ophelia, Baldwin contends, insofar as both rely upon a "medieval morality" that understands the world to be divided cleanly into good and evil, innocent and guilty. Such a morality unfailingly provides right answers without considering their relevance in the lives of human beings who reside in the more complicated realm that is somewhere between heaven and hell. Inadequate to the task of grappling with either slavery or racial injustices, this moral vision copes with their existence by assigning individuals and their behavior to simple categories and mouthing moral formulas. The protest novel proclaims its good intentions but does so by providing so flat a picture of the evil it aims to overcome that readers are not required to recognize racial injustice in their own lives.

Although Baldwin was only twenty-four when he wrote "Everybody's Protest Novel," the essay announces his presence as a critic to be reckoned with. In it, he declares a lifelong assault not only on protest novels but also on any attempt to effect social change through the reduction of individual women and men to symbols of a social wrong. In its insistence that such efforts contribute to the dehumanization of African Americans, "Everybody's Protest Novel" attacks the producers and products of the myth of innocence.

> The "protest" novel, so far from being disturbing, is an accepted and comforting aspect of the American scene, ramifying that framework we believe to be so necessary. Whatever unsettling questions are raised are evanescent, titillating; remote, for this has nothing to do with us, it is safely ensconced in the social arena, where, indeed, it has nothing to do with anyone, so that finally we receive a very definite thrill of virtue from the fact that we are reading such a book at all. This report from the pit reassures us of its reality and its darkness and of our own salvation. ("Everybody's," 19)

Baldwin's critique is not purely an aesthetic one. His opposition stems from his observation that protest novels, far from encouraging self-examination or radical criticism, generate the sort of indignation that comforts the comfortable in the righteousness of their opinions and the necessity of the existing moral framework. Just as the novels stretch the bounds of credibility, Baldwin asserts, the standards that undergird them prove their unreality and lose their power as guides to ethical behavior.

Protest novels, according to Baldwin, refuse to acknowledge the fundamental difficulties of moral improvement. With regard to issues of racial injustice, they have nothing to say to the question of why white Americans have behaved so brutally for so long. Instead, they offer "a mirror of our confusion, dishonesty, panic, trapped and immobilized in the sunlit prison of the American dream" ("Everybody's," 19). Left unasked are hard questions about the prospects for multiracial democracy: What must be given up—by black and white Americans—in the definition of a common and equal citizenry? Is it possible that the women and men whose enslavement was justified by the claim that they were less than human could become, by fiat, fully human, either in the eyes of their oppressors or in their own?

Baldwin gives good reason to think that the answer to the first question is "More than we can now imagine," and the answer to the second question is "No":

> It is the peculiar triumph of society—and its loss—that it is able to convince those people to whom it has given inferior status of the reality of this decree; it has the force and the weapons to translate its dictum into fact, so that the allegedly inferior are actually made so, insofar as the societal realities are concerned. This is a more hidden phenomenon now than it was in the days of serfdom, but it is no less implacable. Now, as then, we find ourselves bound, first without, then within, by the nature of our categorization. And escape is not effected through a bitter railing against this trap; it is as though this very striving were the only motion needed to spring the trap upon us. ("Everybody's," 20)

That the decree of black inferiority is not only hidden but also internalized by black and white Americans indicates the depth of the harm of racial injustice and the difficulty of extirpating such injustice. According to Baldwin, genuine opposition to entrenched racial inequalities requires no less than a transformation—of Americans' understanding of themselves and of the society in which they live.

Baldwin concludes "Everybody's Protest Novel" with a plea that establishes his vision of the purpose of his writing: "Our humanity is our burden, our life; we need not battle for it; we need only do what is infinitely more difficult—that is, accept it. The failure of the protest novel lies in its rejection of life, the human being, the denial of his beauty, dread, power, in its insistence that it is his categorization alone which is real and which cannot be transcended" ("Everybody's," 23). Although Baldwin's language suggests a disavowal of political struggle in a traditional sense, Irving Howe's conclusion that the substitution of *acceptance* for *battle* aligns Baldwin with "a post-war liberalism not very different from conservatism" strikes me as unfair. Howe, defending Richard Wright against challenges by Baldwin and Ralph Ellison, paraphrases Wright to say that "only through struggle could men with black skins, and, for that matter, all the oppressed of the world, achieve their humanity."[3] Rather than counseling quietism, however, Baldwin's attack on the protest novel reminds his readers, first, of the dangers of defining struggle too narrowly, and, second, of the reductionism involved in tying the humanity of "men with black skins" to that struggle. In response, Baldwin might also call Howe's attention to the concluding paragraph of "Notes of a Native Son," where he asserts that the idea of acceptance is always to be accompanied by its twin: the idea of equal power.[4]

The project that Baldwin sets for himself in "Everybody's Protest Novel" is daunting. Simultaneously declaring the equal humanity of black and white Americans and undermining the assumption that the meaning of this claim is self-evident, Baldwin both speaks in the name of democratic principles and unsettles received understandings of those principles. The challenge "Everybody's Protest Novel" implicitly poses for democratic theory is also daunting. If the failure of protest novels resides in the preference for categories over human experiences, then one might expect theoretical accounts of democratic life to be even more remote from those experiences. Part of the task of theory, after all, is to make general claims. But Baldwin's example suggests how democratic theorists might shift attention away from moral formulas and precepts, which too often carry the weight of the neatly framed mottoes that he scorns, to the furnished rooms in which they hang.

By examining Baldwin's struggle to breathe new life into familiar words so that they will respond to his experiences, this chapter suggests how his essays assist his readers in uncovering the habits of thought and the "habits of the heart" that either stymie or nurture democratic possibilities. First, I explore Baldwin's ambivalence about the words of his own language. Then, I consider the story Baldwin tells in *The Fire Next Time* about two of those words, two preeminent principles of democratic theory: equality and freedom. Toward the end of *The Fire Next Time*, Baldwin muses that "people are not . . . terribly anxious to be equal (equal, after all, to what and to whom?)." Later, in the same paragraph, he notes, "I have met only a very few people—and most of these were not Americans—who had any real desire to be free. Freedom is hard to bear."[5] What Baldwin means by these claims and how they bear on thinking about democratic promises in a race-conscious society illuminate the difficulty of defining equality and freedom in a way that makes space for experiences of individuals who have never taken their value for granted.

"To Shape a Silence While Breaking It"[6]

When the Ebonics debate erupted nearly a decade after his death, Baldwin's thoughts about the uses and limits of language made news. Commentators cited his 1979 essay "If Black English Isn't a Language, Then Tell Me, What Is?" to explain what was at stake in the controversy over the use of black English in American schools. Baldwin's argument—that black English reflects the experiences of African Americans in a way that "standard" English does not—might strike a reader as somewhat dishonest.[7] Baldwin, after all, renders his own experiences in uncommonly beautiful "standard" English. Yet the fluency of Baldwin's prose disguises a deep ambivalence about the language of his inheritance. As a racial outsider to the American "mainstream," Baldwin is wary about embracing a language that has functioned as an instrument of his subjugation. As an artist, he grapples with the inadequacy of any language to convey the full force of experience. As a moralist, he wrestles with the problem of expressing his convictions without sacrificing nuance. Combined, these ambivalences suggest why, as Toni Morrison observes, "In spite of its implicit and explicit acknowledgment, 'race' is still a virtually unspeakable thing."[8] And they indicate the sheer difficulty of imagining alternatives to race-blind discourse that do not, at some level, reproduce discredited assumptions about racial difference. Briefly, I will consider the interlocking dimensions of Baldwin's struggle to find his own words as a black man in a white-dominated society, as an artist, and as a moralist, recognizing all the while that it is impossible to separate any single dimension, definitively, from the others.

Baldwin's dispute with his native tongue resides in the suspicion that the language has not done justice to his experiences as a marginal American. Yet because the language that he distrusts is also, inescapably, *his*, he responds by claiming it and molding it to serve a critical purpose. "If the language was not my own," he muses, "it might be the fault of the language; but it might also be my fault. Perhaps the language was not my own because I had never attempted to use it, had only learned to imitate it."[9] Given Baldwin's distrust of the English language, it is no accident that "unspeakable" and "unspeakably" appear so often in his essays.[10] Words such as these acknowledge the fundamental elusiveness of human experiences, which, as he notes in his rejection of protest novels, strain human capacity for expression in *any* language. But Baldwin's emphasis on the "unspeakable" also conveys his sense of the costs of putting into words the hurts of racial injustice. When he writes, "for the horrors of the American Negro's life there has been almost no language," Baldwin means that American public discourse has not generally accommodated stories that so deeply undercut the assumption that democratic ideals have been, for the most part, realized ("Down," 69). And he recognizes that the "privacy" of black experiences protects even as it marginalizes. To break silence, he knows, is to risk exposing the details of those experiences to public scrutiny with no assurance that they will be understood as he intends. He knows as well that the very act of finding a receptive white audience may spell his own alienation from other black Americans. Baldwin believes that everything is at stake in choosing to write. Language, for him, "is the most vivid and crucial key to identity: It reveals the private identity, and connects one with, or divorces one from, the larger, public, or communal identity."[11]

As a writer, Baldwin strains for the words that will move his readers without making them conscious of his efforts or presuming to control exactly how they will respond. To that end, Baldwin writes most effectively when he focuses on the smallest details, the moments that reach beyond themselves. Referring to the powerful imagery of "Notes of a Native Son," Alfred Kazin remarks that "there is a certain law for art: not to know as you're writing what everything means. It's being impressed with the fact, not with the significance of the fact."[12] Baldwin thus makes the most of the incompleteness implied by the name "essay," embracing the uncertainty it entails. He uses his gifts as a reporter of overlooked detail to craft his narratives, leaving it to the reader to discern and absorb their significance. Although Baldwin described himself as a novelist and dreamed of being a great playwright, his development, in the essays, of the persona of James Baldwin may stand as his greatest literary accomplishment. By creating and recreating from his life a figure whose loneliness nearly grabs the reader from the page and whose struggles against despair express a broader, human struggle, Baldwin exemplifies the force of the personal essay. He explores the force of what he calls "the living word"[13] and makes good on the aim to "render the transient eternal."[14]

Baldwin the moralist has a point to make. And he wrestles with the desire to simplify for the sake of making his point compelling. While he probably does not accord *Uncle Tom's Cabin* adequate respect for its part in precipitating the Civil War, his critique of the protest novel nevertheless expresses a valid anxiety about the costs of moral or political persuasion. Causes, he notes, "are notoriously bloodthirsty" ("Everybody's," 15). And crucial to their bloodthirstiness is the reduction of human complexity. Commenting on Cassius's glorification of the killing of Caesar in Shakespeare's *Julius Caesar*, Baldwin writes, "This single-mindedness, which we think of (why?) as ennobling, also operates, and much more surely, to distort and diminish a man—to distort and diminish us all, even, or perhaps especially, those whose needs and whose energy made the overthrow of the State inevitable, necessary and just."[15]

Related to this dilemma of the costs of persuasion and political action is the writer's awareness of the malleability of words that persuade. Even the most admirable ideals can be perverted without losing their formal meaning. Listen, for example, to Václav Havel, who is himself a fighter for the values of the French Revolution, as he describes the multiple meanings possible through the "mysterious, ambiguous, ambivalent, and perfidious phenomenon" of words: "*Liberté, Egalité, Fraternité*—what superb words! And how terrifying their meaning can be. Freedom: the shirt unbuttoned before execution. Equality: the constant speed of the guillotine's fall on different necks. Fraternity: some dubious paradise ruled by a Supreme Being!"[16] Havel's point is not to discount the value or the possibility of liberty, equality, or fraternity. Rather, his emphasis on the multivalence of the words is an appeal to vigilance. It provides a reminder that the proclamation of principle is no guarantee of its meaning. If the perversion Havel describes is extreme, it cannot be explained away as simply an example of the costs of revolutionary zeal. It speaks to one of Baldwin's great worries—the ease with which moral and political ideals become twisted in the course of everyday life.

Compounding Baldwin's worry is his prescience about who is likely to suffer when the political redefinition of democratic ideals involves issues of race. In this regard, he resembles Maurice Merleau-Ponty, who notes that principles can be "instruments of oppression" and who uses as his example the French depiction of Toussaint-L'Ouverture's liberation of Haiti from colonial rule as a counterrevolutionary undertaking.[17] Baldwin's concerns are of particular notice because they have been borne out in American political life in the post–civil rights era. The use of the term "civil rights" in the title of California's Proposition 209 (the "California Civil Rights Initiative"), banning affirmative action, provides one instance of the metamorphosis Baldwin fears. And the prevalence in public discourse of the phrase "reverse discrimination" provides another, indicating how easily the idea of discrimination can be stripped of its historical association with systematic oppression.

Baldwin conveys his own sense of the dilemmas that arise from the inseparable and yet frequently contradictory forces that shape his efforts to break silence in "The Northern Protestant," an essay about a meeting with Ingmar Bergman. Baldwin notes, almost as an aside, that he envies the Swede's unqualified love for his home and his ability to live and work there. As soon as Baldwin makes the admission, however, he allows that maybe he does not really envy Bergman after all. There is no point in wishing for a different home, Baldwin realizes; "everything in a life depends on how that life accepts its limits: it would have been like envying [Bergman] his language."[18]

This line from "The Northern Protestant," while it touches directly on neither political life nor matters of race, goes to the heart of Baldwin's convictions about the possibility of fulfilling the promise of American democratic ambitions. No matter how brilliantly the political institutions are conceived, the success of a democratic experiment depends upon the people (which is not to say that institutions are unimportant); and even the best aspirations of the people are dependent on values, beliefs, and prejudices inculcated in them from birth. That this holds true for the dispossessed as well as the privileged means that the terms according to which change is envisioned are absorbed, ineluctably, from one's surroundings. "It must be remembered that the oppressed and the oppressor are bound together within the same society," Baldwin contends, and

neither the oppressed nor their oppressors can hope realistically to
be free of the other. "Within this cage it is romantic, more, meaningless, to speak of a 'new' society as the desire of the oppressed, for
that shivering dependence on the props of reality which he shares
with the *Herrenvolk* makes a truly new society impossible to con-
ceive" ("Everybody's," 21). Thus, Baldwin apprehends the tension
between a reliance on the traditions and history that form identity
and the aspiration to challenge the status quo. If it is impossible to
transcend completely the assumptions of one's society, it is nevertheless morally and politically necessary to question those assumptions. The act of recognizing and responding to one's "dependence
on the props of reality," in other words, is revolutionary.

Equality and Freedom, Down at the Cross

In order assess how well Baldwin meets the challenge of fashion-
ing new possibilities from the conceptual tools of his inheritance, I
turn now to *The Fire Next Time.* Although this piece has been unfa-
vorably compared to earlier essays,[19] I contend that it succeeds as an
extended example of how Baldwin makes the English language his
own and how, at the same time, he invests it with new critical
power. A critical meditation on the concepts of equality and freedom, *The Fire Next Time* makes a twofold contribution to the task
of understanding the meaning of those principles: through its preci-
sion of language, *The Fire Next Time* evokes their lived meanings to
readers who are not themselves touched by the everydayness of
racial injustice and gives shape to the experiences of those who are;
at the same time, it calls attention to the limits of expression, insisting that change can and must be conceived within those limits.

The Fire Next Time is actually two essays—"My Dungeon Shook:
Letter to My Nephew on the One-Hundredth Anniversary of the
Emancipation" and "Down at the Cross: Letter from a Region in My
Mind." The latter essay first appeared in the 17 November 1962 issue of the *New Yorker*, its twenty thousand words consuming
nearly the entire issue and boosting sales of the magazine dramati-
cally; the former, a much shorter piece, was published in the *Progressive* that December.[20] Most of my comments here focus on

"Down at the Cross," but I read them together as parts of a whole. In "My Dungeon Shook" Baldwin explains to his nephew, who is also named James, why he is growing up in poverty and why his prospects appear so limited. The essay then counsels the nephew to reject the white world's definition of him and urges him to make the notion of freedom real. In "Down at the Cross," Baldwin interweaves a narrative about his early encounters with Christianity with an account of the Nation of Islam and an exposure of the emptiness of white liberal commitments. The points of connection between the two essays are many. Both are written as open letters, although one is addressed to his nephew and the other is addressed to no one in particular, coming from an unspecified region in Baldwin's mind.[21] The nephew to whom Baldwin addresses his thoughts in "My Dungeon Shook" is about fourteen years old, the older Baldwin's age in the opening section of "Down at the Cross." And as the ensuing discussion aims to demonstrate, the notes that Baldwin strikes in the shorter essay are elements of more elaborated themes in "Down at the Cross."

Equality, as it is represented from the opening paragraph of the "Down at the Cross," is terrifying. According to Baldwin, the summer he turned fourteen was one of crisis. It was the summer he "discovered God" and the summer that the onset of puberty convinced him of his damnation. Intertwined with these developments was another: during the summer of 1938, Baldwin recognized in the men and women in his neighborhood the future toward which he seemed inevitably to be hurtling. "What I saw around me that summer in Harlem was what I had always seen; nothing had changed. But now, without any warning, the whores and pimps and racketeers on the Avenue had become a personal menace. It had not before occurred to me that I could become one of them, but now I realized that we had been produced by the same circumstances" ("Down," 16). The essay continues, drawing out what it was in Baldwin's surroundings that suddenly appeared so menacing. Clearly, the dread Baldwin describes is religious. But it is not only the fear of damnation that emerges in the opening paragraph of the essay. The observation that "in the same way that the girls were destined to gain as much weight as their mothers, the boys, it was clear, would rise no higher than their fathers" (18) indicates how the kind of equality evident in the streets of Harlem in 1938 might feel like a trap to an ambitious fourteen-year-old boy. If the men and women who struggled not to be eaten away by "the incessant and gratuitous humiliation and danger one encountered every working day" (19) and those who had long since given up the struggle and succumbed to the lure of "the Avenue" were the examples against which Baldwin measured his own prospects, and if he could see nothing standing between their present and his future, equality could only look frightening.

Against this backdrop, the notion of individual agency and the significance accorded to choice seem irrelevant. According to Baldwin, the only imaginable escape from the ghetto and the certainty of sharing the fate of those around him was to find a "gimmick." Among the gimmicks he reports having considered that summer were prizefighting, singing, dancing, and preaching ("Down," 24). Baldwin does not represent his election of the pulpit over the other options as a righteous one; becoming one of the men and women "on the Avenue" was, morally, no worse than any other fate. As he tells the story, he was essentially seduced into his preaching career when a woman pastor greeted him by asking, "Whose little boy are you?"—precisely the same question used by the street hustlers asking him to join *them* (29, 63).[22] Baldwin's calling to the pulpit was contrived, a flight from the alternatives: "Out of a deep, adolescent cunning I do not pretend to understand, I realized immediately that I could not remain in the church merely as another worshiper. I would have to give myself something to do, in order not to be too bored and find myself among all the wretched unsaved of the Avenue." Irreverent toward his own success as a preacher, Baldwin undercuts the moral authority of the role; his self-mocking description of "what we might call my heyday" relates how he used that authority to win an adolescent battle for power over an overbearing father (32–33). In contrast to the wisdom of the improving mottoes he derides in "Everybody's Protest Novel," Baldwin's retelling of his embrace of and by the church proffers no "neatly framed and incontestable moral." The fact that the arms into which he fell were those of the church was sheer luck; his evasion of the trap of a criminal career was narrow and arbitrary.

Although the principle of equal opportunity, of careers open to talent and hard work, provides the basis for a critique of precisely the sort of restricted future Baldwin describes, his retelling of his fourteenth summer casts even this ideal in a sinister light. His story evokes the power of boundaries more impermeable than the physical barriers of dividing Harlem's Fifth Avenue from the shops and museums downtown. Baldwin conveys his premonition of the unimaginably awful implications of presuming he could realize the same dreams as any other child:

> The fear that I heard in my father's voice . . . when he realized that I really *believed* I could do anything a white boy could do, and had every intention of proving it, was not at all like the fear I heard when one of us was ill or had fallen down the stairs or strayed too far from the house. It was another fear, a fear that the child, in challenging the white world's assumptions, was putting himself in the path of destruction. ("Down," 26–27)[23]

By capturing the dread consequences of believing in equal opportunity in a society not prepared for the full inclusion of African Americans, Baldwin's makes it plain how, for some citizens, the most cherished democratic ideals can be experienced as ambiguous, dangerous, and real.

Does Baldwin's unsettling narrative recommend the abandonment of equality as a political principle? Not at all. In fact, Baldwin's critique is made in the name of the equal humanity of all persons, regardless of race, and of the equal entitlement of all Americans to the basic rights of citizenship. Still, what Baldwin calls for is equality radically reconceived. He penetrates the idea of equality, understanding its multiple meanings, understanding that not all of them are positive. He is wary, for example, of the proximity between equality and conformity. Noting that "the American ideal, after all, is that everyone should be as alike as possible,"[24] he worries about the costs of inclusion to men and women who are marked as different. Baldwin also uses the idea of equality as a critical device. By comparing institutions and principles not generally thought to be alike and showing them to be moral equals, he demonstrates the appeal, and the shortcomings, that they share. Baldwin uses this sort of critical equation to great effect by showing the limitations of all "totems, taboos, crosses, blood sacrifices, steeples, mosques, races, armies, flags, nations" or through his depiction of the similarities between Christianity, American nationalism, and the Black Muslim movement ("Down," 91).

Equality radically reconceived, then, requires grappling with the question "equal . . . to what and to whom?" Baldwin's response is to show that the inclusion of all Americans as equal citizens means reexamining the status of those already recognized as "equals." Taking the notion seriously, he avers, requires that privileged Americans recognize their equals in the men and women "on the Avenue." At the same time, it demands the same from the excluded, who have good reason not to view the men and women who have excluded them as *their* equals. Simply to declare the equality of all citizens or to assume it to have been achieved is to fail to grapple with the difficulty of these demands. "It is easy to proclaim all souls equal in the sight of God," Baldwin notes, in a critique of Harriet Beecher Stowe. But, he adds, "It is hard to make men equal on earth, in the sight of men."[25]

This comment calls for another look at a rhetorical question quoted in the previous chapter. When Michael Walzer traces a transformation of the concept of equality from a limited, bourgeois notion of juridical equality and equality of opportunity to a more radical notion that challenges the inherently unequal structure of capitalist societies, he asks: "How can [the workers] be wrong about the value and significance of equality in their own lives?"[26] Offered, rightly, as a counter to the presumption that false consciousness compromises the workers' sense of their own interests, Walzer's question nonetheless neglects the matter of *what* the workers think and feel about "the value and significance of equality in their own lives." To whom would they call themselves equal? Part of the difficulty of thinking about equality in a race-conscious society is that, in addition to coping with the political and economic faces of equality, one must also address the social barriers that continue to prevent the inclusion of even the most prosperous African Americans.[27] Baldwin's radicalism consists in prying open the questions that are sealed when their answers are assumed to be uncontroversial.

In lieu of reassuring questions, Baldwin prefers those that disrupt the order of things. Hence, he relays approvingly a question raised by the Tunisians in 1956: "Are the *French* ready for self-government?" ("Down," 52). The Tunisians' query could be extended to the American case in the following way: Are white Americans ready for equality? Or, alternatively, "Do I really *want* to be integrated into a burning house?" ("Down," 52, 94).[28] Baldwin asserts that the fundamental difficulty, for white Americans, of seeing blacks as their equals resides in an unwillingness to think through how that equality requires a revaluation of white identities and whites' stake in persistent racial inequalities. He reveals how the idea that moral progress involves the inclusion of black Americans in an ever-expanding circle of people deserving of respect or recognition leaves the center of the circle unexamined and preserves the assumption that that center contains some value worth having or emulating. This idea, Baldwin declares, "is revealed in all kinds of striking ways, from Bobby Kennedy's assurance that a Negro can become President in forty years to the unfortunate tone of warm congratulation with which so many liberals address their Negro equals." For black Americans, who are hardly newcomers to the United States, Kennedy's assurance insults. "It is the Negro, of course, who is presumed to have become equal—an achievement that not only proves the comforting fact that perseverance has no color but also overwhelmingly corroborates the white man's sense of his own value" (94–95). Equality thus extended to the formerly unequal is robbed of its critical potential, for its extension leaves unaddressed the question of what allows white Americans to see black Americans as their inferiors in the first place.

Corresponding to an unwillingness among white Americans to see in black Americans human beings like themselves, Baldwin identifies an unwillingness by black Americans to see whites as capable of rehabilitation. Indeed, he notes that many African Americans view their white neighbors as "slightly mad victims of their own brainwashing" ("Down," 102). The source of the resistance to equality, however, is not the same. In his own life, Baldwin writes, the everydayness of race-based humiliation and the possibility of brutality means that "it begins to be almost impossible to distinguish a real from a fancied injury." Furthermore, protecting oneself against such injuries can, without one's realizing it, engender a hostile outlook toward white Americans. "Most Negroes cannot risk assuming that the humanity of white people is more real to them than their color," Baldwin explains. "And this leads, imperceptibly but inevitably, to a state of mind in which, having long ago learned to expect the worst, one finds it very easy to believe the worst" (68). Baldwin's recollection of dinner at Nation of Islam headquarters indicates just how entrenched such a state of mind can be. Baldwin describes how he groped, unsuccessfully, for a way to counter Elijah Muhammad's rejection of any kind of interracial future. "In the eeriest way possible," he remembers, "I suddenly had a glimpse of what white people must go through at a dinner table when they are trying to prove that Negroes are not subhuman. I had almost said, after all, 'Well, take my friend Mary,' and very nearly descended to a catalogue of those virtues that gave Mary the right to be alive" (73).

Furthermore, Baldwin's conviction that racial hierarchies dehumanize the privileged as much as the oppressed reveals how the premise that blacks aim to be whites' equals demeans African Americans. He captures this sentiment using a device that he deploys in several essays. Compressing a long history into a few moments that expose the connections between past and present, he undermines the attempt to locate racial subjugation in the past or to deny that its residues continue to thwart American democratic possibilities:

> The Negro came to the white man for a roof or for five dollars or for a letter to the judge; the white man came to the Negro for love. But he was not often able to give what he came seeking. The price was too high; he had too much to lose. And the Negro knew this, too. When one knows this about a man, it is impossible for one to hate him, but unless he becomes a man—becomes equal—it is also impossible for one to love him.[29]

This reflection, which appears just before the conclusion of "Down at the Cross," casts equality in an even more unattractive light than do Baldwin's comments at the essay's opening. If the idea that the same conditions had created both him and the men and women "on the Avenue" was frightening to the fourteen-year-old Baldwin, the possibility of being the equal of creatures capable of the kind of baseness described above was nearly inconceivable. Despite the gloominess of this conclusion, however, Baldwin advances an alternative to despair—acceptance.

Acceptance, as noted above, does not connote passivity or fatalism. Instead, it entails an active opposition to innocence, engagement with life's harshest truths. In advancing this notion of acceptance Baldwin casts doubt on other interpretations of *what* it is that needs to be accepted and *by whom*. He departs from received narratives in which outsiders become members by accepting the standards of the inside, and the insiders, in turn, accept the formerly excluded as their fellow citizens, and explores instead the difficulties of expanding the company of equals. When the experiences of African Americans are taken into consideration, he shows, the standards for inclusion appear, at best, incompletely realized, and at worst, fundamentally compromised. By casting his account in the light of those experiences, Baldwin provides an explanation of why black and white Americans are largely ill prepared to achieve the ideal of equality they profess. But acceptance is not only the key to equality for Baldwin; it is also the key to freedom. Indeed, acceptance is the hinge between equality and freedom.

What is political freedom for Baldwin? Baldwin's report of his visit to Nation of Islam headquarters suggests just how difficult it is to formulate a precise answer. In Baldwin's retelling of his conversation there, he maintains a tenuous line, repeating Elijah Muhammad's diagnosis of American racial ills, with which Baldwin agrees, and challenging the proscribed course of treatment, with which he cannot agree. Baldwin understands the conviction that, without land or sovereign power, black Americans have no reason to expect recognition as human beings or inclusion in American prosperity. Yet he cannot endorse the call for a separate black nation. No matter how unlikely the possibility that African Americans will be able to travel or speak publicly or reside or get an education as freely as white Americans, Baldwin objects to an ideal of freedom based on the assumption that blackness and whiteness are internally unified and externally divisible properties. According to Baldwin, this sort of freedom merely displaces the white world's constraints through an illusion. And, like the gimmick that kept Baldwin off the streets as a teenager, it is ultimately as binding as the constraints it succeeds in breaking.

Much of Baldwin's treatment of freedom is negative. By this I do not mean "freedom from," as it is most famously articulated by Isaiah Berlin.[30] Rather, I mean simply that Baldwin dedicates more energy to the task of recounting what freedom is not than he does to the elaboration of what freedom is. His essays emphasize the rarity of freedom. This rarity is evident not only in his descriptions of the lives of women and men trapped in the ghetto but also in the arbitrariness of his own escape.[31] The rarity or even absence of freedom is demonstrated, moreover, by the racial innocence of white Americans.[32] In contrast to this innocence, Baldwin maintains that freedom requires the exercise of moral agency in the face of disagreeable truths. Hence, when Baldwin defines freedom positively, he describes it as "maturity" or "flexibility" or the state of being "present" or "the fire which burns away illusion."

Baldwin's exchange with a young Black Muslim, who escorts him from Nation of Islam headquarters to his next appointment ("Down," 78),[33] suggests what Baldwin means by freedom and why he maintains that it is "hard to bear." During the ride, he engages his driver in a discussion of the prospects of a separate black nation. And afterward, Baldwin writes that

> the boy could see that freedom depended on the possession of land; he was persuaded that, in one way or another, Negroes must achieve this possession. In the meantime, he could walk the streets and fear nothing, because there were millions like him, coming soon, now, to power. He was held together, in short, by a dream—though it is just as well to remember that some dreams come true—and was united with his "brothers" on the basis of their color. Perhaps one cannot ask for more. People always seem to band together in accordance to a principle . . . that releases them from personal responsibility. ("Down," 80–81)

By framing the discussion in personal terms, Baldwin does not underestimate the significance of the political freedom demanded by his driver or by Elijah Muhammad. What he sees instead is that this dream of self-determination is a fantasy. It is a fantasy, moreover, that relies on the same racial logic that makes escape from the United States seem imperative. Given the fundamental interrelation of black and white Americans, neither the nationalist dream of separation (which Baldwin likens to "amputation") nor the liberal notion of integration without fundamental change ("gangrene," in Baldwin's parlance) grasps reality.[34]

Hence, Baldwin's appeal to "personal responsibility." The term, as Baldwin uses it, clearly bears little connection to contemporary political usage. Understanding that individuals are always enmeshed in a larger social and historical context, Baldwin rejects the sort of up-by-the-bootstraps individualism that is often associated with the term. His is not the responsibility that demands the identification of a discrete agent for every hurt or injustice.[35] Personal responsibility, as Baldwin uses it, involves the honest appraisal of the historical roots, as well as the current conditions, of one's situation.

The idea of freedom as the acceptance of responsibility appears at the conclusion of "My Dungeon Shook," preparing the way for the longer treatment in "Down at the Cross." Baldwin proceeds from a piece of advice to his nephew about how to cope with a white world that believes that its acceptance of blacks into the fold is a prize— "The really terrible thing, old buddy, is that *you* must accept *them*"—to the claim that "we cannot be free until they are free."[36] In "Down at the Cross," Baldwin inverts this statement when he asserts that "the price of the liberation of the white people is the liberation of the blacks—the total liberation, in the cities, in the towns, before the law, and in the mind" ("Down," 97). This inversion indicates the elusiveness of "freedom." Baldwin's writing takes aim, simultaneously, at an unjust social structure ("the price of the liberation of the white people is the liberation of the blacks") and at the assumptions and fears that undergird it ("we cannot be free until they are free," and "the total liberation . . . in the mind"). The confusion here is not causal, although his language implies that it is. Rather, it indicates that Baldwin is demanding everything—the freedom of blacks and the freedom of whites—and all at once.

Underlying Baldwin's demand is a deep existentialism, an acknowledgment of the boundedness of human achievement. Freedom, thus, is "hard to bear" precisely because it involves facing the terrifying fact that "the earth turns and the sun inexorably rises and sets, and one day, for each of us, the sun will go down for the last, last time" and salvaging the will to act in spite of it.

> It is the responsibility of free men to trust and to celebrate what is constant—birth, struggle, and death are constant, and so is love, though we may not always think so—and to apprehend the nature of change, to be able and willing to change. I speak of change not

on the surface but in the depths—change in the sense of renewal. But renewal becomes impossible if one supposes things to be constant that are not—safety, for example, or money, or power. One clings then to chimeras, by which one can only be betrayed, and the entire hope—the entire possibility—of freedom disappears. ("Down," 91–92)

Among the chimeras to which Americans cling, he insists, is the idea that pronouncements about the "race problem" can serve as a substitute for confronting the fact of human finitude.

From this existential innocence grows another form of innocence, one with concrete political implications: the evasion, by citizens, of responsibility for the gaps between democratic principles and the quality of so many Americans' lives. Consciously or not, Americans rely on race as a kind of explanatory crutch. It satisfies nagging questions about why, in a democratic nation of unprecedented prosperity, infant mortality, childhood poverty, and incarceration levels are as high as they are for black citizens. In spite of legal and social prohibitions against overt racial discrimination, the tacit acceptance of racial division props up American confidence in the realization of democratic principles. It can, moreover, stifle the generation of political will by either the privileged or the disadvantaged. "Nothing is more desirable than to be released from an affliction," Baldwin writes, "but nothing is more frightening than to be divested of a crutch."[37] Baldwin's job as an essayist is to convince his readers that they are not walking at all, until they try to move without the crutch of race; but, at the same time, he warns that no American can imagine what that kind of walking would feel like without interrogating their reliance on the crutch in the first place. That the effort to do so is imperative, Baldwin leaves little doubt: "Everything now, we must assume, is in our hands" ("Down," 105).

Finding the Words

Color is not a human or a personal reality; it is a political reality. But this is a distinction so extremely hard to make that the West has not been able to make it yet. And at the center of this dreadful storm, this vast confusion, stand the black people of this nation, who must now share the fate of a nation that has never accepted them, to which they were brought in chains. Well, if this is so, one has no choice but to do all in one's power to change that fate, and at no matter what risk—eviction, imprisonment, torture, death. For the sake of one's children, in order to minimize the bill that *they* must pay, one must be careful not to take refuge in any delusion—and the value placed on the color of the skin is always and everywhere and forever a delusion. I know that what I am asking is impossible. But in our time, as in every time, the impossible is the least that one can demand. ("Down," 104)[38]

The first sentence of this passage from the penultimate paragraph of "Down at the Cross" is surprising. What is Baldwin's message, if it is not that color is a human or a personal reality, and that those realities and political realities are thoroughly entangled with each other? But the statement that "color is not a human or a personal reality; it is a political reality" does not indicate a lapse in Baldwin's thinking about race blindness. It captures the tension that Baldwin strives to maintain. "The value placed on the color of the skin," while a delusion, has real effects on individual experiences. Or, although whiteness and blackness have no meaning in themselves, they are significant in the context of racial domination. Because that significance cannot be wished away, to demand the impossible is to aspire to change society fundamentally without either valorizing race or denying the value attached to it.[39]

Thus, "Down at the Cross" brings together the two senses of race consciousness defined in the first chapter. The message of the essay is that overcoming the damaging effects of race consciousness, in the descriptive sense, involves becoming race conscious in the normative sense. Baldwin both insists that racial assumptions, which serve to perpetuate racial hierarchy, pervade American society to a degree that defies simple abolition and urges that Americans acknowledge the ways in which those assumptions shape their experience, their identities, their language. Race blindness is, by this account, an attempt at escaping the horrors of American history. Even if escape is undertaken in the name of the ideals that that history is supposed to represent, it is a costly innocence. Race consciousness, on the other hand, requires that one "strive to become . . . tough and philosophical concerning destruction and death."[40]

Of course, becoming "tough and philosophical" is not a specific plan of action. But perhaps it is this attitude that Baldwin has in mind when he speaks of "the relatively conscious whites and the relatively conscious blacks" and that he finds in the blues ("Down," 105, 100). It is this attitude as well that Baldwin detects in the students braving angry mobs in their attempts to break down southern segregation. They are, he says, "the only genuine aristocrats this country has produced" (100).[41] Baldwin's own experiences testify to the personal toll of adhering to a standard that precludes him from taking refuge in either dreams of racial harmony or fantasies of racial revenge. His struggles also indicate why battles over discourse are real battles, and why racial dialogue is such a demanding endeavor. This is not to say that all matters of language are political or that dialogue is a substitute for other forms of political action. What emerges from Baldwin's essays, rather, is an appreciation of the risks of genuine engagement with questions about the meaning of democratic principles. Too much attention to the more frightening connotations of equality or to the rarity of freedom might simply lead to despair. Too little, he warns, simply perpetuates the empty profession of principle.

"How stunning is the achievement of those who have searched for and mined a shareable language for the words to say it."[42] Toni Morrison's tribute, while not directed specifically at Baldwin, captures his gift to the society he criticized throughout his life as a writer.[43] By trying to find the words, both to make his own experiences real for those to whom the message of those experiences was inaudible and to re-form the language to accommodate the stories that had not been given expression, Baldwin puts flesh on those democratic values he criticizes so relentlessly. The words—equality, freedom, democracy—are part of Baldwin's inheritance. His achievement consists in the ways that he seized that inheritance and that he bequeathed it, changed, to subsequent generations.

Baldwin and the Search for a Majority

The primary aim of this book has been to think through the implications, for democratic life and for democratic theory, of the persistence of the color line in the post–civil rights era. Sifting through the evidence of things not said, I show how attention to the specificity of black Americans' experiences exposes both the hollowness of claims for race blindness and the difficulty of developing a public discourse that does not rely on degrading racial assumptions. Baldwin's essays, I maintain, offer invaluable guidance for the task of investigating the silences and listening for the echoes that, by revealing how race gets noticed, reveal as well the deeper reservoirs of assumptions and anxieties beneath such noticing. Throughout the preceding chapters, I have highlighted Baldwin's insistence that those assumptions and anxieties are fundamental to Americans' sense of identity even though they do not exhaust that identity. By inhabiting and describing the spaces between principle and practice, Baldwin's writing lays critical groundwork for the construction of political theories that tackle the challenges of race consciousness. He develops a vivid moral psychology to suggest why racial injustices have survived the public rejection of racism and conveys how those are injustices are felt at the level of the individual. In so doing, he provides a crucial reminder of the peculiar vulnerability of democratic societies to the prejudices of their members.

What all of these chapters attest to is the vibrancy of Baldwin's legacy as a democratic thinker. Baldwin's democratic commitments are evident in his celebration of individuality, but his individualism is not romantic. It is tied indivisibly to a sense of history that foregrounds injustice. Nor is it abstract. Through attention to the details of the lives of the disesteemed and to the innocence of the privileged, Baldwin conveys the relationship between the internal life and concrete disparities of power and resources. Without abandoning his commitment to the fundamental democratic ideals of freedom and equality, he demonstrates how they must be reexamined. Without claiming that the suffering of African Americans has exceeded all others, Baldwin nonetheless requires that the achievements of American democracy be appraised in the light of black experiences.

Naturally, there are pitfalls in appropriating a body of work that was largely produced in the postwar era to illuminate the dilemmas of the post–civil rights period. Does the growth of Latino and Asian-American populations, for example, spell the obsolescence of the black-white paradigm Baldwin explores? My provisional answer would be yes and no. It is inadequate to reduce all racial matters to those relating to the black-white color line—it always has been. Still, troubling evidence that the equal humanity of African Americans is implicitly questioned in countless everyday encounters indicates the continuing need for Baldwin's penetrating account of the sources of race consciousness. Such recent trends as the increasing segregation by race in American schools and the dismantling of affirmative action do not only harm black Americans.[1] But the harm that they endure and the innocence that undergirds these developments ought to be of concern to all citizens.

One would also want to say more about the "America" Baldwin hopes to remake. Does it make sense even to talk about *American* democracy in a time of such enormous economic and political interpenetration of national borders? Does it undermine Baldwin's critique that he relies so heavily on a concept that is itself predicated on racial exploitation and conquest? Baldwin's essays do display a kind of American exceptionalism, investing hope in the possibility that the United States is uniquely positioned to overcome racial injustice and to create a new, more democratic way of life. Still, he applies his ambivalence even here and leaves open-ended the question of what that "America" will be.[2] Writing in the late 1960s, Baldwin muses that the new consciousness brought about by the struggle for black freedom signals "either the beginning or the end of America."[3] Or, in George Shulman's formulation, Baldwin urges the cultivation of "practices of citizenship that defeat idealization but not aspiration."[4] While he locates the United States at the center of his analysis, because it is the society he knows most intimately, Baldwin recognizes that the constitution of America is itself undefined territory whose contours cannot be mapped in advance of social change.

Above all, he aims to create a new majority. The majority Baldwin seeks cannot be defined in terms of numbers or political power. Rather, it is one of "moral influence."[5] Baldwin's majority is unafraid of the ambiguity of democratic ideals and willing to risk everything for them. Echoing the words of another passionate democrat, Henry David Thoreau, Baldwin insists that "we must dare to take another view of majority rule, disengaging it from anything resembling a popularity contest; taking it upon ourselves to become the majority by changing the moral climate."[6] Recognizing that any call to racial dialogue is meaningless if it serves merely as an alternative to concrete change, his aim is to wake his readers from their dreams of innocence, to alert them to their responsibilities as human beings and as citizens.

It is telling that so many of Baldwin's most powerful essays are those he offers as letters. Whether written "from Harlem," or "from the South," or "from a region in my mind," Baldwin's essays comprise a legacy of love letters to a home in which he could not live but, nonetheless, could never leave. He uses the intimacy of the epistolary form to build bridges—between himself and his neighbors and between the scene of a crime or a hurt or an injustice and the often more comfortable environment of his audience. The continuity implied in the notion of a correspondence spans the distance between the angry critic and people he tries to reach. Part of the force of Baldwin's letters consists in his generosity in continuing the correspondence even when the evidence of its effectiveness is weak.

As much as he demands from his readers, he also gives to them in presuming that they will be able to read what he has to say. As writer John Edgar Wideman notes, "when you write a letter, you not only perform an act of self-revelation, but you are simultaneously making somebody else, you're making your correspondent by what you choose to say and how you say it."[7] By touching individual readers, "making" them one at a time, Baldwin aims to bring about a societal change in consciousness.

A call to consciousness is not especially satisfying as a political agenda. And Baldwin offers little concrete guidance about the mechanisms of social transformation. He has virtually nothing to say about how to construct more just political institutions and policies. Further, his essays challenge most solutions by revealing levels of complexity unnoticed by would-be problem solvers. To strategic questions about the relative merits of grassroots organizing, legal struggle, or electoral politics as avenues to social change, he adds little. What he contributes instead is a reminder of the significance to the polity of the interior lives of its citizens and a model of how Americans might develop richer accounts of injustice. He further understands that the realization of democratic promise requires an extraordinary, sustained exercise of will.

As I note in chapter 1, Baldwin managed to dissatisfy people across the political spectrum and across the racial divide; he was dismissed by some critics as an assimilationist and by others as a militant unable to acknowledge the progress that took place during his lifetime. Yet his message is more radical than either critique suggests. The radicalism of Baldwin's essays consists in their capacity to trace the workings of race consciousness at so many levels of American experience. It consists as well in Baldwin's acknowledgment of the inescapable tension between human beings' dependence on the circumstances that have made them and the aspiration to create something truly new. For Baldwin apprehends the depth of the transformation that would be required to become race conscious, in the normative sense, and to realize the promise of multiracial democracy:

The possibility of liberation which is always real is also always painful, since it involves such an overhauling of all that gave us

our identity. The Negro who will emerge out of this present struggle—whoever, indeed, this dark stranger may prove to be—will not
be dependent, in any way at all, on any of the many props and
crutches which help form our identity now. And neither will the
white man. We will need every ounce of moral stamina we can
find. For everything is changing, from our notion of politics to our
notion of ourselves, and we are certain, as we begin history's
strangest metamorphosis, to undergo the torment of being forced
to surrender far more than we ever realized we had accepted.[8]

NOTES

Chapter One. Speaking of Race

1. By referring to "race" without setting the word off in quotation marks I do not aim to reinforce the idea that it stands for some static or readily definable property. Rather, the intention of this project is to undermine such assumptions.

2. Felicia Lee, "The Honest Dialogue That Is Neither," *New York Times*, 7 December 1997.

3. Lani Guinier, *The Tyranny of the Majority: Fundamental Fairness in Representative Democracy* (New York: The Free Press, 1994), 20.

4. I generally refer to the United States as "America" where such a reference relies on or alludes to another author's use of the name and employ the terms "American" and "Americans" for lack of adequate substitutes, but I recognize the exclusion inherent in conflating the United States and "America." For an account of the political issues involved in these questions of language and how they are implicated in debates about the meaning of the term "African-American," see Michael Hanchard, "Identity, Meaning and The African-American," *Social Text* 24 (Spring 1990): 31–42.

5. I use the terms "black Americans" and "African Americans" to refer

to Americans of African descent unless discussing a quotation in which another word is used. The choice of terminology is a difficult one because the words themselves are politically charged and carry deep personal significance for so many people. Because the terms continue to evolve, I have chosen to opt for anachronism (for example, using the word "African American" in the context of debates that preceded its widespread use) over inconsistency.

6. For a measure of racial inequalities in a variety of domains—economic, educational, judicial, political—see *A Common Destiny: Blacks and American Society*, ed. Gerald David Jaynes and Robin M. Williams (Washington, D.C.: National Academy Press, 1989).

7. See Donald R. Kinder and Lynn M. Sanders, *Divided by Color: Racial Politics and Democratic Ideals* (Chicago: University of Chicago Press, 1996); and Lawrence D. Bobo and Ryan A. Smith, "From Jim Crow Racism to Laissez-Faire Racism: The Transformation of Racial Attitudes," in *Beyond Pluralism: The Conception of Groups and Group Identities in America*, ed. Wendy F. Katkin, Ned Landsman, and Andrea Tyree (Urbana: University of Illinois Press, 1998), 182–220.

8. For three defenses of deliberation as a basic democratic norm, see Amy Gutmann and Dennis Thompson, *Democracy and Disagreement* (Cambridge: Harvard/Belknap, 1996), esp. 11–51; Jürgen Habermas, "Three Normative Models of Democracy," in *Democracy and Difference: Contesting the Boundaries of the Political*, ed. Seyla Benhabib (Princeton: Princeton University Press, 1996), 21–30; and Joshua Cohen, "Procedure and Substance in Deliberative Democracy," in *Democracy and Difference*, ed. Benhabib, 95–119.

9. For a classic argument linking deliberation to the transformation of interests, see Jean-Jacques Rousseau, *On the Social Contract*, ed. Roger D. Masters, trans. Judith R. Masters (New York: St. Martin's Press, 1978).

10. Writing in 1993, sociologists Douglas Massey and Nancy Denton conclude that "no group in the history of the United States has ever experienced the sustained high level of residential segregation that has been imposed on blacks in large American cities for the past fifty years" (Douglas S. Massey and Nancy A. Denton, *American Apartheid: Segregation and the Making of the Underclass* [Cambridge: Harvard University Press, 1993], 2.) For a summary of recent empirical studies of discrimination and segregation, see Lawrence D. Bobo, "The Color Line, the Dilemma, and the Dream: Race Relations in America at the Close of the Twentieth Century," in *Civil Rights and Social Wrongs: Black-White Relations Since World War II*, ed. John Higham (University Park, Pa.: Penn State Press, 1997), 30–55. See also A. Leon

Higginbotham, Jr., *Shades of Freedom: Racial Politics and Presumptions of the American Legal Process* (New York: Oxford University Press, 1996), 3–17.

11. Kimberlé Williams Crenshaw, "Color-blind Dreams and Racial Nightmares: Reconfiguring Racism in the Post–Civil Rights Era," in *Birth of a Nation'hood: Gaze, Script, and Spectacle in the O. J. Simpson Case*, ed. Toni Morrison and Claudia Brodsky Lacour (New York: Pantheon Books, 1997), 109.

12. See Kimberlé Crenshaw, "Race, Reform, and Retrenchment: Transformation and Legitimation in Antidiscrimination Law," *Harvard Law Review* 101 (May 1988): 1331–87.

13. Alexis de Tocqueville, *Democracy in America*, vol. 1, ed. J. P. Mayer, trans. George Lawrence (New York: Harper and Row, 1969), 356.

14. James Baldwin, "The Crusade of Indignation" (1956), in *The Price of the Ticket: Collected Nonfiction, 1948–1985* (New York: St. Martin's/Marek), 157. The initial reference to any essay from this collection will include the original date of publication in parentheses.

15. There are several related but different ways of defining and using the term. In the context of discussion of policy measures to combat racial inequalities (e.g., affirmative action programs and political redistricting), "race consciousness" connotes the deliberate use of race as a consideration. Race consciousness can also signify the appreciation of the distinctive identity and character of racial communities. For an exploration of the first use, see Guinier, *Tyranny of the Majority*, 119–56; for an example of the second, see Gary Peller, "Race-Consciousness," in *Critical Race Theory: The Key Writings That Formed the Movement*, ed. Kimberlé Crenshaw, Neil Gotanda, Gary Peller, and Kendall Thomas (New York: The New Press, 1995), 127–58.

16. Hortense Spillers, "Mama's Baby, Papa's Maybe: An American Grammar Book," *Diacritics* 17 (Summer 1987): 67.

17. Thus understood, race consciousness calls to mind Hans-Georg Gadamer's notion of prejudices. Prejudices, according to Gadamer, "are simply conditions whereby we experience something—whereby what we encounter says something to us." They are not mistaken or groundless judgments but prejudgments that reflect the workings of history and tradition in human consciousnesses (Hans-Georg Gadamer, "The Universality of the Hermeneutical Problem," in *Philosophical Hermeneutics*, trans. and ed. David E. Linge [Berkeley: University of California Press, 1976], 9).

18. Michael Omi and Howard Winant, *Racial Formation in the United States: From the 1960s to the 1980s* (New York: Routledge and Kegan Paul, 1986), 62.

19. Baldwin, "Words of a Native Son" (1964), in *Price of the Ticket*, 395–96.

20. Charles R. Lawrence III, "The Id, the Ego, and Equal Protection: Reckoning with Unconscious Racism," *Stanford Law Review* 39 (January 1987): 331.

21. I am grateful to one of the readers at Cornell University Press for helping me to clarify this point.

22. For an illuminating discussion of the sources and effects of unconscious racism, see Lawrence, "The Id, the Ego, and Equal Protection."

23. Lawrence Bobo and Ryan Smith use the term "laissez-faire racism" to describe this phenomenon (Lawrence Bobo and Ryan Smith, "From Jim Crow Racism to Laissez-Faire Racism," 182–220).

24. James Baldwin, "An Open Letter to My Sister, Angela Y. Davis," in *If They Come in the Morning: Voices of Resistance* (New York: Signet, 1971), 23.

25. James Baldwin, *The Fire Next Time* (New York: Vintage International, 1993), 105.

26. Antonio Gramsci, *Selections from the Prison Notebooks*, trans. and ed. Quinton Hoare and Geoffrey Nowell Smith (New York: International Publishers, 1971), 324.

27. Baldwin, quoted in Jane Howard, "'The Doom and Glory of Knowing Who You Are,'" *Life*, 24 May 1963, 89.

28. Amy Gutmann, "Responding to Racial Injustice," in K. Anthony Appiah and Amy Gutmann, *Color Conscious: The Political Morality of Race* (Princeton: Princeton University Press, 1996), 112–13.

29. See Michael B. Katz, "The Urban 'Underclass' as a Metaphor of Social Transformation," in *The Underclass Debate: Views from History*, ed. Michael B. Katz (Princeton: Princeton University Press, 1993), 3–23.

30. The historical literature is too large to be adequately summarized here. For two accounts of the relationship between black Americans and the definition of citizenship, see A. Leon Higginbotham, Jr., *In the Matter of Color: Race and the American Legal Process: The Colonial Period* (New York: Oxford University Press, 1978), and *Shades of Freedom*. For a political theorist's perspective, see Judith N. Shklar, *American Citizenship: The Quest for Inclusion* (Cambridge: Harvard University Press, 1991).

31. Because Baldwin always refers to David Baldwin—who adopted him in 1927—as his "father," I will follow suit.

32. That Baldwin says very little about the Harlem Renaissance and the gay subculture that flourished in Harlem during his childhood may be a reflection of the religious community of which his family was a part

and which isolated Baldwin from the world around him. For an account of Harlem's "gay neighborhood enclave" in the interwar years, see George Chauncey, *Gay New York: Gender, Urban Culture, and the Making of the Gay Male World, 1890–1940* (New York: Basic Books, 1994), 227–67.

33. Rather than providing a full biographical sketch, I will refer to events in Baldwin's life as they illuminate the meaning of his writing. In addition to Baldwin's own telling and retelling of his story in his essays and extensive interviews, several book-length biographies have been published since his death. They include Randall Kenan, *James Baldwin* (New York: Chelsea House, 1994), which was written for secondary school students as part of the series Lives of Notable Gay Men and Lesbians; David Leeming, *James Baldwin: A Biography* (New York: Alfred A. Knopf, 1994); James Campbell, *Talking at the Gates: A Life of James Baldwin* (New York: Penguin Books, 1991); and W. J. Weatherby, *James Baldwin: Artist on Fire* (New York: Donald I. Fine, 1989). Fern Marja Eckman's *The Furious Passage of James Baldwin* (New York: M. Evans and Company, 1966) continues to shed light on his development as a writer.

34. James Baldwin, *No Name in the Street* (New York: Dial Press, 1972), 95.

35. For an account of King's transformation, see James H. Cone, *Martin and Malcolm and America: A Dream or a Nightmare* (Maryknoll, N.Y.: Orbis Books, 1991).

36. Henry Louis Gates, Jr., "The Fire Last Time," *New Republic* 206 (1 July 1992): 38.

37. Baldwin, *The Fire Next Time*, 94 (emphasis in the original). Baldwin does not cite the source of this question, although it may be Lorraine Hansberry, according to whom it was on the minds of "all Negro intellectuals, . . . all politically-conscious Negroes" in the early 1960s (Lorraine Hansberry, quoted in "The Negro in American Culture," *Cross Currents* 11 [Summer 1961]: 222).

38. James Baldwin, "Autobiographical Notes," in *Notes of a Native Son* (Boston: Beacon Press, 1984), 9.

39. Baldwin's published works include the following novels: *Go Tell It on the Mountain* (1953), *Giovanni's Room* (1956), *Another Country* (1962), *Tell Me How Long the Train's Been Gone* (1968), *If Beale Street Could Talk* (1974), and *Just Above My Head* (1979). His essay collections and book-length essays are *Notes of a Native Son* (1955), *Nobody Knows My Name: More Notes of a Native Son* (1961), *The Fire Next Time* (1963), *No Name in the Street* (1972), *The Devil Finds Work* (1976), *The Evidence of Things Not Seen* (1985), and *The Price of the*

Ticket: Collected Non-Fiction, 1948–1985 (1985). Other writings include *Going to Meet the Man* (1965), a collection of stories; *Blues for Mister Charlie* (1964) and *The Amen Corner* (1968), plays; *One Day, When I Was Lost: A Scenario Based on "The Autobiography of Malcolm X"* (1972), a screenplay; *Little Man, Little Man: A Story of Childhood* (1976), a children's book; and *Jimmy's Blues: Selected Poems* (1983). For a complete bibliography of Baldwin's published writings, see Leeming, *James Baldwin*, 405–17.

40. Darryl Pinckney, "The Magic of James Baldwin," *New York Review of Books* 45 (19 November 1998), 70.

41. Baldwin, "The Harlem Ghetto," in *Notes of a Native Son*, 64.

42. Baldwin, *No Name in the Street*, 194.

43. Baldwin, "The Creative Process" (1962), in *Price of the Ticket*, 316.

44. Baldwin, "Many Thousands Gone," in *Notes of a Native Son*, 33.

45. Baldwin, quoted in Julius Lester, "Some Tickets Are Better: The Mixed Achievement of James Baldwin," in *Critical Essays on James Baldwin*, ed. Fred L. Standley and Nancy V. Burt (Boston: G. K. Hall, 1988), 245.

46. Baldwin, quoted in Margaret Mead and James Baldwin, *A Rap on Race* (New York: Dell Publishing, 1992), 48. The pagination of this edition, which is a reprint of the original edition (Philadelphia: J. B. Lippincott, 1971), is slightly different from that of the original.

47. Theodor W. Adorno, "The Essay as Form," in *Notes to Literature*, vol. 1, ed. Rolf Tiedemann, trans. Shierry Weber Nicholsen (New York: Columbia University Press, 1991), 10–11.

48. For further discussion, see chapter 2.

49. Stuart Hall, quoted in Cornel West, "The New Cultural Politics of Difference," in *Keeping Faith: Philosophy and Race in America* (New York: Routledge, 1993), 19.

50. See David R. Roediger, *The Wages of Whiteness: Race and the Making of the American Working Class*, rev. ed. (New York: Verso, 1999), 12.

51. Nancy Fraser and Linda Nicholson coin this expression to describe sexism, but it precisely identifies the tension between generality and specificity that exists in critiques of racial injustice as well (Nancy Fraser and Linda J. Nicholson, "Social Criticism without Philosophy: An Encounter between Feminism and Postmodernism," in *Feminism/Postmodernism*, ed. Linda J. Nicholson [New York: Routledge, 1990], 34).

52. One of the most forceful scenes in *Go Tell It on the Mountain*, Baldwin's first novel, displays his understanding of both the appeal and the illusory nature of the idea that it is possible for people simply to rise above the circumstances that made them. In the scene, the fourteen-

year-old protagonist escapes his Harlem home to climb his favorite hill in Central Park. From its summit, the boy achieves a momentary sense of mastery, feeling himself to be a "giant who might crumble the city with his anger" or "a long-awaited conqueror at whose feet flowers would be strewn" (James Baldwin, *Go Tell It on the Mountain* [New York: Signet Books, 1953], 30). He does not long remain master of what he surveys, however. If the view looking north to Harlem is bleak, the dazzling view of the skyline to the south reminds him that the New Yorkers hurrying along the streets of New York cannot see him, have not ever seen him, or, when they have, have never shown him any sign of welcome. Commenting on the scene, Cornel West once remarked that it is akin to Moses seeing Egypt on both sides of the Red Sea.

53. Baldwin, "White Man's Guilt" (1965), in *Price of the Ticket*, 410.

54. Baldwin, "Autobiographical Notes," in *Notes of a Native Son*, 9.

55. Baldwin, "Every Good-Bye Ain't Gone" (1977), in *Price of the Ticket*, 643 (emphasis added).

56. For the limitations of Tocqueville on this point, see Rogers M. Smith, "Beyond Tocqueville, Myrdal, and Hartz: The Multiple Traditions in America," *American Political Science Review* 87 (September 1993): 549–66.

57. Laurence Thomas discerns three sources of vulnerability experienced by individuals who belong to "downwardly constituted social categories": the constant effort to prove that degrading social assumptions are untrue; knowing there is virtually no way to prove them false; and the twofold worry that, if one does not speak out, no one else will counter these assumptions, and if one speaks out too often, the message will lose its audience (Laurence Thomas, "Moral Deference," *Philosophical Forum* 24 [Fall-Spring 1992–93]: 240).

58. Annette C. Baier, "Trust and Antitrust," in *Moral Prejudices: Essays on Ethics* (Cambridge: Harvard University Press, 1994), 98.

59. Ibid., 120.

60. Patricia J. Williams, *The Alchemy of Race and Rights: Diary of a Law Professor* (Cambridge: Harvard University Press, 1991), 163.

61. By focusing on the United States, I do not mean to suggest that it provides a model for democracy in general or that black Americans' experiences are not part of a broader diasporic context. For two illuminating *global* treatments of the interrelation of race, politics, and modernity, see Paul Gilroy, *The Black Atlantic: Modernity and Double Consciousness* (Cambridge: Harvard University Press, 1993), and Charles Mills, *The Racial Contract* (Ithaca: Cornell University Press, 1997).

62. Baldwin, "Autobiographical Notes," in *Notes of a Native Son*, 9.

63. Judith N. Shklar, *The Faces of Injustice* (New Haven: Yale University Press, 1990).

64. Hampshire is describing the drama of the ancients and the modern novel, which he calls "the necessary arts of the moralist." I would argue that the personal essay could be added to this list (Stuart Hampshire, *Innocence and Experience* [Cambridge: Harvard University Press, 1989], 105).

65. Hans-Georg Gadamer, *Truth and Method*, 2nd rev. ed., trans. Joel Weinsheimer and Donald G. Marshall, (New York: Continuum, 1993), 270.

66. Baldwin, "Everybody's Protest Novel," in *Notes of a Native Son*, 20.

67. Michael Walzer, *The Company of Critics: Social Criticism and Political Commitment in the Twentieth Century* (New York: Basic Books, 1988), 235.

68. See chapter 4 for a critique of Walzer's racial innocence.

69. James Baldwin, "The Discovery of What It Means to Be an American," in *Nobody Knows My Name: More Notes of a Native Son* (New York: Dial Press, 1961), 10.

70. Chapter 5 examines Baldwin's notion of acceptance more closely.

71. Baldwin, "The Discovery of What It Means to Be an American," in *Nobody Knows My Name*, 11.

72. Baldwin, "The Creative Process," in *Price of the Ticket*, 317.

73. In distinguishing among three paths in moral philosophy, Walzer contends that the path of interpretation is not so much superior to the paths of discovery (for which Thomas Nagel's formulation, "the view from nowhere," serves as a shorthand) and invention (represented by John Rawls and Jürgen Habermas) as it is the *only* available way for human beings to reflect on moral commitments. "The moralities we discover and invent," he observes, "always turn out, and always will turn out, remarkably similar to the morality we already have" (Michael Walzer, *Interpretation and Social Criticism* [Cambridge: Harvard University Press, 1987], 20–21).

74. In other words, his essays constitute what Nancy Fraser calls a "contextualizing historical narrative that genealogizes norms and thereby situates them more precisely" (Nancy Fraser, "False Antitheses: A Response to Seyla Benhabib and Judith Butler," in *Justice Interruptus: Critical Reflections on the "Post-Socialist" Condition* [New York: Routledge, 1997], 212).

75. Baldwin, *No Name in the Street*.

76. Cruse is quoting a phrase used by Baldwin in a profile in *Esquire* (Harold Cruse, *The Crisis of the Black Intellectual: A Historical Analysis of the Failure of Black Leadership* [New York: Quill, 1967], 193–95).

77. See Campbell, *Talking at the Gates*, 181.

78. Ella Baker, quoted in Joanne Grant, *Ella Baker: Freedom Bound* (New York: John Wiley and Sons, 1998), 218–19 (emphasis in the original).

79. Baldwin, *The Fire Next Time*, 88–89.

80. Baldwin, "Stranger in the Village," in *Notes of a Native Son*, 159. All future references in this chapter to this essay (abbreviated "Stranger") appear in the text.

81. "Weight" is a term that recurs throughout Baldwin's writing, both his essays and his fiction. The word, as he uses it here, signifies value or substance. But he also uses it to mean influence, power, and, in some cases, oppression.

82. Cf. Frantz Fanon, *Black Skin, White Masks*, trans. Charles Lam Markmann (New York: Grove Weidenfeld, 1967), 110.

83. Ralph Ellison also makes this point in "What Would America Be Like without Blacks," in *Going to the Territory* (New York: Random House, 1986), 104–12.

84. Emphasis added.

85. Baldwin, quoted in *Rap on Race*, 66.

86. Lani Guinier, "Reframing the Affirmative Action Debate," *Kentucky Law Journal* 86 (1997–98): 505–25.

87. Baldwin, "Many Thousands Gone," in *Notes of a Native Son*, 45.

Chapter Two. "A Most Disagreeable Mirror"

1. Baldwin, "Stranger in the Village," in *Notes of a Native Son*, 168.

2. Ibid., 164.

3. Richard Rorty, "Solidarity," in *Contingency, Irony, and Solidarity* (Cambridge: Cambridge University Press, 1989), 190.

4. Ibid., 192 (emphasis added).

5. One way of tracing these consequences in contemporary society is investigating what Adrian Piper calls "higher-order discrimination," a "funhouse worldview" in which a universalist ethic is conjoined with an unadmitted view of the superiority of certain kinds of people. Piper argues that such a world-view is much more difficult to identify than overt or "first-order discrimination," for it attaches judgment to preferences or behaviors that appear unconnected to traits such as race or gender or sexual orientation. The implication is that higher-order discrimination may well flourish unnoticed and operate indirectly among those of "us" most committed to ending racism (Adrian M. S. Piper, "Higher-Order Discrimination," in *Identity, Character, and Morality: Essays in Moral Psychology*, ed. Owen Flanagan and Amélie Oksenberg Rorty [Cambridge: MIT Press, 1990], 285–309).

6. W. E. B. Du Bois, *The Souls of Black Folk* (New York: Penguin Books, 1989), 1. All future references in this chapter to this book (abbreviated *Souls*) appear in the text.

7. The more significant caution against bringing double consciousness into contemporary debates is that its misuses reinforce rather than undermine the idea that African Americans are a "problem" people. Adolph Reed argues that the term is resonant in contemporary American discourse because it confirms the assumption that African Americans have a special incapacity for fitting into the American mainstream. Other critics, including Malcolm X, reject double consciousness altogether, identifying the problem of twoness with African Americans who bend to white supremacy by striving for both black and white approval without receiving satisfaction in either (Adolph Reed Jr., "Du Bois's 'Double Consciousness': Race and Gender in Progressive Era American Thought," *Studies in American Political Development* 6 [Spring 1992]: 95; Cornel West, "Malcolm X and Black Rage," in *Race Matters* [Boston: Beacon Press, 1993], 96–97).

8. There is a good deal of scholarly disagreement about the intellectual origins of the term "double consciousness." I note only three helpful treatments of the issue. In *The Art and Imagination of W. E. B. Du Bois*, Arnold Rampersad suggests that Du Bois's meaning reflects the influence of turn-of-the-century psychology, including the writings of "his favorite professor," William James. David Levering Lewis, on the other hand, contends that the influence of James's *Principles of Psychology*, is unclear. Lewis also notes that Du Bois's account of twoness suggests the impact of the fiction of Goethe and Charles Chesnutt and, possibly, of Emerson's lecture, "The Transcendentalist." A third argument, made by Shamoon Zamir, is that the idea of double consciousness, and indeed *Souls* as a whole, is best understood as a reworking of Hegel's *Phenomenology* (see Arnold Rampersad, *The Art and Imagination of W. E. B. Du Bois* [New York: Schocken Books, 1990], 74; David Levering Lewis, *W. E. B. Du Bois: Biography of a Race, 1868–1919* [New York: Henry Holt, 1993], 96, 280–83; Shamoon Zamir, *Dark Voices: W. E. B. Du Bois and American Thought, 1888–1903* [Chicago: University of Chicago Press, 1995], 113–68).

9. I am grateful to Robert Gooding-Williams for pointing out that the image of "the swarthy spectre" is that of Shakespeare's Banquo. The allusion to *Macbeth* suggests that Du Bois offers an alternative reading of the American founding narrative that casts doubt on the legitimacy of the United States and explains the hold of racial guilt on white American consciences.

10. It is perhaps eerier still that such tacit rules continue to function as

what Omi and Winant call a "racial etiquette"—a code based on racialized expectations of behavior that govern everyday interactions in the contemporary United States (see Michael Omi and Howard Winant, *Racial Formation in the United States*, 62).

11. Du Bois captures this phenomenon even more eloquently in the 1904 essay "The Development of a People." As in *Souls*, Du Bois takes his readers South to show them the imprint of the color line on the physical and spiritual worlds of the people whose lives are circumscribed by that line (W. E. B. Du Bois, "The Development of a People," in *The Souls of Black Folk*, ed. David W. Blight and Robert Gooding-Williams [Boston: Bedford Books, 1997], 238–54).

12. Baldwin, "Notes of a Native Son," in *Notes of a Native Son*, 93.

13. Baldwin, *The Fire Next Time*, 26 (emphasis in the original).

14. Baldwin, "Encounter on the Seine," in *Notes of a Native Son*, 122–23.

15. Baldwin's vehemence about this point reflects, in part, a belief that the Middle Passage represents a complete rupture with any African past. Du Bois, in contrast, maintains a strong sense of the links between Africa and diasporic black cultures. For an account of Du Bois's "cultural ideal of double consciousness" that develops its relationship to Africa, see Eric J. Sundquist, *To Wake the Nations: Race in the Making of American Literature* (Cambridge: Harvard/Belknap, 1993).

16. Baldwin, "Encounter on the Seine," in *Notes of a Native Son*, 123.

17. Baldwin, "Princes and Powers," in *Nobody Knows My Name*, 20–21 (emphasis added).

18. Baldwin, "Stranger in the Village," in *Notes of a Native Son*, 172. The complexity of this legacy is similarly expressed in the writing of Patricia Williams, who reveals her ambivalence about claiming her connection to a long line of (white) lawyers, one of whom impregnated her great-great-grandmother Sophie: "Reclaiming that from which one has been disinherited is a good thing. . . . Yet claiming for myself a heritage the weft of whose genesis is my own disinheritance is a profoundly troubling paradox" (Williams, *Alchemy of Race and Rights*, 217).

19. Baldwin, "White Man's Guilt," in *Price of the Ticket*, 409.

20. This strategy—which Baldwin deploys in several of his early essays—could be criticized as an attempt by Baldwin to situate himself "above the veil" to appeal to the white editors and readers of *Partisan Review*, where "Many Thousands Gone" first appeared. One example of this kind of criticism is Orlando Patterson's assessment in *New Left Review*. Patterson argues that Baldwin attempts to speak as "a White liberal with a difference, namely, a Negro experience," and succeeds

only in spreading confusion. Yet Baldwin's unsparing treatment of white hypocrisies implies that Baldwin's end is to trouble rather than to curry favor. And his attention to the impact of the color line on black consciousnesses rebuts Patterson's contention that Baldwin is "not content to speak to a Black audience" (H. Orlando Patterson, "The Essays of James Baldwin," *New Left Review* [Summer 1964]: 33).

21. Baldwin, "Many Thousands Gone," in *Notes of a Native Son*, 24 (emphasis in the original). All future references in this chapter to this essay (abbreviated "Many") appear in the text.

22. Baldwin alludes to the passage that concludes Richard Wright's 1940 essay "How 'Bigger' Was Born." In the essay, Wright observes that, despite the general drabness of the United States as a young, industrial society, "we . . . have in the Negro the embodiment of a past tragic enough to appease the spiritual hunger of even a James; and we have in the oppression of the Negro a shadow athwart our national life dense and heavy enough to satisfy even the gloomy broodings of a Hawthorne. And if Poe were alive, he would not have to invent horror; horror would invent him" (Richard Wright, "How 'Bigger' Was Born," in *Native Son*, restored edition [New York: HarperPerennial, 1993], 540).

23. Irving Howe, "Black Boys and Native Sons," *Dissent* (Autumn 1963): 354. "Many Thousands Gone" is not the only Baldwin essay that examines *Native Son* and explores the significance of Bigger Thomas in American imaginations; another, "Everybody's Protest Novel," is discussed in chapter 5. Baldwin addresses *Native Son* (and *Uncle Tom's Cabin*) as early as 1947 in a review for *New Leader* of Chester Himes's *Lonely Crusade*. Interestingly, the "we" deployed by Baldwin in this review is not the ambiguous "we" of "Many Thousands Gone" but refers more exclusively to white Americans. For example, Baldwin writes that "the minstrel man is gone and Uncle Tom is no longer to be trusted. Even Bigger Thomas is becoming irrelevant; we are faced with a black man as many faceted as we ourselves are, as individual, with our ambivalences and insecurities and our struggles to be loved" (James Baldwin, "History as Nightmare," *New Leader* 30 [25 October 1947]: 15).

24. Emphasis added.

25. I refer to doublenesses rather than enumerating the number of dimensions of identity in question (threeness, fourness, and so on) because it allows me to hold two dimensions in tension and investigate the relationship between them. Yet the imprecision of the term—for there are never only two dimensions—serves as a reminder that an accurate accounting of all of the relevant facets of an individual's

identity and their relation to each other is not possible. For a forceful caution against the dangers of "additive analyses," see Elizabeth V. Spelman, *Inessential Woman: Problems of Exclusion in Feminist Thought* (Boston: Beacon Press, 1988).

26. See Baldwin, "Nobody Knows My Name," in *Nobody Knows My Name*, 98–116.

27. See Baldwin, "The Creative Process," in *Price of the Ticket*, 315–18; James Baldwin, "Mass Culture and the Creative Artist: Some Personal Notes," in *Culture for the Millions? Mass Media in Modern Society*, ed. Norman Jacobs (Boston: Beacon Press, 1964), 120–23.

28. At one point Baldwin goes so far as to proclaim that "artists are the only people in a society who can tell that society the truth about itself" (Baldwin, "Words of a Native Son," in *Price of the Ticket*, 396).

29. For a particularly poignant recollection of a how an unwanted suit, given to a childhood friend, becomes a marker of the gulf between Baldwin and the world from which he came, see Baldwin, *No Name in the Street*, 9–22.

30. See Robert J. Corber, *Homosexuality in Cold War America: Resistance and the Crisis of Masculinity* (Durham, N.C.: Duke University Press, 1997); and Michael S. Sherry, *In the Shadow of War: The United States Since the 1930s* (New Haven: Yale University Press, 1995), esp. 156–77.

31. Baldwin's forthrightness about his sexuality was nonetheless ground-breaking, and his example continues to inspire black gay men (see *Brother to Brother: New Writings by Black Gay Men*, ed. Essex Hemphill [Boston: Alyson Publications, 1991], esp. essays by Hemphill and Joseph Beam).

32. In an essay that provides a much more extended treatment of this topic, Kendall Thomas explores how a "heteronormative logic" undergirded attacks on Baldwin's racial authenticity when he was alive and inform attempts to "neuter" Baldwin in the making of his memory (see Kendall Thomas, " 'Ain't Nothing Like the Real Thing' ": Black Masculinity, Gay Sexuality, and the Jargon of Authenticity," in *The House That Race Built: Black Americans, U.S. Terrain*, ed. Wahneema Lubiano [New York: Pantheon Books, 1997], 116–35).

33. James Baldwin, quoted in James Mossman, "Race, Hate, Sex, and Colour: A Conversation with James Baldwin and Colin MacInnes," in *Conversations with James Baldwin*, ed. Fred L. Standley and Louis H. Pratt (Jackson: University Press of Mississippi, 1989), 54.

34. James Baldwin, *Tell Me How Long the Train's Been Gone* (New York: Dial Press, 1968), 345.

35. See Chauncey, *Gay New York*, 12–23.

36. Although always wary of the reductionism required by slogans, Baldwin is more comfortable with the use of racial slogans for the purpose of political mobilization than he is with sexual ones. Writing about "Black Power," for instance, he admits the importance of the phrase as "a political necessity," a means of providing a positive self-image to Americans from whom it has been denied. Even so, he refuses to endorse any positive image that relies on the dehumanization of members of other groups (see James Baldwin, "Anti-Semitism and Black Power," letter to "Reader's Forum," *Freedomways* 7 [Winter 1967]: 75–77; for further discussion of Baldwin's suspicion of slogans, see chapter 5).

37. Baldwin's interest in the potential of genuine sexual love to overcome individuals' estrangement from one another—which is suggested by the image of the lovers in the closing passage of *The Fire Next Time* (quoted in chapter 1 of this book)—receives more explicit attention in Baldwin's fiction than in his essays. *Another Country* provides the most extended exploration of the possibilities for and obstacles to connections across the divides of race and gender. By coupling and uncoupling the main characters in a variety of sexual relationships (but none of them lesbian), Baldwin probes the fears that divide them and the needs that they share.

38. Baldwin, "The Male Prison," in *Nobody Knows My Name*, 156.

39. James Baldwin, quoted in Richard Goldstein, "'Go the Way Your Blood Beats': An Interview with James Baldwin," in *James Baldwin: The Legacy*, ed. Quincy Troupe (New York: Simon and Schuster/Touchstone, 1984), 174.

40. In an interview with one of his biographers, Baldwin notes that his complaints about Gide were really directed at himself and his own defensiveness about his sexuality (Eckman, *The Furious Passage of James Baldwin* [1966], 135–36).

41. Baldwin, "The Male Prison," in *Nobody Knows My Name*, 157; cf. Michel Foucault, *The History of Sexuality*, vol. 1, trans. Robert Hurley (New York: Vintage, 1980).

42. James Baldwin, "Preservation of Innocence," *Zero* 2 (Summer 1949): 16.

43. Ibid., 17.

44. Baldwin, "Here Be Dragons" (1985), in *Price of the Ticket*, 690.

45. In "The Male Prison," Baldwin does call his own critique into question by asserting that the existence of two sexes is "one of the facts of life" (Baldwin, "The Male Prison," in *Nobody Knows My Name*, 161).

46. Eldridge Cleaver, "Notes on a Native Son," in *Soul on Ice* (New York: Dell Publishing, 1968), 97.

47. Ibid., 100.

48. Ibid., 98.

49. That the same criticism can be made of Du Bois indicates something about the masculinity of the qualities he associates with American citizenship. Although the civic virtues mentioned in *Souls* are distinctly manly, Du Bois is in fact more attuned to the particular connections between the situation of black women and "the problem of the color-line" than Baldwin. For a fuller expression of Du Bois's feminism, see "The Damnation of Women," in *W. E. B. Du Bois: A Reader*, ed. David Levering Lewis (New York: Henry Holt, 1995), 299–312.

50. Not using "Preservation of Innocence," Kaplan overstates Baldwin's binary opposition between men and women in what is otherwise a very helpful account of gender and sexual tensions in Baldwin's work (Cora Kaplan, " 'A Cavern Opened in My Mind': The Poetics of Homosexuality and the Politics of Masculinity in James Baldwin," in *Representing Black Men*, ed. Marcellus Blount and George P. Cunningham [New York: Routledge, 1996], 27–54).

51. Baldwin, *No Name in the Street*, 62. For a general critique of the exclusion of black women's interests in anti-racist critiques of interracial rape, see Kimberlé Williams Crenshaw, "Mapping the Margins: Intersectionality, Identity Politics, and Violence against Women of Color," in *Critical Race Theory: The Key Writings That Formed the Movement*, ed. Kimberlé Crenshaw, Neil Gotanda, Gary Peller, and Kendall Thomas (New York: The New Press, 1995), 357–83.

52. "Revolutionary Hope: A Conversation between James Baldwin and Audre Lorde," *Essence* 15 (December 1984): 72–74, 129–33; see also James Baldwin and Nikki Giovanni, *A Dialogue* (London: Michael Joseph, 1975).

53. Baldwin, "Princes and Powers," in *Nobody Knows My Name*, 42–43 (emphasis added).

54. Charles Taylor, "The Politics of Recognition," in *Multiculturalism: Examining the Politics of Recognition*, 2nd ed., ed. Amy Gutmann (Princeton: Princeton University Press, 1994).

55. Baldwin, quoted in Goldstein, " 'Go the Way Your Blood Beats,' " 181.

56. Taylor, "Politics of Recognition," in *Multiculturalism*, ed. Gutmann, 25–26.

57. Taylor sometimes understates this point. Using the example of women's and blacks' writings about the effects of degrading stereotypes, in an essay on Canadian struggles with the question of identity, Taylor observes that the absence of recognition "is portrayed as an act of aggression or domination so that the accent is displaced from the

human need itself to the interhuman drama of power and exploitation." The displaced accent, Taylor writes, may be explained by the fact that making a claim for recognition entails an acknowledgment of vulnerability. But the writers Taylor chooses as his example *are* already publicly vulnerable. Although I share Taylor's suspicions about the inadequacy of a politics of antidiscrimination to address or to overcome deep social divisions, his choice of examples shows that Taylor misses how opposing power and exploitation, even through a language of justice and rights, reflects a "human need." Further, he overlooks the possibility that it is the vulnerability of the privileged, the reliance of their sense of self on an unjust status quo, which requires public exposure (Charles Taylor, "Impediments to a Canadian Future," in *Reconciling the Solitudes: Essays on Canadian Federalism and Nationalism*, ed. Guy Laforest [Montreal: McGill-Queens University Press, 1993], 190–93).

58. While most white Americans are committed to the principle of equal opportunity in housing, 60 percent of those polled in 1980 would have voted for a law that allowed individuals to refuse to sell their homes to someone on the grounds of race (although such a law would be prohibited by the Fair Housing Act of 1968) (Massey and Denton, *American Apartheid*, 92).

59. Taylor, "Politics of Recognition," in *Multiculturalism*, ed. Gutmann, 38.

60. Ibid., 63. Paul Gilroy uses the term "double consciousness" to capture the ambivalence that black peoples on both sides of the Atlantic feel in their relationship with societies of the modern West. For Gilroy, the black diaspora has no true center, because black cultures emerge as a response to perpetual homelessness (Gilroy, *Black Atlantic*).

61. Emphasis in the original.

62. See James Baldwin, "Pour libérer les Blancs," interview with François Bondy, *Preuves* (October 1963): 11–12.

63. Baldwin, "Every Good-Bye Ain't Gone," in *Price of the Ticket*, 643 (emphasis in the original).

64. Amélie Oksenberg Rorty, "The Hidden Politics of Cultural Identification," *Political Theory* 22 (February 1994): 158.

65. Ross Posnock, *Color and Culture: Black Writers and the Making of the Modern Intellectual* (Cambridge: Harvard University Press, 1998), 221.

66. Baldwin, *No Name in the Street*, 18.

67. Virginia Woolf, *A Room of One's Own* (San Diego: Harcourt Brace Jovanovich, 1981), 36.

Chapter Three. Blessed Are the Victims?

1. Baldwin, "Many Thousands Gone," in *Notes of a Native Son*, 44. I want to thank George Shulman for prodding me to think through the implications of this chapter and suggesting how to strengthen it.
2. Vincent Descombes, "Is There a Politics of Authenticity?" trans. Daniel Weinstock, *Raritan* 13 (Spring 1994): 108–9, emphasis in the original.
3. Baldwin, "On Catfish Row" (1956), in *Price of the Ticket*, 181.
4. Fanon, *Black Skin, White Masks*, 112.
5. Daryl Michael Scott, *Contempt and Pity: Social Policy and the Image of the Damaged Black Psyche, 1880–1996* (Chapel Hill: University of North Carolina Press, 1997).
6. Williams, *Alchemy of Race and Rights*, 156.
7. Glenn Loury, "Beyond Victimhood," *Times Literary Supplement* (10 June 1994): 15.
8. Clarence Thomas, quoted in "Excerpts from Senate's Hearings on the Thomas Nomination," *New York Times*, 12 October 1991.
9. Clarence Thomas, quoted in U.S. Congress, Senate Committee on the Judiciary, *Hearings on the Nomination of Judge Clarence Thomas to be Associate Justice of the Supreme Court*, 102nd Cong., 1st sess., 1991, pt. 4, 203.
10. Wendy Brown, *States of Injury: Power and Freedom in Late Modernity* (Princeton: Princeton University Press, 1995), 27.
11. Brown, *States of Injury*, 64–65. The masculinism that appears in Baldwin's writing (discussed in chapter 2) corroborates this idea. However, as I will argue in this chapter, Baldwin provides a basis for a humanism that discredits the ideal of the white, male, middle-class, heterosexual individual but also respects the role such an ideal has played in his own experience and in his formulation of a possible emancipatory future. It cannot, in other words, simply be rooted out as a form of false consciousness.
12. Stanley Crouch, *Notes of a Hanging Judge: Essays and Reviews, 1979–89* (New York: Oxford University Press, 1990), esp. 202–3, 231–36.
13. Jerry Gafio Watts, *Heroism and the Black Intellectual: Ralph Ellison, Politics, and Afro-American Intellectual Life* (Chapel Hill: University of North Carolina Press, 1994), 9.
14. Watts, *Heroism and the Black Intellectual*, 17–20.
15. In his review of *Roots*, for instance, Baldwin writes about white Americans: "They need the moral authority of their former slaves, who are the only people in the world who know anything about them

and who may be, indeed, the only people in the world who really care anything about them." Similarly, in his last completed book, *The Evidence of Things Not Seen*, he "speak[s] with the authority of the issue of the slave born in the country once believed to be *the last best hope of earth*" (Baldwin, "A Review of *Roots*" [1976], in *Price of the Ticket*, 554; James Baldwin, *The Evidence of Things Not Seen* [New York: Holt, Rinehart and Winston, 1985], 125, emphasis in the original).

16. Albert Murray, *The Omni-Americans: Black Experience and American Culture* (New York: Outerbridge and Dienstfrey, 1970), 158.

17. Baldwin, *Evidence of Things Not Seen*, 78.

18. Baldwin, "Princes and Powers," in *Nobody Knows My Name*, 36.

19. Reviewing *Nobody Knows My Name*, Alfred Kazin concurs, "Of all the many things I admire about Baldwin's essays, I think what I admire most is this: more than any other Negro writer whom I, at least, have ever read, he wants to describe the exact place where private chaos and social outrage meet. He wants to know just how far *he* is responsible for his unhappiness" (Alfred Kazin, "Close to Us," *The Reporter* 25 [17 August 1961]: 60 [emphasis in the original]).

20. Sheldon Wolin, "Political Theory as a Vocation," in *Machiavelli and the Nature of Political Thought*, ed. Martin Fleisher (New York: Atheneum, 1972), 23–75.

21. James Baldwin, "As Much Truth as One Can Bear," *New York Times Book Review* (14 January 1962): 38; see also Horace Porter, *Stealing the Fire: The Art and Protest of James Baldwin* (Middletown, Conn.: Wesleyan University Press, 1989), 30.

22. Baldwin, "Notes of a Native Son," in *Notes of a Native Son*, 85. All future references in this chapter to this essay (abbreviated "Notes") appear in the text.

23. Baldwin, "Stranger in the Village," in *Notes of a Native Son*, 165.

24. Emphasis added.

25. Emphasis in the original.

26. Shklar, *Faces of Injustice*, 35.

27. Ibid., 7.

28. Ibid., 108.

29. Thomas, "Moral Deference," 233–50.

30. Miriam Nissim-Sabat further complicates this picture, noting how capitalist societies distinguish between those misfortunes that are recognized to be impersonal in their origin (such as earthquakes or hurricanes) and those that are traced to a deficiency in the victim (poverty or unemployment) (Miriam Nissim-Sabat, "Victim No More," *Radical Philosophy Review* 1 [1998]: 17–34).

31. Judith N. Shklar, "*The Education of Henry Adams*, by Henry Adams," in *Redeeming American Political Thought*, ed. Stanley Hoffmann and Dennis F. Thompson (Chicago: University of Chicago Press, 1998), 83; see also Shklar, *Faces of Injustice*, 1–2, "Positive Liberty, Negative Liberty in the United States," trans. Stanley Hoffmann, in *Redeeming American Political Thought*, 111–26, and *American Citizenship*.

32. Baldwin, "A Question of Identity," in *Notes of a Native Son*, 124.

33. For a powerful example, see "Sonny's Blues," in *Going to Meet the Man*, 86–122.

34. Baldwin, "The Discovery of What It Means to Be an American," in *Nobody Knows My Name*, 12.

35. Feminist theorists, according to Carole Pateman, ask "why the patriarchal character of the separation of a depoliticized public sphere from private life is so easily 'forgotten.'" This "forgetting" both encourages the persistence of the notion that power relations in the private sphere are not matters of public or political concern and compromises women's participation in public life (Carole Pateman, "Feminist Critiques of the Public/Private Dichotomy," in *The Disorder of Women: Democracy, Feminism and Political Theory* [Stanford: Stanford University Press, 1989], 118–40).

36. Spillers, "Mama's Baby, Papa's Maybe," 65.

37. Baldwin, "A Talk to Teachers" (1963), in *Price of the Ticket*, 329.

38. Baldwin, "The Price of the Ticket," in *Price of the Ticket*, xvii.

39. Williams, *Alchemy of Race and Rights*, 151.

40. Cheryl I. Harris, "Whiteness as Property," *Harvard Law Review* 106 (June 1993): 1761–66.

41. Mari J. Matsuda, "Public Response to Racist Speech: Considering the Victim's Story," in *Words That Wound: Critical Race Theory, Assaultive Speech, and the First Amendment*, by Mari J. Matsuda, Charles R. Lawrence III, Richard Delgado, and Kimberlé Crenshaw (Boulder, Colo.: Westview Press, 1993), 18.

42. Crenshaw, "Race, Reform, and Retrenchment," 1359–60.

43. Baldwin, "Many Thousands Gone," in *Notes of a Native Son*, 41. For an account of the availability of such images in the context of the trial of the officers who beat Rodney King, see Thomas L. Dumm, "Rodney King, or the New Enclosures," in *united states* (Ithaca: Cornell University Press, 1994), 88–113.

44. Baldwin, "Many Thousands Gone," in *Notes of a Native Son*, 27.

45. This chapter will not attempt to provide a complete accounting of the origins of the riot or of its relationship to the Detroit riot that took place in July 1943 and the Harlem riot of 1935. But it is worth noting

three events in the first seven months of 1943, which, according to Dominic Capeci, particularly angered black New Yorkers: the decision to rent facilities at Hunter College to the navy despite its policy of racial segregation, the closing of the Savoy Ballroom in Harlem on dubious charges of prostitution, and Mayor La Guardia's approval of the building of Stuyvesant Town, a whites-only housing project on the Lower East Side (Dominic J. Capeci, Jr., *The Harlem Riot of 1943* [Philadelphia: Temple University Press, 1977], 136–41).

46. See Capeci, *Harlem Riot of 1943*, 115–33; Nat Brandt, *Harlem at War: The Black Experience in WWII* (Syracuse: Syracuse University Press, 1996), 211.

47. Robert Gooding-Williams, " 'Look, A Negro!' " in *Reading Rodney King, Reading Urban Uprising* (New York: Routledge, 1993), 169–71.

48. Tocqueville, *Democracy in America*, vol. 1, 341.

49. Sheldon S. Wolin, "Injustice and Collective Memory," in *The Presence of the Past: Essays on the State and the Constitution* (Baltimore: Johns Hopkins University Press, 1989), 35.

50. Ibid., 38.

51. Baldwin, "A Fly in Buttermilk," in *Nobody Knows My Name*, 96–97 (emphasis in the original).

52. Baldwin, "The Creative Process," in *Price of the Ticket*, 318.

53. Ralph Ellison similarly links the image of black male criminality to Americans' fear of chaos and that fear to an "anti-tragic approach to experience" (Ralph Ellison, "Change the Joke and Slip the Yoke," in *Shadow and Act* [New York: Vintage Books, 1972], 48).

54. Baldwin, *The Fire Next Time*, 9.

55. James Baldwin, "The White Problem," in *100 Years of Emancipation*, ed. Robert A. Goldwin (Chicago: Rand McNally, 1964), 84.

56. Baldwin, "White Man's Guilt," in *Price of the Ticket*, 410.

57. Baldwin, "Encounter on the Seine," *Notes of a Native Son*, 120–21.

58. Michel Foucault, *Discipline and Punish: The Birth of the Modern Prison*, trans. Alan Sheridan (New York: Vintage Books, 1979), 31.

59. James Baldwin, *The Devil Finds Work* (New York: Dial Press, 1976), 110.

60. Baldwin, "Fifth Avenue, Uptown," in *Nobody Knows My Name*, 71.

Chapter Four. Presumptions of Innocence

1. Baldwin, "Fifth Avenue, Uptown," in *Nobody Knows My Name*, 67–68.

2. Ibid., 68.

3. Baldwin, "A Question of Identity," in *Notes of a Native Son*, 133.

4. Among his novels, *Giovanni's Room* is Baldwin's most masterful exploration of the contours of innocence.

5. My use of the term "critical geography" is slightly different from Toni Morrison's in the opening essay of *Playing in the Dark*. There, Morrison writes, "I want to draw a map, so to speak, of a critical geography and use that map to open as much space for discovery, intellectual adventure, and close exploration as did the original charting of the New World—without the mandate for conquest." Whereas Morrison's enterprise is to chart new territory, tracing the presence of blacks in the fiction of white Americans, the accent of my reading of Baldwin is on the enclosedness of the territory Americans inhabit (Toni Morrison, *Playing in the Dark: Whiteness and the Literary Imagination* [Cambridge: Harvard University Press, 1992], 3).

6. Baldwin, "Fifth Avenue, Uptown," in *Nobody Knows My Name*, 57–58.

7. Ibid., 56. According to Baldwin, the construction of the Riverton housing project in Harlem was intended as a response to the outcry over the city's involvement in the construction of the all-white Stuyvesant Town complex downtown.

8. Ibid., 60.

9. Ibid., 66.

10. Baldwin, "White Man's Guilt," in *Price of the Ticket*, 410.

11. Baldwin, *No Name in the Street*, 87.

12. Harris, "Whiteness as Property"; Roediger, *The Wages of Whiteness*; George Lipsitz, *The Possessive Investment in Whiteness: How White People Profit from Identity Politics* (Philadelphia: Temple University Press, 1998).

13. Harris, "Whiteness as Property," 1782. Harris notes that even Supreme Court decisions in favor of affirmative action have allowed that it burdens "innocent whites."

14. Shelby Steele, *The Content of Our Character: A New Vision of Race in America* (New York: St. Martin's Press, 1990), esp. chapters 1 and 5.

15. Baldwin, "Words of a Native Son," in *Price of the Ticket*, 400.

16. James Baldwin, "The Negro at Home and Abroad," *The Reporter* (27 November 1951): 37.

17. Baldwin, "Many Thousands Gone," in *Notes of a Native Son*, 25–26.

18. James Baldwin, "Too Late, Too Late," *Commentary* (January 1949): 98.

19. Baldwin, "Notes of a Native Son," in *Notes of a Native Son*, 91.

20. Thomas, "Moral Deference," 239.

21. Baldwin, *The Fire Next Time*, 55.

22. See John Rawls, *Political Liberalism* (New York: Columbia University Press, 1993), 43–46.

23. Hampshire, *Innocence and Experience*, 12.

24. Jane Flax, *Disputed Subjects: Essays on Psychoanalysis, Politics and Philosophy* (New York: Routledge, 1993), esp. 131–47.

25. Dumm, *united states*, 16–17.

26. Seyla Benhabib, "Feminism and Postmodernism: An Uneasy Alliance," in *Feminist Contentions: A Philosophical Exchange* (New York: Routledge, 1995), 28.

27. Baldwin, "The Black Boy Looks at the White Boy," in *Nobody Knows My Name*, 218.

28. Baldwin, "A Question of Identity," in *Notes of a Native Son*, 136.

29. Walzer, *Interpretation and Social Criticism*, 21. All future references in this chapter to this book (abbreviated *Interpretation*) appear in the text.

30. This chapter will not attempt to provide a comprehensive account of Walzer's political and moral thought. That having been said, I will not restrict myself to Walzer's two books on social criticism but will make use of other pieces where they illuminate aspects of these books.

31. Walzer, *Company of Critics*, 231.

32. Walzer uses John Rawls's idea of the original position as his example in making the hotel room/home distinction, although he admits that the account is a caricature and further qualifies it by adding, in a footnote, that his target is not Rawls so much as Rawlsians.

33. Emphasis in the original.

34. Baldwin, *The Fire Next Time*, 54–55 (emphasis in the original).

35. Baldwin, "Faulkner and Desegregation," in *Nobody Knows My Name*, 117.

36. Michael Walzer, *Spheres of Justice: A Defense of Pluralism and Equality* (New York: Basic Books, 1983), 31. Because Walzer's work focuses on members of "political communities," I will use the words "member" and "citizen" interchangeably in this discussion.

37. Although my discussion focuses on the experiences of American citizens, it is informed by recent debates about Walzer's notion of membership and its implications for international obligations (see Veit Bader, "Citizenship and Exclusion: Radical Democracy, Community, and Justice: Or, What Is Wrong with Communitarianism?" *Political Theory* 23 [May 1995]: 211–46; and William James Booth, "Foreigners: Insiders, Outsiders, and the Ethics of Membership," *Review of Politics* 59 [Spring 1997]: 259–92).

38. Michael Walzer, *Thick and Thin: Moral Argument at Home and Abroad* (Notre Dame: University of Notre Dame Press, 1994), 12–13.

39. The characterization of the United States as an "immigrant society," which appears frequently in Walzer's recent writings (although not in the two books on social criticism), hinders his capacity to think critically about the situation of African Americans, Native Americans, and others whose incorporation into American society could not be described as chosen. When he links a presumption of voluntary citizenship to an argument that the United States ought to be "rigorously neutral" in mediating among different American racial and ethnic groups, he forgets his observation that "societies are necessarily particular because they have members and memories, members *with* memories not only of their own but also of their common life." Such a claim raises questions about whose memories, and which ones, are honored (Walzer, *Thick and Thin*, quotations from 82 and 8 [emphasis in the original], respectively).

40. Walzer, *Company of Critics*, 140, and *Interpretation and Social Criticism*, 59.

41. In a discussion of affirmative action, Walzer explicitly denies the significance or even the existence of racial borders. When people compete for a position, he argues, the only line that may defensibly be drawn to exclude individuals from equal consideration is the line between insiders and outsiders. What he calls the "reservation of office" for certain kinds of individuals "is possible only after boundaries have been drawn between members and strangers. *In American society today, there are no such boundaries.*" Moving quickly from the assertion that only one kind of preference is morally justifiable to the assertion that the conditions for such a preference do not exist within the United States, Walzer overlooks the experiences of many African Americans and others who testify to the robustness of the boundaries he denies. Moreover, his repeated use of the word "natural" to describe the ways in which jobs are generally distributed, neighborhoods populated, and so forth, implies that such boundaries as do exist are those that result from the natural groupings of like with like (Walzer, *Spheres of Justice*, 148–54 [emphasis added]).

42. Ibid., 74 (emphasis added).

43. Walzer, *Company of Critics*, 158.

44. Michael Walzer, "The Obligations of Oppressed Minorities," in *Obligations: Essays on Disobedience, War, and Citizenship* (Cambridge: Harvard University Press, 1970), 58 (emphasis in the original).

45. Ibid., 49 (emphasis in the original).

46. Ibid., 51.

47. See Michael Walzer, "Shared Meanings in a Poly-Ethnic Democratic Setting: A Response," *Journal of Religious Ethics* 22 (Fall 1994): 401–5.

48. Walzer, *Company of Critics*, 44, and *Interpretation and Social Criticism*, 60.

49. This requirement distinguishes the social critic from the activists described in "The Obligations of Oppressed Minorities."

50. Walzer, *Company of Critics*, 237.

51. Walzer's distinction between prophet and priest owes a great deal to Max Weber. For further discussion of the elements of Weber's argument that Walzer uses and those he rejects, see Lawrie Balfour, "The Appeal of Innocence: Baldwin, Walzer, and the Bounds of Social Criticism," *The Review of Politics* 61 (Summer 1999): 373–401; cf. Max Weber, *Ancient Judaism*, trans. and ed. Hans H. Gerth and Don Martindale (Glencoe, Ill.: The Free Press, 1952), esp. 267–335; Max Weber, *Economy and Society*, vol. 1, ed. Guenther Roth and Claus Wittich (Berkeley: University of California Press, 1978), esp. 439–68; and Max Weber, "Politics as a Vocation," *From Max Weber: Essays in Sociology*, ed. and trans. H. H. Gerth and C. Wright Mills (New York: Oxford University Press, 1946), 79–80; Walzer, *Interpretation and Social Criticism*, 70 and 82, n. 15.

52. Michael Walzer, "Political Action: The Problem of Dirty Hands," in *War and Moral Responsibility*, ed. Marshall Cohen, Thomas Nagel, and Thomas Scanlon (Princeton: Princeton University Press, 1974), 63.

53. Walzer, *Company of Critics*, 81.

54. Walzer, "Political Action," 63–64.

55. Ibid., 76.

56. Baldwin's assessment of black leadership is as much a class-based critique as a critique of the temptations of political power. Musing that it is, "perhaps, the most unlucky bourgeoisie in the world's entire history," Baldwin sees the black middle class from which the leadership emerges as "trapped . . . in a no-man's-land between black humiliation and white power." The result of this bind, Baldwin contends, is that the appeal of innocence is particularly strong among middle-class African Americans, for their ascending status requires that they not see how the social structure is predicated on the humiliation of black citizens (Baldwin, "The Dangerous Road before Martin Luther King," in *Price of the Ticket*, 260).

57. Walzer, *Company of Critics*, 238.

58. Emphasis added.

59. See Michael Walzer, *Radical Principles: Reflections of an Unreconstructed Democrat* (New York: Basic Books, 1980), 15.

60. At the conclusion of "Nobody Knows My Name," Baldwin uses language very similar to Walzer's: "Any honest examination of the national life proves how far we are from the standard of human freedom

with which we began. The recovery of this standard demands of every-one who loves this country a hard look at himself" (Baldwin, "Nobody Knows My Name," in *Nobody Knows My Name*, 116). This passage reflects a recurrent tension in Baldwin's thought between his opposition to self-delusion (including the delusion that Americans have ever known a "standard of freedom" worth wholehearted celebration) and his investment in an *American* democracy. In offering a reading of Baldwin's use of "freedom" in chapter 5, I aim to show that it is more importantly understood as a kind of responsibility that Americans have never fully accepted than a standard to be recovered.

61. Walzer similarly misses racial meanings in his account of how the principle of equal treatment came to be recognized as part of American public life. Retelling the story of how white Americans revolted against the Conscription Act of 1863 (in which exemptions from the Civil War draft could be bought for $300), Walzer does not mention that the violence was racial. He describes the riots as "the resistance and resentment of masses of citizens that drew the line between what could be sold and what could not" and adds that "we acknowledge now the principle of equal treatment—because of the political struggles of 1863." In an account of the same events, Ronald Takaki relates that the immediate target of the violence—which he also depicts as an example of working-class outrage at the privileges of the rich—was New York's black population. In addition to burning a black orphan-age, destroying black homes, and assaulting African Americans, the ri-oters cried, "Vengeance on every nigger in New York." The point here is not that the story has nothing to teach about equal treatment, but that "the political struggles of 1863" offer a cautionary example of the way the expansion of some citizens' rights has been intertwined with the oppression of others and a reminder of the invisibility of racial identity when the violence is the work of the "majority" (Walzer, *Spheres of Justice*, 99; Ronald Takaki, *A Different Mirror: A History of Multicultural America* [Boston: Little, Brown, 1993], 152–53).

62. See Baldwin, "As Much Truth as One Can Bear," *New York Times Book Review* (14 January 1962): 1.

63. Baldwin, "They Can't Turn Back" (1960), in *Price of the Ticket*, 228.

64. Baldwin, "A Question of Identity," in *Notes of a Native Son*, 136–37.

65. Baldwin was commissioned by Philip Rahv, the editor of *Partisan Review*, to join a fray that had already erupted in response to Faulkner's comments (Campbell, *Talking at the Gates*, 98–100).

66. William Faulkner, quoted in Russell Warren Howe, "A Talk with William Faulkner," *The Reporter* 14 (22 March 1956): 19 (emphasis added).

67. Faulkner, quoted in Baldwin, "Faulkner and Desegregation," in *Nobody Knows My Name,* 121.
68. Ibid., 121.
69. Ibid., 122; cf. Du Bois, *Souls of Black Folk,* 164–65.
70. Martin Luther King, Jr., "Letter from Birmingham City Jail," in *A Testament of Hope: The Essential Writings and Speeches of Martin Luther King, Jr.,* ed. James M. Washington (New York: HarperCollins, 1986), 292–93.
71. Harris notes that the Supreme Court's order that schools be desegregated "with all deliberate speed" in *Brown II* (the 1955 decision that set the plan for implementing the desegregation called for in *Brown v. Board of Education*) marks a departure from earlier approaches to violations of constitutional rights. She argues that white resistance, rather than the rights of black students, dictated the pace of reform (Harris, "Whiteness as Property," 1754–56).
72. At the conclusion of his beautiful memoir about returning to Mississippi, Anthony Walton similarly observes the entanglement of time and place and innocence: "We Americans love to think ourselves innocent of the tragedies—personal and public—that the past and our compulsions have visited upon us, all of us. Most of all, we want to be innocent of how much the ghosts and bones of our beautiful landscape have shaped and twisted virtually everything that has happened here; and we want to remain ignorant of how costly our innocence is to our government, our communities and our hearts" (Anthony Walton, *Mississippi: An American Journey* [New York: Vintage Books, 1996], 274–75).
73. Baldwin, "Faulkner and Desegregation," in *Nobody Knows My Name,* 117.
74. Benhabib, "Feminism and Postmodernism," 28.
75. Baldwin, "Every Good-Bye Ain't Gone," in *Price of the Ticket,* 645–46.

Chapter Five. The Living Word

1. This discussion will not assess either Baldwin's relationship to Wright or his reading of Stowe.
2. Baldwin, "Everybody's Protest Novel," in *Notes of a Native Son,* 13. All future references in this chapter to this essay (abbreviated "Everybody's") appear in the text. For a fuller account of the sinister effect of such moralizing mottoes, see Baldwin's description of the Grimes family's living-room mantel in *Go Tell It on the Mountain.* There, the

narrator reports, hang two examples of such mottoes—a hackneyed poem written in pink and blue and an excerpt from the Gospel of John "in letters of fire against a background of gold." For the novel's primary character, John Grimes, the juxtaposition of the mottoes with a green metal serpent, and, more important, with an environment in which neither the saccharine poem of welcome nor the claim that "God so loved the world . . ." bears any relation to the isolation of the family living there, produces an even profounder feeling of isolation and fear (Baldwin, *Go Tell It on the Mountain*, 25–26).

3. Howe, "Black Boys and Native Sons," esp. 360.
4. Baldwin, "Notes of a Native Son," in *Notes of a Native Son*, 113–14.
5. Baldwin, "Down at the Cross," in *The Fire Next Time*, 88. All future references in this chapter to this essay (abbreviated "Down") appear in the text.
6. Toni Morrison, "Unspeakable Things Unspoken: The Afro-American Presence in American Literature," *Michigan Quarterly Review* 28 (Winter 1989): 23.
7. Baldwin, "If Black English Isn't a Language, Then Tell Me, What Is?"(1979), in *Price of the Ticket*, 649–52.
8. Morrison, "Unspeakable Things Unspoken," 3.
9. Baldwin, "Why I Stopped Hating Shakespeare," *The Observer* (19 April 1964): 21.
10. Josh Kun provides an important reminder that another explanation for Baldwin's emphasis on the "unspeakable" is his conviction that music, particularly the blues, captures what the written or spoken word cannot (see Josh Kun, "Life according to the Beat: James Baldwin, Bessie Smith, and the Perilous Sounds of Love," in *James Baldwin Now*, ed. Dwight A. McBride [New York: New York University Press, 1999], 307–28).
11. Baldwin, "If Black English Isn't a Language, Then Tell Me, What Is?" in *Price of the Ticket*, 650.
12. Alfred Kazin, quoted in "The Negro in American Culture," *Cross Currents* 11 (Summer 1961): 213. Other participants in the discussion, which was broadcast on public radio in New York City, were Baldwin, Lorraine Hansberry, Emile Capouya, and Langston Hughes. Nat Hentoff moderated the event.
13. Baldwin, quoted in *A Dialogue*, 89.
14. Adorno, "Essay as Form," in *Notes to Literature*, vol. 1, 11.
15. Baldwin, "Why I Stopped Hating Shakespeare," 21.
16. Václav Havel, "Words on Words," *New York Review of Books* 36 (18 January 1990): 6.
17. Maurice Merleau-Ponty, "A Note on Machiavelli," in *Signs*, trans.

Richard C. McCleary (Evanston, Ill.: Northwestern University Press, 1964), 220.

18. Baldwin, "The Northern Protestant," in *Nobody Knows My Name*, 176.

19. For example, in a review originally published as the cover article of the inaugural issue of the *New York Review of Books*, F. W. Dupee criticizes Baldwin for replacing the acute analysis and critique of his earlier essays with more grandiose prophetic claims (F. W. Dupee, "James Baldwin and 'The Man,'" in *James Baldwin*, ed. Harold Bloom [New York: Chelsea House Publishers, 1986], 11–15).

20. According to David Leeming, an editor at Dial Press understood the link between the two essays and recommended publishing them together (Leeming, *James Baldwin*, 211–13). Because the two essays collected as *The Fire Next Time* are examined more closely in this chapter than in preceding chapters, I cite them by name.

21. James Campbell notes that the *New Yorker* format required that Baldwin's essay be entitled "Letter from. . . ." Nevertheless, as I point out in my afterword, many of Baldwin's essays are written as "letters from . . ." (see Campbell, *Talking at the Gates*, 160).

22. This question, he reports, is the same one that the men on "the Avenue" used in suggesting he join them, and it is implicit in Elijah Muhammad's smile upon meeting Baldwin. In any case, the question evokes such a strong response, a yearning for belonging to something or someone, that Baldwin finds it hard to resist no matter what its source.

23. Emphasis in the original.

24. Baldwin, "The Harlem Ghetto," in *Notes of a Native Son*, 65.

25. Baldwin, "The Crusade of Indignation," in *Price of the Ticket*, 158.

26. Walzer, *Interpretation and Social Criticism*, 44.

27. See, for example, Lucius J. Barker, "Limits of Political Strategy: A Systemic View of the African American Experience," *American Political Science Review* 88 (March 1994): 11.

28. Emphasis in the original.

29. Baldwin uses this narrative strategy to similar effect when he makes his own genealogy emblematic of centuries of African American history: "I am called Baldwin because I was either sold by my African tribe or kidnapped out of it into the hands of a white Christian named Baldwin . . . and this is what it means to be an American Negro, this is who he is—a kidnapped pagan, who was sold like an animal and treated like one, who was once defined by the American Constitution as 'three-fifths' of a man, and who, according to the Dred Scott decision, had no rights that a white man was bound to respect." By enlarg-

ing his own life in this way, Baldwin conveys the personal impact of that history, its centrality to his sense of identity (Baldwin, "Down at the Cross," in *The Fire Next Time*, 102, and 84, respectively).

30. That having been said, however, Baldwin does provide a powerful definition of negative freedom, as "freedom from . . . ," in the American context: "they, the blacks, simply don't wish to be beaten over the head by the whites every instant of our brief passage on this planet" (see Isaiah Berlin, "Two Concepts of Liberty," in *Four Essays on Liberty* [London: Oxford University Press, 1969], 118–72; Baldwin, "Down at the Cross," in *The Fire Next Time*, 21–22).

31. Although Baldwin did eventually make his escape through his writing—an eventuality that he claims did not appear possible to him as a child—his account of how he managed to prevent himself from turning to a criminal career by preaching a gospel he could not fully believe is reminiscent of W. E. B. Du Bois's claim that "the price of culture is a Lie." (See chapter 2 for further discussion.)

32. In an interview with David Leeming, Baldwin remarks that "freedom and innocence are antithetical" (Baldwin, quoted in David Adams Leeming, "An Interview with James Baldwin on Henry James," *Henry James Review* 8 [Fall 1986]: 54).

33. As he wryly observes: "I was . . . going to have a drink with several white devils on the other side of town."

34. Baldwin, "Notes of a Native Son," in *Notes of a Native Son*, 112.

35. For an incisive discussion of the oppressive consequences of a "strong doctrine of responsibility" and of the relationship between the desire to identify a discrete, responsible party for every evil and the unwillingness to confront the unavoidability of the human condition, see William E. Connolly, *Identity\Difference: Democratic Negotiations of Political Paradox* (Ithaca: Cornell University Press, 1991), 95–122.

36. Baldwin, "My Dungeon Shook," in *The Fire Next Time*, 8–10 (emphasis in the original).

37. Baldwin, introduction to *Nobody Knows My Name*, xii.

38. Emphasis in the original.

39. Stephen Spender's complaint that *The Fire Next Time* counsels despair by "postulating a quite impossible demand as the only way of dealing with a problem that has to be solved" misses the point in two respects. First, by saying Baldwin offers his "impossible demand" as the *only* way to deal with racial inequality, Spender mistakes Baldwin's criticism of incremental change for the assertion that such change is not an improvement. And, more important, the assertion that the "problem has to be solved" does not mean that it is as suscep-

tible to solution as Spender intimates (Stephen Spender, "James Baldwin: Voice of a Revolution," *Partisan Review* 30 [Summer 1963]: 257–58).

40. Baldwin, "My Dungeon Shook," in *The Fire Next Time*, 5.

41. Perhaps the most compelling depiction of this attitude toward life is his portrait of "G.," a southern teenager determined to "make it" at a high school in which he is the only black student (see "A Fly in Buttermilk," in *Nobody Knows My Name*, 83–97).

42. Morrison, *Playing in the Dark*, xiii.

43. Morrison does offer such a tribute elsewhere (see Toni Morrison, "Life in His Language," in *James Baldwin: The Legacy*, ed. Quincy Troupe [New York: Simon and Schuster, 1989], 75–78).

Afterword: Baldwin and the Search for a Majority

1. See Gary Orfield and John T. Yun, *Resegregation in American Schools*, Harvard University, Civil Rights Project (June 1999).

2. In one essay, for example, he describes "America" as "a new, almost completely undefined and extremely controversial proper noun" (Baldwin, "The Discovery of What It Means to Be an American," in *Nobody Knows My Name*, 3).

3. Baldwin, "An Open Letter to My Sister, Angela Davis," 23.

4. George Shulman, "Race and the Romance of American Nationalism in Martin Luther King, Norman Mailer, and James Baldwin," in *Cultural Studies and Political Theory*, ed. Jodi Dean (Ithaca: Cornell University Press, 2000), 227.

5. Baldwin, "In Search of a Majority," in *Nobody Knows My Name*, 127–37.

6. James Baldwin, "Envoi," in *A Quarter Century of un-Americana*, ed. Charlotte Pomerantz (New York: Marzani and Munsell, 1963), 127.

7. John Edgar Wideman, quoted in *Black Writers Redefine the Struggle: A Tribute to James Baldwin*, ed. Jules Chametzky (Amherst, Mass.: Institute for Advanced Study in the Humanities, 1989), 64.

8. Baldwin, "The Dangerous Road before Martin Luther King," in *Price of the Ticket*, 262.

BIBLIOGRAPHY

Works by James Baldwin

This list comprises only the works cited in the text. It is neither a complete record of Baldwin's published writings nor an exhaustive list of those that shaped this book.

Baldwin, James. *Another Country.* New York: Dell Publishing, 1962.
——. "Anti-Semitism and Black Power." *Freedomways* 7 (Winter 1967): 75–77.
——. "As Much Truth as One Can Bear." *New York Times Book Review* (14 January 1962): 1, 38.
——. *Conversations with James Baldwin.* Edited by Fred L. Standley and Louis H. Pratt. Jackson: University Press of Mississippi, 1989.
——. *The Devil Finds Work.* New York: Dial Press, 1976.
——. "Envoi." In *A Quarter Century of un-Americana.* Edited by Charlotte Pomerantz. New York: Marzani and Munsell, 1963.
——. *The Evidence of Things Not Seen.* New York: Holt, Rinehart and Winston, 1985.
——. *The Fire Next Time.* 1963. Reprint. New York: Vintage International, 1993.

——. *Giovanni's Room*. New York: Dell Publishing, 1956.

——. *Go Tell It on the Mountain*. New York: Signet Books, 1952.

——. *Going to Meet the Man*. New York: Dell Publishing, 1965.

——. "History as Nightmare." *New Leader* 30 (25 October 1947): 11, 15.

——. "Mass Culture and the Creative Artist: Some Personal Notes." In *Culture for the Millions? Mass Media in Modern Society*. Edited by Norman Jacobs. Boston: Beacon Press, 1964.

——. "The Negro at Home and Abroad." *The Reporter* (27 November 1951): 37.

——. *Nobody Knows My Name: More Notes of a Native Son*. New York: Dial Press, 1961.

——. *Notes of a Native Son*. 1955. Reprint. Boston: Beacon Press, 1984.

——. "On the Painter Beauford Delaney." *Transition* 4 (1965): 45.

——. "An Open Letter to My Sister, Angela Y. Davis." In *If They Come in the Morning: Voices of Resistance*. New York: Signet, 1971.

——. "Pour libérer les Blancs." Interview with François Bondy. *Preuves* (October 1963): 3–17.

——. "Preservation of Innocence." *Zero* 2 (Summer 1949): 14–22.

——. *The Price of the Ticket: Collected Nonfiction, 1948–85*. New York: St. Martin's/Marek, 1985.

——. *Tell Me How Long the Train's Been Gone*. New York: Dial, 1968.

——. "Too Late, Too Late." *Commentary* (January 1949): 96–99.

——. "What Price Freedom?" *Freedomways* 4 (Spring 1964): 191–95.

——. "The White Problem." In *100 Years of Emancipation*. Edited by Robert A. Goldwin. Chicago: Rand McNally, 1964.

——. "Why I Stopped Hating Shakespeare." *The Observer* (19 April 1964): 21.

Baldwin, James, and Nikki Giovanni. *A Dialogue*. London: Michael Joseph, 1975.

Baldwin, James, and Audre Lorde. "Revolutionary Hope: A Conversation between James Baldwin and Audre Lorde." *Essence* 15 (December 1984): 72–74, 129–33.

Leeming, David Adams. "An Interview with James Baldwin on Henry James." *Henry James Review* 8 (Fall 1986): 47–56.

"Liberalism and the Negro: A Roundtable Discussion." *Commentary* 37 (March 1964): 25–42.

Mead, Margaret, and James Baldwin. *A Rap on Race*. New York: Dell Publishing, 1992.

"The Negro in American Culture." *Cross Currents* 11 (Summer 1961): 205–24.

Other Works

Adorno, Theodor W. "The Essay as Form." *Notes to Literature*. Vol. 1. Edited by Rolf Tiedemann. Translated by Shierry Weber Nicholsen. New York: Columbia University Press, 1991.

Allen, Ernest, Jr. "On the Reading of Riddles: Rethinking Du Boisian Double Consciousness." In *Existence in Black: An Anthology of Black Existential Philosophy*. Edited by Lewis R. Gordon. New York: Routledge, 1997.

Bader, Veit. "Citizenship and Exclusion: Radical Democracy, Community, and Justice. Or What Is Wrong with Communitarianism?" *Political Theory* 23 (May 1995): 211–46.

Baier, Annette. *Moral Prejudices: Essays on Ethics*. Cambridge: Harvard University Press, 1994.

Barker, Lucius J. "Limits of Political Strategy: A Systemic View of the African American Experience." *American Political Science Review* 88 (March 1994): 1–13.

Bell, Derrick. *And We Are Not Saved: The Elusive Quest for Racial Justice*. New York: Basic Books, 1987.

——. *Race, Racism and American Law*. Boston: Little, Brown, 1973.

Benhabib, Seyla. "Feminism and Postmodernism: An Uneasy Alliance." In *Feminist Contentions: A Philosophical Exchange*. New York: Routledge, 1995.

Black Writers Redefine the Struggle: A Tribute to James Baldwin. Edited by Jules Chametzky. Amherst: Institute for Advanced Study in the Humanities, 1989.

Blight, David W. "W. E. B. Du Bois and the Struggle for Historical Memory." In *History and Memory in African-American Culture*. Edited by Geneviève Fabre and Robert O'Meally. New York: Oxford University Press, 1994.

Bobo, Lawrence D. "The Color Line, the Dilemma, and the Dream: Race Relations in America at the Close of the Twentieth Century." In *Civil Rights and Social Wrongs: Black-White Relations Since World War II*. Edited by John Higham. University Park, Pa.: Penn State Press, 1997.

Bobo, Lawrence D., and Ryan A. Smith. "From Jim Crow Racism to Laissez-Faire Racism: The Transformation of Racial Attitudes." In *Beyond Pluralism: The Conception of Groups and Group Identities in America*. Edited by Wendy Katkin, Ned Landsman, and Andrea Tyree. Urbana: University of Illinois Press, 1998.

Booth, William James. "Foreigners: Insiders, Outsiders, and the Ethics of Membership." *Review of Politics* 59 (Spring 1997): 259–92.

Branch, Taylor. *Parting the Waters: America in the King Years, 1954–63.* New York: Simon and Schuster, 1988.

Brandt, Nat. *Harlem at War: The Black Experience in WWII.* Syracuse: Syracuse University Press, 1996.

Brother to Brother: New Writings by Black Gay Men. Edited by Essex Hemphill. Boston: Alyson Publications, 1991.

Brown, Wendy. *States of Injury: Power and Freedom in Late Modernity.* Princeton: Princeton University Press, 1995.

Campbell, James. *Talking at the Gates: A Life of James Baldwin.* New York: Penguin Books, 1991.

Capeci, Dominic J., Jr. *The Harlem Riot of 1943.* Philadelphia: Temple University Press, 1977.

Clark, Kenneth B. *King, Malcolm, Baldwin: Three Interviews by Kenneth B. Clark.* Middletown, Conn.: Wesleyan University Press, 1985.

Carby, Hazel V. "The Multicultural Wars." In *Black Popular Culture.* Edited by Gina Dent. Seattle: Bay Press, 1992.

Champion, Ernest A. *Mr. Baldwin, I Presume: James Baldwin–Chinua Achebe: A Meeting of the Minds.* Lanham, Md.: University Press of America, 1995.

Chauncey, George. *Gay New York: Gender, Urban Culture, and the Making of the Gay Male World, 1890–1930.* New York: Basic Books, 1994.

Cleaver, Eldridge. *Soul on Ice.* New York: Dell Publishing, 1968.

Cohen, Joshua. "Procedure and Substance in Deliberative Democracy." In *Democracy and Difference: Contesting the Boundaries of the Political.* Edited by Seyla Benhabib. Princeton: Princeton University Press, 1996.

Committee on the Judiciary, U.S. Senate. *The Nomination of Clarence Thomas to Be Associate Justice of the Supreme Court of the United States.* Washington, D.C.: U.S. Government Printing Office, 1993.

A Common Destiny: Blacks and American Society. Edited by Gerald David Jaynes and Robin M. Williams. Washington, D.C.: National Academy Press, 1989.

Cone, James H. *Martin and Malcolm and America: A Dream or a Nightmare.* Maryknoll, N.Y.: Orbis Books, 1991.

Connolly, William E. *Identity\Difference: Democratic Negotiations of Political Paradox.* Ithaca: Cornell University Press, 1991.

——. *Politics and Ambiguity.* Madison: University of Wisconsin Press, 1987.

Cooper, Anna Julia. *A Voice from the South.* New York: Oxford University Press, 1988.

Corber, Robert J. *Homosexuality in Cold War America: Resistance and the Crisis of Masculinity.* Durham, N.C.: Duke University Press, 1997.

Court of Appeal: The Black Community Speaks Out on the Racial and Sexual Politics of Thomas vs. Hill. Edited by *The Black Scholar* [Robert Chrisman and Robert L. Allen]. New York: Ballantine Books, 1992.

Crenshaw, Kimberlé Williams. "Color-blind Dreams and Racial Nightmares: Reconfiguring Racism in the Post–Civil Rights Era." In *Birth of a Nation'hood: Gaze, Script, and Spectacle in the O. J. Simpson Case.* Edited by Toni Morrison and Claudia Brodsky Lacour. New York: Pantheon Books, 1997, 97–168.

——. "Mapping the Margins: Intersectionality, Identity Politics, and Violence against Women of Color." In *Critical Race Theory: The Key Writings That Formed the Movement.* Edited by Kimberlé Crenshaw, Neil Gotanda, Gary Peller, and Kendall Thomas. New York: The New Press, 1995.

——. "Race, Reform, and Retrenchment: Transformation and Legitimation in Antidiscrimination Law." *Harvard Law Review* 101 (May 1988): 1331–87.

Critical Essays on James Baldwin. Edited by Fred L. Standley and Nancy V. Burt. Boston: G. K. Hall, 1988.

Crouch, Stanley. *Notes of a Hanging Judge: Essays and Reviews, 1979–89.* New York: Oxford University Press, 1990.

Cruse, Harold. *The Crisis of the Negro Intellectual.* New York: Quill, 1967.

Davis, Angela Y. *Women, Race and Class.* New York: Vintage Books, 1981.

Descombes, Vincent. "Is There a Politics of Authenticity?" Translated by Daniel Weinstock. *Raritan* 13 (Spring 1994): 102–23.

Dolan, Frederick M. *Allegories of America: Narratives, Metaphysics, Politics.* Ithaca: Cornell University Press, 1994.

Du Bois, W. E. B. *Black Reconstruction in America.* 1935. Reprint. New York: Atheneum, 1962.

——. "The Development of a People." *In The Souls of Black Folk.* Edited by David W. Blight and Robert Gooding-Williams. Boston: Bedford Books, 1997.

——. *Dusk of Dawn: An Essay toward an Autobiography of a Race Concept.* New Brunswick, N.J.: Transaction Publishers, 1984.

——. *The Souls of Black Folk.* 1903. Reprint. New York: Penguin Books, 1989.

——. *W. E. B. Du Bois: A Reader.* Edited by David Levering Lewis. New York: Henry Holt, 1995.

Dumm, Thomas L. *united states.* Ithaca: Cornell University Press, 1994.

Dupee, F. W. "James Baldwin and 'The Man.'" In *James Baldwin.* Edited by Harold Bloom. New York: Chelsea House, 1986.

Dworkin, Ronald. "To Each His Own." *New York Review of Books* (14 April 1983): 4–6.

Eckman, Fern Marja. *The Furious Passage of James Baldwin.* New York: M. Evans and Company, 1966.

Edsall, Thomas Byrne, and Mary D. Edsall. *Chain Reaction: The Impact of Race, Rights, and Taxes on American Politics.* New York: Norton, 1992.

Ellison, Ralph. *Going to the Territory.* New York: Random House, 1986.

——. *Invisible Man.* New York: Vintage Books, 1972.

——. *Shadow and Act.* New York: Vintage Books, 1972.

Emerson, Ralph Waldo. *Emerson: Essays and Lectures.* Edited by Joel Porte. New York: Library of America, 1983.

Euben, J. Peter. *The Tragedy of Political Theory: The Road Not Taken.* Princeton: Princeton University Press, 1990.

"Excerpts from Senate's Hearings on the Thomas Nomination." *New York Times,* 12 October 1991.

Fanon, Frantz. *Black Skin, White Masks.* Translated by Charles Lam Markmann. New York: Grove Weidenfeld, 1967.

Faulkner, William. "A Talk with William Faulkner." Interview by Russell Warren Howe. *The Reporter* (22 March 1956): 18–20.

Fields, Barbara Jeanne. "Slavery, Race and Ideology in the United States of America." *New Left Review* 181 (May-June 1990): 95–118.

Flax, Jane. *Disputed Subjects: Essays on Psychoanalysis, Politics and Philosophy.* New York: Routledge, 1993.

Foucault, Michel. *Discipline and Punish: The Birth of the Prison.* Translated by Alan Sheridan. New York: Vintage Books, 1977.

——. *History of Sexuality.* Vol. 1. Translated by Robert Hurley. New York: Vintage, 1980.

Frankenberg, Ruth. *White Women, Race Matters: The Social Construction of Whiteness.* Minneapolis: University of Minnesota Press, 1993.

Franklin, John Hope. *The Color Line: Legacy for the Twenty-First Century.* Columbia: University of Missouri Press, 1993.

Fraser, Nancy. *Justice Interruptus: Critical Reflections on the "Postsocialist" Condition.* New York: Routledge, 1997.

Fraser, Nancy, and Linda J. Nicholson. "Social Criticism without Philosophy: An Encounter between Feminism and Postmodernism." In *Feminism/Postmodernism.* Edited by Linda J. Nicholson. New York: Routledge, 1990.

Gadamer, Hans-Georg. *Philosophical Hermeneutics.* Translated and edited by David E. Linge. Berkeley: University of California Press, 1976.

——. *Truth and Method.* 2nd rev. ed. Translated by Joel Weinsheimer and Donald G. Marshall. New York: Continuum, 1993.

Gates, Henry Louis, Jr. "The Fire Last Time." *New Republic* (1 July 1992): 37–43.

———. "Introduction: On Bearing Witness." In *Bearing Witness: Selections from African-American Autobiography in the Twentieth Century*. Edited By Henry Louis Gates, Jr. New York: Pantheon Books, 1991.

Gayle, Addison, Jr. "A Defense of James Baldwin." *CLA Journal* 10 (March 1967): 201–8.

Gibson, Donald B. "Ralph Ellison and James Baldwin." In *The Politics of Twentieth-Century Novelists*. Edited by George A. Panichas. New York: Hawthorne Books, 1971.

Gilroy, Paul. *The Black Atlantic: Modernity and Double Consciousness*. Cambridge: Harvard University Press, 1993.

Gooding-Williams, Robert. "'Look, a Negro!'" In *Reading Rodney King, Reading Urban Uprising*. Edited by Robert Gooding-Williams. New York: Routledge, 1993.

Gordon, Lewis R. *Bad Faith and Antiblack Racism*. Atlantic Highlands, N.J.: Humanities Press, 1995.

———. "Existential Dynamics of Theorizing Black Invisibility." In *Existence in Black: An Anthology of Black Existential Philosophy*. Edited by Lewis R. Gordon. New York: Routledge, 1997.

———. *Fanon and the Crisis of European Man: An Essay on Philosophy and the Human Sciences*. New York: Routledge, 1995.

Gramsci, Antonio. *Selections from the Prison Notebooks*. Translated and edited by Quinton Hoare and Geoffrey Nowell Smith. New York: International Publishers, 1971.

Grant, Joanne. *Ella Baker: Freedom Bound*. New York: John Wiley and Sons, 1998.

Greenberg, Cheryl Lynn. *"Or Does It Explode?" Black Harlem in the Great Depression*. New York: Oxford University Press, 1991.

Guinier, Lani. "Reframing the Affirmative Action Debate." *Kentucky Law Journal* 86 (1997–98): 505–25.

———. *The Tyranny of the Majority: Fundamental Fairness in Representative Democracy*. New York: The Free Press, 1994.

Gutmann, Amy. "Responding to Racial Injustice." In K. Anthony Appiah and Amy Gutmann, *Color Conscious: The Political Morality of Race*. Princeton: Princeton University Press, 1996.

Gutmann, Amy, and Dennis Thompson. *Democracy and Disagreement*. Cambridge: Harvard/Belknap, 1996.

Habermas, Jürgen. "Three Normative Models of Democracy." In *Democracy and Difference: Contesting the Boundaries of the Political*. Edited by Seyla Benhabib. Princeton: Princeton University Press, 1996.

Hacker, Andrew. *Two Nations: Black and White, Separate, Hostile, Un-equal*. New York: Ballantine Books, 1992.

Hampshire, Stuart. *Innocence and Experience*. Cambridge: Harvard University Press, 1989.

Hanchard, Michael. "Identity, Meaning and the African-American." *Social Text* 24 (Spring 1990): 31–42.

Harding, Vincent. *There Is a River: The Black Struggle for Freedom in America*. New York: Harcourt Brace Jovanovich, 1981.

Harris, Cheryl I. "Whiteness as Property." *Harvard Law Review* 106 (June 1993): 1707–91.

Harris, Trudier. *Black Women in the Fiction of James Baldwin*. Knoxville: University of Tennessee Press, 1985.

Havel, Václav. "Words on Words." *New York Review of Books* 36 (18 January 1990): 5–6, 8.

Higginbotham, A. Leon. *In the Matter of Color: Race and the American Legal Process. The Colonial Period*. New York: Oxford University Press, 1978.

——. *Shades of Freedom: Racial Politics and Presumptions of the American Legal Process*. New York: Oxford University Press, 1996.

Horkheimer, Max, and Theodor Adorno. *Dialectic of Enlightenment*. Translated by John Cumming. New York: Herder and Herder, 1972.

Howard, Jane. " 'The Doom and Glory of Knowing Who You Are.' " *Life* (24 May 1963): 86–90.

Howe, Irving. "Black Boys and Native Sons." *Dissent* (Autumn 1963): 353–68.

——. "James Baldwin: At Ease in the Apocalypse." *Harper's* (September 1968): 92–100.

Huggins, Nathan Irvin. "The Deforming Mirror of Truth." New introduction to reissued edition of *Black Odyssey: The African-American Ordeal in Slavery*. New York: Vintage Books, 1990.

James Baldwin. Edited by Harold Bloom. New York: Chelsea House, 1986.

James Baldwin. Edited by Keith Kinnamon. Englewood Cliffs, N.J.: Prentice-Hall, 1974.

James Baldwin: A Critical Evaluation. Edited by Therman B. O'Daniel. Washington, D.C.: Howard University Press, 1977.

James Baldwin: The Legacy. Edited by Quincy Troupe. New York: Simon and Schuster, 1989.

James Baldwin Now. Edited by Dwight A. McBride. New York: New York University Press, 1999.

Jones, LeRoi (Amiri Baraka). *Home: Social Essays*. New York: William Morrow, 1966.

Kaplan, Cora. " 'A Cavern Opened in My Mind': The Poetics of Homosexuality and the Politics of Masculinity in James Baldwin." In *Representing Black Men*. Edited by Marcellus Blount and George P. Cunningham. New York: Routledge, 1996.

Karst, Kenneth L. *Law's Promise, Law's Expression: Visions of Power in the Politics of Race, Gender, and Religion*. New Haven: Yale University Press, 1993.

Kateb, George. *The Inner Ocean: Individualism and Democratic Culture*. Ithaca: Cornell University Press, 1992.

Katz, Michael B. "The Urban 'Underclass' as a Metaphor of Social Transformation." In *The Underclass Debate: Views from History*. Edited by Michael B. Katz. Princeton: Princeton University Press, 1993.

Kazin, Alfred. "Close to Us." *The Reporter* 25 (17 August 1961): 58–60.

Kenan, Randall. *James Baldwin*. New York: Chelsea House, 1994.

Kinder, Donald R., and Lynn M. Sanders. *Divided by Color: Racial Politics and Democratic Ideals*. Chicago: University of Chicago Press, 1996.

King, Martin Luther, Jr. *A Testament of Hope: The Essential Writings and Speeches of Martin Luther King, Jr.* Edited by James M. Washington. New York: HarperCollins, 1986.

Kun, Josh. "Life according to the Beat: James Baldwin, Bessie Smith, and the Perilous Sounds of Love." In *James Baldwin Now*. Edited by Dwight A. McBride. New York: New York University Press, 1999.

Lawrence, Charles, III. "The Id, the Ego, and Equal Protection: Reckoning with Unconscious Racism." *Stanford Law Review* 39 (January 1987): 317–88.

Lee, Felicia. "The Honest Dialogue That Is Neither." *New York Times*, 7 December 1997.

Leeming, David. *James Baldwin: A Biography*. New York: Alfred A. Knopf, 1994.

Lefort, Claude. *Democracy and Political Theory*. Translated by David Macey. Minneapolis: University of Minnesota Press, 1988.

Lewis, David Levering. *W. E. B. Du Bois: Biography of a Race, 1868–1919*. New York: Henry Holt, 1993.

Lipsitz, George. *The Possessive Investment in Whiteness: How White People Profit from Identity Politics*. Philadelphia: Temple University Press, 1998.

Lorde, Audre. *Sister Outsider: Essays and Speeches*. Freedom, Calif.: The Crossing Press, 1984.

Loury, Glenn. "Beyond Victimhood." *Times Literary Supplement* (10 June 1994): 15.

Lubiano, Wahneema. "Shuckin' Off the African-American Native Other:

What's 'Po-Mo' Got to Do with It?" *Cultural Critique* (Spring 1991): 149–86.

Lure and Loathing: Essays on Race, Identity, and the Ambivalence of Assimilation. Edited by Gerald Early. New York: Allen Lane, 1993.

Macebuh, Stanley. *James Baldwin: A Critical Study*. New York: The Third Press, 1973.

Massey, Douglas S. "Residential Segregation and Persistent Urban Poverty." In *Civil Rights and Social Wrongs: Black-White Relations since World War II*. Edited by John Higham. University Park, Pa.: Penn State Press, 1997.

Massey, Douglas S., and Nancy A. Denton. *American Apartheid: Segregation and the Making of the Underclass*. Cambridge: Harvard University Press, 1993.

Matsuda, Mari J., Charles R. Lawrence III, Richard Delgado, and Kimberlé Williams Crenshaw. *Words That Wound: Critical Race Theory, Assaultive Speech, and the First Amendment*. Boulder, Colo.: Westview Press, 1993.

Merleau-Ponty, Maurice. *Signs*. Translated by Richard C. McCleary. Evanston, Ill.: Northwestern University Press, 1964.

Mills, Charles W. *Blackness Visible: Essays on Philosophy and Race*. Ithaca: Cornell University Press, 1998.

——. *The Racial Contract*. Ithaca: Cornell University Press, 1997.

Morrison, Toni. "Home." In *The House That Race Built: Black Americans, U.S. Terrain*. Edited by Wahneema Lubiano. New York: Pantheon Books, 1997.

——. "Life in His Language." In *James Baldwin: The Legacy*. Edited by Quincy Troupe. New York: Simon and Schuster, 1989.

——. *Playing in the Dark: Whiteness and the Literary Imagination*. Cambridge: Harvard University Press, 1992.

——. "The Site of Memory." In *Inventing the Truth: The Art and Craft of Memoir*. Edited by William Zinsser. Boston: Houghton Mifflin, 1987.

——. "Unspeakable Things Unspoken: The Afro-American Presence in American Literature." *Michigan Quarterly Review* 28 (Winter 1989): 1–34.

Murray, Albert. *The Omni-Americans: New Perspectives on Black Experience and American Culture*. New York: Outerbridge and Dienstfrey, 1970.

Myrdal, Gunnar. *An American Dilemma: The Negro Problem and Modern Democracy*. New York: Harper and Brothers, 1944.

Nissim-Sabat, Miriam. "Victim No More." *Radical Philosophy Review* 1 (1998): 17–34.

Nkosi, Lewis. "The Mountain." *Transition* 79 (1999): 102–25.

Omi, Michael, and Howard Winant. *Racial Formation in the United States: From the 1960s to the 1980s.* New York: Routledge and Kegan Paul, 1986.

Orfield, Gary, and John T. Yun. *Resegregation in American Schools.* Harvard University, Civil Rights Project (June 1999).

Pateman, Carole. *The Disorder of Women: Democracy, Feminism and Political Theory.* Stanford: Stanford University Press, 1989.

Patterson, H. Orlando. "The Essays of James Baldwin." *New Left Review* (Summer 1964): 31–38.

Peller, Gary. "Race-Consciousness." In *Critical Race Theory: The Key Writings That Formed the Movement.* Edited by Kimberlé Crenshaw, Neil Gotanda, Gary Peller, and Kendall Thomas. New York: The New Press, 1995.

Pinckney, Darryl. "The Magic of James Baldwin." *New York Review of Books* 45 (19 November 1998): 64–74.

Piper, Adrian M. S. "Higher-Order Discrimination." In *Identity, Character, and Morality: Essays in Moral Psychology.* Edited by Owen Flanagan and Amélie Oksenberg Rorty. Cambridge: MIT Press, 1990.

Plato. *The Republic.* Translated by G. M. A. Grube. Revised by C. D. C. Reeve. Indianapolis: Hackett Publishing, 1992.

Porter, Horace A. *Stealing the Fire: The Art and Protest of James Baldwin.* Middletown, Conn.: Wesleyan University Press, 1989.

Posnock, Ross. *Color and Culture: Black Writers and the Making of the Modern Intellectual.* Cambridge: Harvard University Press, 1998.

Pratt, Louis H. *James Baldwin.* Boston: G. K. Hall, 1978.

Race-ing Justice, En-gendering Power: Essays on Anita Hill, Clarence Thomas, and the Construction of Social Reality. Edited by Toni Morrison. New York: Pantheon Books, 1992.

Rampersad, Arnold. *The Art and Imagination of W. E. B. Du Bois.* New York: Schocken Books, 1990.

Rawls, John. *Political Liberalism.* New York: Columbia University Press, 1993.

———. *A Theory of Justice.* Cambridge: Harvard University Press, 1971.

Reed, Adolph, Jr. "Du Bois's 'Double Consciousness': Race and Gender in Progressive Era American Thought." *Studies in American Political Development* 6 (Spring 1992): 92–139.

Rocco, Christopher. "Between Modernity and Postmodernity: Reading *Dialectic of Enlightenment* against the Grain." *Political Theory* 22 (February 1994): 71–97.

Roediger, David R. *The Wages of Whiteness: Race and the Making of the American Working Class.* Rev. ed. New York: Verso, 1999.

Rogin, Michael. *Blackface, White Noise: Jewish Immigrants in the Hollywood Melting Pot.* Berkeley: University of California Press, 1996.

Rorty, Amélie Oksenberg. "The Hidden Politics of Cultural Identification." *Political Theory* 22 (February 1994): 152–66.

Rorty, Richard. *Contingency, Irony, and Solidarity.* Cambridge: Cambridge University Press, 1989.

——. *Objectivity, Relativism, and Truth.* Cambridge: Cambridge University Press, 1991.

Ross, Marlon B. "White Fantasies of Desire: Baldwin and the Racial Identities of Sexuality." In *James Baldwin Now.* Edited by Dwight A. McBride. New York: New York University Press, 1999.

Rousseau, Jean-Jacques. *On the Social Contract.* Edited by Roger D. Masters. Translated by Judith R. Masters. New York: St. Martin's Press, 1978.

Sartre, Jean-Paul. *Anti-Semite and Jew.* Translated by George J. Becker. New York: Schocken Books, 1948.

——. *Orphée Noir.* In *Anthologie de la nouvelle poésie nègre et malagache de langue française.* Edited by Léopold Sédar Senghor. Paris: Presses Universitaires de France, 1969.

Scott, Daryl Michael. *Contempt and Pity: Social Policy and the Image of the Damaged Black Psyche, 1880–1996.* Chapel Hill: University of North Carolina Press, 1997.

Shapiro, Ian. *Political Criticism.* Berkeley: University of California Press, 1990.

Sherry, Michael S. *In the Shadow of War: The United States since the 1930s.* New Haven: Yale University Press, 1995.

Shklar, Judith. *American Citizenship: The Quest for Inclusion.* Cambridge: Harvard University Press, 1991.

——. *The Faces of Injustice.* New Haven: Yale University Press, 1990.

——. *Ordinary Vices.* Cambridge: Harvard University Press, 1984.

——. *Redeeming American Political Thought.* Edited by Stanley Hoffmann and Dennis F. Thompson. Chicago: University of Chicago Press, 1998.

Shulman, George. "American Political Culture, Prophetic Narration, and Toni Morrison's *Beloved.*" *Political Theory* 24 (May 1996): 295–314.

——. "Race and the Romance of American Nationalism in Martin Luther King, Norman Mailer, and James Baldwin." In *Cultural Studies and Political Theory.* Edited by Jodi Dean. Ithaca: Cornell University Press, 2000.

Smith, Rogers M. "Beyond Tocqueville, Myrdal, and Hartz: The Multiple Traditions in America." *American Political Science Review* 87 (September 1993): 549–66.

Spelman, Elizabeth V. *Inessential Woman: Problems of Exclusion in Feminist Thought*. Boston: Beacon Press, 1988.

Spender, Stephen. "James Baldwin: Voice of a Revolution." *Partisan Review* 30 (Summer 1963): 256–60.

Spillers, Hortense. "Mama's Baby, Papa's Maybe: An American Grammar Book." *Diacritics* 17 (Summer 1987): 65–81.

Steele, Shelby. *The Content of Our Character: A New Vision of Race in America*. New York: St. Martin's Press, 1990.

Stepto, Robert B. *From behind the Veil: A Study of Afro-American Narrative*. Urbana: University of Illinois Press, 1991.

Stovall, Tyler. *Paris Noir: African Americans in the City of Light*. New York: Houghton Mifflin, 1996.

Sundquist, Eric J. *To Wake the Nations: Race in the Making of American Literature*. Cambridge: Harvard/Belknap, 1993.

Takaki, Ronald. *A Different Mirror: A History of Multicultural America*. Boston: Little, Brown, 1993.

Taylor, Charles. *The Ethics of Authenticity*. Cambridge: Harvard University Press, 1992.

——. "The Politics of Recognition." In *Multiculturalism: Examining the Politics of Recognition*. 2nd ed. Edited by Amy Gutmann. Princeton: Princeton University Press, 1994.

——. *Reconciling the Solitudes: Essays on Canadian Federalism and Nationalism*. Montreal: McGill-Queens University Press, 1993.

Thelwell, Ekwueme Michael. "A Prophet Is Not without Honor." *Transition* 58 (1992): 90–113.

Thomas, Kendall. "'Ain't Nothing Like the Real Thing': Black Masculinity, Gay Sexuality, and the Jargon of Authenticity." In *The House That Race Built: Black Americans, U.S. Terrain*. Edited by Wahneema Lubiano. New York: Pantheon Books, 1997.

Thomas, Laurence. "Moral Deference." *Philosophical Forum* 24 (Fall-Spring 1992–93): 233–50.

Thoreau, Henry David. *Walden and Other Writings*. Edited by Joseph Wood Krutch. New York: Bantam Books, 1962.

Thorsen, Karen (director and producer). *James Baldwin: The Price of the Ticket*. San Francisco: California Newsreel, 1990.

Tocqueville, Alexis de. *Democracy in America*. Edited by J. P. Mayer. Translated by George Lawrence. New York: Harper and Row, 1969.

U.S. Congress. Senate. Committee on the Judiciary. *Hearings on the Nomination of Judge Clarence Thomas to be Associate Justice of the Supreme Court*. 102nd Cong., 1st sess., 1991, pt. 4.

Walton, Anthony. *Mississippi: An American Journey*. New York: Vintage Books, 1996.

Walzer, Michael. *The Company of Critics: Social Criticism and Political Commitment in the Twentieth Century.* New York: Basic Books, 1988.

——. *Exodus and Revolution.* New York: Basic Books, 1985.

——. *Interpretation and Social Criticism.* Cambridge: Harvard University Press, 1987.

——. *Obligations: Essays on Disobedience, War, and Citizenship.* Cambridge: Harvard University Press, 1970.

——. "Political Action: The Problem of Dirty Hands." In *War and Moral Responsibility.* Edited by Marshall Cohen, Thomas Nagel, and Thomas Scanlon. Princeton: Princeton University Press, 1974.

——. *Radical Principles: Reflections of an Unreconstructed Democrat.* New York: Basic Books, 1980.

——. "Response to Veit Bader." *Political Theory* 23 (May 1995): 247–52.

——. "Shared Meanings in a Poly-Ethnic Democratic Setting: A Response." *Journal of Religious Ethics* 22 (Fall 1994): 401–5.

——. *Spheres of Justice: A Defense of Pluralism and Equality.* New York: Basic Books, 1983.

——. *Thick and Thin: Moral Argument at Home and Abroad.* Notre Dame: University of Notre Dame Press, 1994.

Warnke, Georgia. "Social Interpretation and Political Theory: Walzer and His Critics." In *Hermeneutics and Critical Theory in Ethics and Politics.* Edited by Michael Kelly. Cambridge: MIT Press, 1990.

Watts, Jerry Gafio. *Heroism and the Black Intellectual: Ralph Ellison, Politics, and Afro-American Intellectual Life.* Chapel Hill: University of North Carolina Press, 1994.

Weatherby, W. J. *James Baldwin: Artist on Fire.* New York: Donald I. Fine, 1989.

Weber, Max. *Ancient Judaism.* Translated and edited by Hans H. Gerth and Don Martindale. Glencoe, Ill.: The Free Press, 1952.

——. *Economy and Society.* Vol. 1. Edited by Guenther Roth and Claus Wittich. Berkeley: University of California Press, 1978.

——. "Politics as a Vocation." *From Max Weber: Essays in Sociology.* Translated and edited by H. H. Gerth and C. Wright Mills. New York: Oxford University Press, 1946.

West, Cornel. *Keeping Faith: Philosophy and Race in America.* New York: Routledge, 1993.

——. *Race Matters.* Boston: Beacon Press, 1993.

Williams, Patricia J. *The Alchemy of Race and Rights: Diary of a Law Professor.* Cambridge: Harvard University Press, 1991.

——. *The Rooster's Egg: On the Persistence of Prejudice.* Cambridge: Harvard University Press, 1995.

Wolin, Sheldon S. "Political Theory as a Vocation." In *Machiavelli and the Nature of Political Thought*. Edited by Martin Fleisher. New York: Atheneum, 1972.

——. *The Presence of the Past: Essays on the State and the Constitution*. Baltimore: Johns Hopkins University Press, 1989.

Woolf, Virginia. *A Room of One's Own*. San Diego: Harcourt Brace Jovanovich, 1981.

Wright, Richard. *Native Son*. Restored edition. New York: HarperPerennial, 1993.

Young, Iris Marion. *Justice and the Politics of Difference*. Princeton: Princeton University Press, 1990.

Zamir, Shamoon. *Dark Voices: W. E. B. Du Bois and American Thought, 1888–1903*. Chicago: University of Chicago Press, 1995.

——. " 'The Sorrow Songs'/'Song of Myself': Du Bois, the Crisis of Leadership, and Prophetic Imagination." In *The Black Columbiad: Defining Moments in African American Literature and Culture*. Edited by Werner Sollors and Maria Diedrich. Cambridge: Harvard University Press, 1994.

INDEX

Acceptance, 22, 128–31
Adorno, Theodor, 15, 120
Affirmative action, 4, 163n. 41
  innocence and, 90–91
  "reverse discrimination" and, 121
  See also Civil Rights Act
African Americans
  history of, 84–86, 106, 109
  leaders of, 105, 164n. 56
American Indians, 85
Amos (prophet), 100–101, 104–7
Androgyny, 53
Another Country (Baldwin), 154n. 37
Artistic consciousness, 50
Asian Americans, 136
Authenticity, racial, 37, 54, 58–59

Baier, Annette, 18–19
Baker, Ella, 23
Baldwin, David, 67–70, 72–75, 144n. 31
Baldwin, James
  on "American Negro past," 84–86, 106, 109

on androgyny, 53
on black English, 118
on black leaders, 105, 164n. 56
Eldridge Cleaver on, 54, 58
as "commuter," 11, 49–50
on double consciousness, 31, 41–55
on equality, 26, 123–28
on Faulkner, 110–12
on freedom, 24, 129–32
on guilt, 91–94
on homophobia, 53
homosexuality of, 10, 51–55
on idea of home, 98–99, 110–12
individualism of, 15, 24–27, 60–61, 136
on innocence, 27–29, 88, 90–91, 132
Robert Kennedy and, 11, 105
narrative "we" of, 31, 43–49, 106
on *Native Son*, 14, 46–48, 60, 80, 113
on *négritude* movement, 54, 58, 66
on personal responsibility, 130–32
on privacy, 52, 77–78, 119
on protest novels, 113–17, 120

Baldwin, James *(continued)*
  on racial images, 31–32, 60–67,
    78–86
  on segregation, 84, 109
  as spokesman, 14–15
  on whiteness, 16, 90–91
  on writer's vocation, 14, 17, 22,
    119–20
  See also specific works
Beauvoir, Simone de, 102
Benhabib, Seyla, 96
Bergman, Ingmar, 121
Berlin, Isaiah, 129
Bill of Rights, 109
Bisexuality, 44. *See also* Homosexual-
    ity
Black English, 118
Blues, 134, 167n. 10
Bobo, Lawrence, 144n. 23
Brown, Wendy, 64
Brown v. Board of Education, 63

California Civil Rights Initiative
    (Proposition 209), 121
Césaire, Aimé, 54, 66
Civil Rights Act (1964), 11, 109
Civil War, 83, 88, 120
Cleaver, Eldridge, 54, 58
Clinton, Bill, 1
Cohen, Joshua, 142n. 8
Colonialism, 66, 121, 126–27
"Color consciousness," 9
Color line, 2–3, 36–43
  crossing of, 43–49
  Du Bois on, 36–40
Communism, 51
Conformity
  equality and, 18, 125
  individuality and, 61
Congress of Racial Equality (CORE),
    11
Connolly, William, 169n. 35
Consciousness
  artistic, 50
  gender, 50–51
  See also Double consciousness; Race
    consciousness
Cowboy-and-Indian stories, 85
Crenshaw, Kimberlé, 4–6, 80, 155n. 51
Crouch, Stanley, 65
Cruse, Harold, 23

Davis, Angela, 8, 11
Democracy
  Baldwin's conception of, 18–30,
    122–32, 135–39
  deliberative theories of, 3
  exclusion and, 29, 35–36
  multiracial, 5–6, 13, 21, 138–39
  racial dialogue and, 1–5, 134
  trust and, 18–19
Denton, Nancy, 142n. 10
Descombes, Vincent, 61
Detroit riot (1943), 67, 159n. 45
Discrimination, 7
  "higher-order," 149n. 5
  "reverse," 121
Double consciousness
  Baldwin on, 31, 41–55
  Du Bois on, 31, 36–41, 111
  Malcolm X on, 150n. 7
  origins of, 150n. 8
  racial images and, 83–84
  sexuality and, 50–55
  See also Race consciousness
"Down at the Cross" (Baldwin),
    122–32
Du Bois, W. E. B.
  "Development of a People," 151n. 11
  on double consciousness, 31, 36–41,
    111
  gender issues and, 155n. 49
  Souls of Black Folk, 31, 36–43
Duke, David, 94
Dumm, Thomas, 96
Dupee, F. W., 168n. 19

Ebonics, 118
Ellison, Ralph, 116, 149n. 83, 160n. 53
Equality
  Baldwin's conception of, 26, 123–28
  conformity and, 18, 125
  Václav Havel on, 120
  limitations of formal, 5, 18, 20–21,
    75–76
  Michael Walzer on, 107–8, 126
Ethnicity, 9
Etiquette, racial, 151n. 10
"Everybody's Protest Novel" (Bald-
    win), 113–17, 120, 124
Exclusion, 25–26
  "us/them" mentality and, 35, 45, 47
  See also Inclusion

Fanon, Frantz, 62, 149n. 82
"Faulkner and Desegregation" (Baldwin), 110–12
"Fifth Avenue, Uptown" (Baldwin), 87–89, 101
Fire Next Time (Baldwin), 8, 11–13, 117, 122–34
  "Down at the Cross" in, 122–34
  "My Dungeon Shook" in, 122–23, 131
Flax, Jane, 96
Foucault, Michel, 105
Fraser, Nancy, 146n. 51, 148n. 74
Freedom
  Baldwin's conception of, 24, 129–32
  Václav Havel on, 120
  self-determination and, 130
Fuhrman, Mark, 94

Gadamer, Hans-Georg, 143n. 17
Gates, Henry Louis, Jr., 12
Gay identity, 51–52. *See also* Homosexuality
Gay rights movement, 51
Gender
  double consciousness and, 50–51
  Du Bois on, 155n. 49
  fluidity of, 53
  race consciousness and, 9
Gide, André, 52
Gilroy, Paul, 147n. 61, 156n. 60
Giovanni's Room (Baldwin), 51, 161n. 4
Gooding-Williams, Robert, 82, 150n. 9
Go Tell It on the Mountain (Baldwin), 146n. 52, 166n. 2
Gramsci, Antonio, 8, 104–5
Great Migration, 67
Greenwich Village, 10–11
Guilt, 91–94
Guinier, Lani, 1–3, 30, 143n. 15
Gutmann, Amy, 9, 142n. 8

Habermas, Jürgen, 142n. 8, 148n. 73
Hall, Stuart, 16
Hampshire, Stuart, 20, 96
Hanchard, Michael, 141n. 4
Hansberry, Lorraine, 145n. 37
Harlem
  coming of age in, 123–24
  gay subculture of, 144n. 32

1943 riot in, 67–68, 71–72, 81, 159n. 45, 161n. 7
Harris, Cheryl, 79, 90, 166n. 71
Havel, Václav, 120
Higginbotham, Leon, 4
Hill, Anita, 63–64
Himes, Chester, 152n. 23
Home
  Baldwin on, 98–99, 110–12
  Michael Walzer on, 98
Homophobia, 53
Homosexuality
  communism and, 51
  double consciousness and, 50–55
  as "problem," 52–53
Horton, Willie, 47, 62
Howe, Irving, 46–47, 116–17

Identity
  double consciousness and, 34–59
  exclusion and, 25–26
  masculine, 53–55
  racial, 58–59, 84
  racial images and, 31–32, 60–62
  sexual, 50–55
"If Black English Isn't a Language, Then Tell Me, What Is?" (Baldwin), 118
Inclusion, privilege of, 18–19, 35. *See also* Exclusion
Individualism, Baldwin's, 15, 24–27, 60–61, 136
Injustice
  misfortune vs., 77, 83
  "passive," 76, 94
  as "personal" problem, 75–82
  Judith Shklar on, 32, 66, 76–77, 94
  See also Racial injustice
Innocence, 4, 27–29, 32, 88, 90–91, 132
  existential, 132
  political theory and, 95–96
  Michael Walzer and, 32–33, 96–110

Jim Crow laws, 8, 50, 70, 88
Jonah (prophet), 100
Joyce, James, 27

Kaplan, Cora, 54
Katz, Michael, 144n. 29
Kazin, Alfred, 119, 158n. 19

Kennedy, Robert, 11, 105, 127
Kinder, Donald, 142n. 7
King, Martin Luther, Jr., 11–12, 104,
    111
King, Rodney, 81–82
Kun, Josh, 167n. 10

Lamming, George, 55
Latinos, 136
"Letter from Birmingham Jail" (King),
    111
Lewis, David Levering, 150n. 8
Lipsitz, George, 90
Lorde, Audre, 54–55
Los Angeles riots (1992), 81–82
Loury, Glenn, 63
Lynchings, 27, 109

MacIntyre, Alasdair, 97
Majority rule, 137
Malcolm X, 11–12
    on double consciousness, 150n. 7
"Many Thousands Gone" (Baldwin),
    31, 36, 43–49, 60, 92
Marginalization. *See* Exclusion
Masculinity
    ideals of, 53–55
    politics of, 54
Massey, Douglas, 142n. 10
Matsuda, Mari, 79–80
Memory, selective
    of Civil War, 83
    history and, 108–9
Merleau-Ponty, Maurice, 121
Mills, Charles, 147n. 61
Morrison, Toni, 118, 134, 161n. 5
Murray, Albert, 65
"My Dungeon Shook" (Baldwin),
    122–23, 131

Nagel, Thomas, 148n. 73
Nation of Islam, 123, 126, 128–30
Native Son (Wright), 14, 46–48, 60, 80,
    113
    Irving Howe on, 46–47, 116–17
Négritude movement, 54, 58
Newton, Huey, 11
Nicholson, Linda, 146n. 51
Nissim-Sabat, Miriam, 158n. 30
Nobody Knows My Name (Baldwin)

    "Faulkner and Desegregation" in,
        110–12
    "Fifth Avenue, Uptown" in, 87–89,
        101
    "Northern Protestant" in, 121
    "Princes and Powers" in, 55
No Name in the Street (Baldwin), 13,
    54
"Normality," 51–53
Notes of a Native Son (Baldwin)
    "Everybody's Protest Novel" in,
        113–17, 120, 124
    "Many Thousands Gone" in, 31, 36,
        43–49, 60, 92
    "Notes of a Native Son" in, 31–32,
        67–75, 81, 93, 119
    "Stranger in the Village" in, 24–30,
        34–35

Omi, Michael, 151n. 10
"Open Letter to My Sister, Angela Y.
    Davis" (Baldwin), 8

Pateman, Carole, 159n. 35
Patterson, Orlando, 151–52n. 20
Peller, Gary, 143n. 15
Personal responsibility, 130–32
Pinckney, Darryl, 12
Piper, Adrian, 149n. 5
Plato, 14
Politics
    Baldwin and, 11–13, 20, 23–24,
        136–39
    of "equal respect," 56
    of masculinity, 54
    of recognition, 57–59
    of *ressentiment*, 64
    of victimhood, 62–65
Posnock, Ross, 58
"Post–civil rights" predicament, 5
Prejudices
    democracy and, 29
    Gadamer on, 21, 143n. 17
"Preservation of Innocence" (Baldwin),
    53
"Princes and Powers" (Baldwin), 55
Privacy
    feminist critiques of, 77–78
    marginalization and, 119
    racial injustice and, 75–82

Prophecy, 100–101, 104–7
Protest novels, 113–17, 120

Race
  "blackness" and, 4, 9
  Clinton's dialogue on, 1–2
  as fiction, 9
  sexuality and, 51–55
Race blindness, 4–6, 36, 57, 135
Race consciousness, definition of, 6–9,
    143n. 15. *See also* Double con-
    sciousness
Racial images, 31–32, 60–62, 75–86
  deindividualizing effects of, 61–62, 79
Racial injustice
  colonialism and, 66
  dialogue on, 1–2, 33
  "personal," 75–82
  victimization and, 62–64
  See also Injustice
Racism
  assumptions of, 6
  Faulkner and, 110–11
  guilt about, 16
Radicalism, Baldwin's, 23, 138
Rage of "disesteemed," 27, 69–71
Rampersad, Arnold, 150n. 8
Rawls, John, 148n. 73, 162nn. 22, 32
Recognition
  limits of, 55–59
  politics of, 57–59
  Charles Taylor on, 56–57
Reed, Adolph, Jr., 150n. 7
Religion, race consciousness and, 9
Responsibility, personal, 131–32
Ressentiment, politics of, 64
Roediger, David, 90
Rorty, Richard, 35
Rousseau, Jean-Jacques, 142n. 9

Sanders, Lynn, 142n. 7
Scott, Daryl Michael, 62
Segregation. *See* Exclusion
Sexual harassment, 63
Sexuality
  identity and, 50–55
  "normal," 51–53
Sexual orientation
  double consciousness and, 50–55
  race consciousness and, 9

Shklar, Judith, 20, 66, 76–77, 94
Shulman, George, 137
Silence
  breaking of, 118–22
  of majority, 1–10
Slavery, 27, 59, 77, 82–83
Smith, Rogers, 147n. 56
Smith, Ryan, 144n. 23
Social criticism
  political theory and, 21–22, 96–
    110
  Michael Walzer on, 97–110
Souls of Black Folk (Du Bois), 31,
    36–43
Spelman, Elizabeth, 152n. 25
Spender, Stephen, 169n. 39
Spillers, Hortense, 78
Stonewall uprising, 51
Stowe, Harriet Beecher, 126
"Stranger in the Village" (Baldwin),
    24–29, 34–35
Student Nonviolent Coordinating
    Committee (SNCC), 11–12
Sundquist, Eric, 151n. 15

Takaki, Ronald, 165n. 61
Taylor, Charles, 55–58
*Tell Me How Long the Train's Been
    Gone* (Baldwin), 51
Thomas, Clarence, 63–64
Thomas, Kendall, 153n. 32
Thomas, Laurence, 76, 93, 147n. 57
Thompson, Dennis, 142n. 8
Thoreau, Henry David, 137
Tocqueville, Alexis de, 5, 18, 29, 82
Toussaint-L'Ouverture, François-Do-
    minique, 121

Uncle Tom's Cabin (Stowe), 113–14,
    120, 152n. 23
"Us/them" mentality, 35, 45, 47. *See
    also* "We"

Victimhood
  images of, 31–32, 62–67, 85
  myths of, 86
  politics of, 31–32, 62–65, 86
Victimization
  experience of, 67–75
  innocence and, 92–93

Voting Rights Act (1965), 2, 11
Vulnerability, equality and, 26

Wallace, George, 94
Walton, Anthony, 166n. 72
Walzer, Michael, 21–22, 32, 89
    on "core" values, 107–9
    Interpretation and Social Criticism,
        97–98, 104, 106, 108
    on membership, 100–103
    "Obligations of Oppressed Minori-
        ties," 102–3
    social criticism of, 97–110
Watts, Jerry Gafio, 65
"We," Baldwin's, 28, 31, 35–36, 43–49,
    106. *See also* "Us/them" mentality
Weber, Max, 105, 164n. 51

West, Cornel, 147n. 52
Whiteness
    innocence and, 27–30, 90–91
    privileges of, 90–91, 127–29
    white supremacy and, 16, 43
Wideman, John Edgar, 138
Williams, Patricia, 19, 63, 79, 151n.
    18
Winant, Howard, 151n. 10
Wolin, Sheldon, 83
Woolf, Virginia, 59
Wright, Richard, 11
    Irving Howe on, 116–17
    Native Son, 14, 46–48, 60, 80, 113

Zamir, Shamoon, 150n. 8